Who Is This Book For?

Visual Studio 2012 Express is available for download **completely free of charge** from Microsoft's web site. You won't need to invest in any other software in order to follow all of the exercises in this book. All you will need is a computer with Microsoft Windows 7 or Windows 8 (recommended).

If you are an absolute beginner and want to master the art of creating interactive data-driven web sites with ASP.NET and C# you've found the right book.

The book will teach you to create and maintain ASP.NET websites, using Visual Studio, the industry-standard development tool. The express version of Visual Studio is used in this book. This can be downloaded **completely free of charge** from Microsoft's web site.

The book begins by showing you how to install Visual Studio 2012 Express and explore some of its most important features. You'll then learn the basic web technologies of HTML, CSS and JavaScript.

With this solid grounding in web technologies, it is then possible for you to understand how C# and ASP.NET 4.5 combine to create dynamic, interactive, data-driven web applications.

Because data-driven web applications require a database, the book will also teach you how to use Microsoft's new LINQ technology to easily integrate a database. The free SQL Server Express database software is automatically installed when you install Visual Studio Express, so everything you need is included.

The emphasis throughout this book is on solid, professional coding practices and techniques. Instead of simple code snippets the book takes you through the process of developing a high-quality, sophisticated web application. By the end of the course you will have a working and complete application that can be used as the basis for your own real-world commercial projects.

This book is for users who:

- Want to take the first step towards a career in web development.
- Are absolute beginners with little or no previous exposure to ASP.NET, C# and other web technologies.
- Are already comfortable with using Windows and a web browser.
- Want to understand the core web technologies of HTML, CSS and JavaScript.
- Want to become proficient with Visual Studio, the industry-standard development tool.
- Want to learn C#, the world's most widely-used professional programming language.
- Want to learn to use ASP.NET 4.5 to create data-driven, dynamic web applications.

Learn ASP.NET 4.5, C# and Visual Studio 2012 Essential Skills with The Smart Method

Simon Smart

Published by:

The Smart Method Ltd
Burleigh Manor
Peel Road
Douglas, IOM,
Great Britain
IM1 5EP

Tel: +44 (0)845 458 3282 Fax: +44 (0)845 458 3281

E-mail: sales@ASPNETCentral.com
Web: www.ASPNETCentral.com (this book's dedicated web site)

FIRST EDITION

International Standard Book Number (ISBN13): 978-1-909253-04-9

1 2 4 6 8 10 9 7 5 4

About the Author

Simon Smart has spent the last 10 years working in almost every aspect of software development, from accounting systems to manufacturing machinery programming. Over the course of his career he has seen software move away from desktop machines and towards web-based applications like the ones covered in this book.

Starting with the earliest versions of ASP he experienced its growth into ASP.NET 4.5, spending many long hours finding out what works and what doesn't.

Simon always found books and documentation about ASP.NET to be of limited use, even to the experienced. In 2011 he set out to write his own book, hoping to pass on the knowledge gained in his years working as a programmer.

In his spare time, Simon can be usually be found in the outdoors, roaming the forests and hills looking for new places to explore. His dad finds this amusing, particularly when it's raining.

Author's Acknowledgements

Kind words can be short and easy to speak, but their echoes are truly endless.

Mother Teresa, Catholic Nun (1910-1997)

Special thanks are due to my father Mike Smart, the founder of The Smart Method, who encouraged me to put my years of experience in .NET programming to use in writing this book.

Special thanks are also due to Jack Smart, Jen Stowell and Gord Hill who provided much useful feedback, improving the book greatly.

Finally, I would like to thank the readers of this book. It is my fondest hope that this book will give many people the first step they need to embark upon a career of web application development.

Contents

Introduction

Welcome to *Learn ASP.NET 4.5, C# and Visual Studio 2012 Essential Skills with The Smart Method*. This book has been designed to enable students to master essential ASP.NET skills by self-study. The book is equally useful as courseware in the classroom.

Smart Method publications are continually evolving as we discover better ways of explaining or teaching the concepts presented.

Feedback

At The Smart Method we love feedback – be it positive or negative. If you have any suggestions for improvements to future versions of this book, or if you find content or typographical errors, the author would always love to hear from you via e-mail to:

feedback@ASPNETCentral.com

Future editions will always incorporate your feedback so that there are never any known errors at time of publication.

If you have any difficulty understanding or completing a lesson, or if you feel that anything could have been more clearly explained, we'd also love to hear from you. We've made hundreds of detail improvements to our books based upon reader's feedback and continue to chase the impossible goal of 100% perfection!

Downloading the sample files

In order to use this book it is sometimes necessary to download sample files from the Internet. The sample files are available from:

http://www.ASPNETCentral.com

Type the above URL into your web browser and you'll see the link to the sample files at the top of the home page.

Problem resolution

If you encounter any problem downloading or using the sample files please send an e-mail to:

feedback@ASPNETCentral.com

We'll do everything possible to quickly resolve the problem.

Typographical Conventions Used In This Book

This guide consistently uses typographical conventions to differentiate parts of the text.

When you see this	Here's what it means
Right-click on *My Project* in the Solution Explorer and then click *Build* from the shortcut menu.	Italics are used to refer to text that appears in a menu, a dialog, or elsewhere within the Visual Studio application. At times, italics may also be used for emphasis or distinction.
Click File→New Project.... File Edit View Project Build Debug Data Tools New Project... Ctrl+Shift+N New Web Site... Shift+Alt+N New File... Ctrl+N	Click on the *File* menu and choose *New Project...* from the drop-down menu.
Click Edit→Outlining→ Collapse To Definitions. Outlining ▶ Toggle Outlining Expansion Ctrl+M, Ctrl+M IntelliSense ▶ Toggle All Outlining Ctrl+M, Ctrl+L RegisterUser.Continue Stop Outlining Ctrl+M, Ctrl+P } Stop Hiding Current Ctrl+M, Ctrl+U protected void RegisterUs Collapse to Definitions Ctrl+M, Ctrl+O	Click on the *Edit* menu and look for the *Outlining* sub-menu. Click the *Outlining* menu and then click on *Collapse to Definitions*.
Click Tools→Options...→Formatting→ Server tag→Assembly definition. 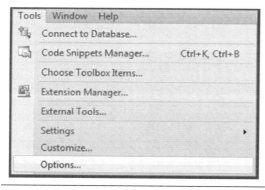	This is a more involved example. 1. Click the *Tools* menu, and then click the *Options...* button. A new dialog pops up. 2. Click on the *Formatting* group in the *Options* dialog. 3. Drop down the *Server Tag* list and click *Assembly definition*.
Type **int X;** on the next line.	Whenever you are asked to actually type something on the keyboard it is shown in bold faced text.
Press <**Ctrl**> + <**Z**>.	You should hold down the **Ctrl** key and then press the **Z** key.

Toolbox

When a lesson tells you to click a button, an image of the relevant button will often be shown either in the page margin or within the text itself.

note

If you switch to *Design* view and click on the properties of an object in the *Properties* window, you'll notice a short description of the property...

If you want to read through the book as quickly as possible, notes which usually expand a little on the lesson text, may be ignored.

important

Do not click the Delete button at this point as to do so would erase the entire table.

Whenever something can easily go wrong, or when the subject text is particularly important, you will see the *important* sidebar.

You should always read important sidebars.

tip

Moving between tabs using the keyboard

You can also use <Ctrl>+<Tab> on the keyboard to cycle through all of the tabs you have open.

Tips add to the lesson text by showing you shortcuts or time-saving techniques relevant to the lesson.

The bold text at the top of the tip box enables you to establish whether the tip is appropriate to your needs without reading all of the text.

In this example you may not be interested in keyboard shortcuts so you do not need to read further.

anecdote

I worked on an ASP.NET project for a gaming company a couple of years ago...

Sometimes I add an anecdote gathered over the years from my work or from other areas of my experience.

If you simply want to learn ASP.NET as quickly as possible, ignore anecdotes.

trivia

The Mosaic browser

Before 1993, the Internet was very different to the way it is today...

Sometimes I indulge myself by adding a little piece of trivia in the context of the skill being taught.

Just like my anecdotes you can ignore these if you want to. They won't help you to learn ASP.NET any better!

If you are not completing the course incrementally use the sample file: **Lesson 5-1** to begin this lesson.

When there is a sample file (or files) to accompany a session, the file name will be shown in a folder icon.

You can download the lesson or file from: *www.ASPNETCentral.com.* Detailed instructions are given in: *Lesson 1-3: Set up the development environment.*

Putting the Smart Method to Work

Visual Studio version and service pack

This edition was written using *Visual Web Developer 2012 Express* running under the *Microsoft Windows 8* operating system. You'll discover how to confirm that your computer is running these versions during *Lesson 1-2: Check your Visual Studio and Windows version.*

If you are using an earlier operating system (such as Windows 7) this book will be equally relevant, but you may notice small differences in the appearance of some of the screen grabs in the book. This will only occur when describing an operating system (rather than a Visual Studio) feature.

This book is written purely for Visual Studio 2012 Express and, due to changes in this version, some features may not be available in earlier or later versions (such as 2008 and 2010).

Sessions and lessons

The book is arranged into Sessions and Lessons. In a *Smart Method* course a Session would generally last for between forty-five and ninety minutes. Each Session would represent a continuous period of interactive instruction followed by a coffee break of ten or fifteen minutes.

When this book is used for self-instruction I recommend that you do the same. You'll learn better if you lock yourself away, switch off your telephone and complete the whole session without interruption. The memory process is associative, and each lesson within each session is very closely coupled (contextually) with the others. By learning the whole session in one sitting, you'll store all of that information in the same part of your memory and should find it easier to recall later.

The experience of being able to remember all of the words of a song as soon as somebody has got you "started" with the first line is an example of the memory's associative system of data storage.

It is highly recommend that you do take a break between sessions and spend it relaxing rather than catching up on your e-mails. This gives your brain a little idle time to do some data sorting and storage.

Read the book from beginning to end

Many books consist of disassociated self-contained chapters, often all written by different authors. This approach works well for pure reference books (such as encyclopedias). The problem with this approach is that there's no concept of building knowledge upon assumed prior knowledge, so the text is either confusing or unduly verbose as instructions for the same skill are repeated in many parts of the book.

This book is more effective as a learning tool because it takes a holistic approach. You will learn ASP.NET 4.0 in the same way you would be taught during one of our *Smart Method* courses.

In our classroom courses it's often the case that a delegate turns up late. One golden rule is that we can't begin until everybody is present, as each hands-on lesson builds upon skills taught in the previous lesson.

I strongly recommend that you read the book from beginning to end in the order in which it is written. Because of the unique presentational style, you'll hardly waste any time reading about things that you already know and even the most advanced ASP.NET developer will find some nugget of extremely useful information in every session.

How this book avoids wasting your time

> Nobody has things just as he would like them. The thing to do is to make a success with what material I have.
>
> *Dr. Frank Crane (1861–1928), American clergyman and journalist*

The only material available to me in teaching you ASP.NET is the written word and sample files. I'd rather have you sitting next to me in a classroom, but Frank Crane would have told me to stop complaining and use the tools I have in the most effective way.

Over the years I have read many hundreds of computer text books. Most of my time was wasted. The main problem with most books is having to wade through thousands of words just to learn one important technique. Not reading everything could mean missing that one essential insight.

This book utilizes some of the tried and tested techniques developed after teaching vast numbers of people during many years of delivering *Smart Method* classroom courses.

As you'll see in this section, many presentational methods are used to help you to avoid reading about things you already know, or things that are of little interest.

Why our classroom courses work so well

In our classroom courses we don't waste time teaching skills that the delegates already know. If it is clear that the delegate already understands a skill no time is wasted explaining it, but if the delegate has difficulty, more information is given until success is demonstrated.

Another key to learning effectively is to teach only the best way to accomplish a task. For example, you can comment code by typing two forward slashes or you can click the shortcut buttons on the toolbar. Because typing forward slashes is the easiest, fastest and most intuitive method, only this is practised in the classroom. In the book we do mention the alternatives, but only in a sidebar.

How this book mimics our classroom technique

Here's a lesson step:

---

tip

Comment shortcuts using the toolbar

You can quickly comment and uncomment code using the comment buttons on the toolbar:

1   Add a basic comment.

1. Add a new line before:

    return RoundNumber(FirstNumber + SecondNumber);

2. Add a comment with the code:

    //Add FirstNumber and SecondNumber

    You'll see that the comment is shown in green.

If you already know how to add a comment, read only the line: *Add a basic comment* and just do it. Don't waste your time reading anything else.

Read the smaller print only when the information is new to you.

If you're in a hurry to learn only the essentials, as fast as possible, don't bother with the sidebars unless they are labeled **important**.

Read the sidebars only when you want not to miss anything and have the time and interest.

Avoiding repetition

2	Open the code-behind file of *default.aspx*.
	You learned how to do this in: *Lesson 1-7: Manage a project with the Solution Explorer.*

In this book (and in our classroom courses) we do not wish to waste your time with reiteration.

In a classroom course, a delegate will sometimes forget something that has already been covered that day. The instructor must then try to get the student to remember and drop little hints reminding them about how they completed the task earlier.

This isn't possible in a book, so I've made extensive use of cross references in the text pointing you back to the lesson in which the relevant skill was learned. The cross references also help when you use this book as a reference work but have forgotten the more basic skills needed to complete each step.

Use of American English

American English (rather than British English) spelling has been used throughout. This is because the help system and screen elements all use American English spelling, making the use of British English confusing.

Examples of differences are the British English spelling: *Colour* and *Dialogue* as opposed to the American English spelling: *Color* and *Dialog*.

Because this book is available worldwide, much care has been taken to avoid any country-specific terminology. For example, in most of the English speaking world, apart from North America, the symbol # is referred to as the **hash sign**, so the term *hash* is used throughout this book.

First page of a session

1/ The first page begins with a quotation, often from an era before the age of the computer, that is particularly pertinent to the session material. As well as being fun, this helps us to remember that all of the real-world problems we solve with technology have been around for a long time.

3/ The session objectives *formally* state the precise skills that you will learn in the session.

At the end of the session you should re-visit the objectives and not progress to the next session until you can honestly agree that you have achieved them.

In a *Smart Method* course we never progress to the next session until all delegates are completely confident that they have achieved the previous session's objectives.

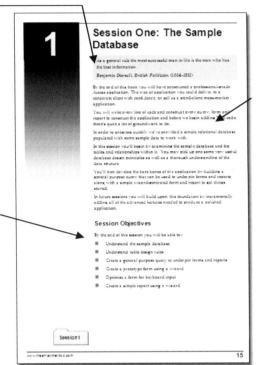

2/ In the next few paragraphs we *informally* summarise why the session is important and the benefits that can be gained.

This is important because without motivation adults do not learn. For adults, learning is a means to an end and not an end in itself.

The aim of the introduction is to motivate your retention of the skills that will be taught in the following session by allowing you to preview the relevance of the material that will be presented. This may subconsciously put your brain into "must remember this" mode—assuming, of course, that the introduction convinces you that the skills will be useful to you!

Every lesson is presented on two facing pages

> Pray this day, on one side of one sheet of paper, explain how the Royal Navy is prepared to meet the coming conflict.
>
> *Winston Churchill, Letter to the Admiralty, Sep 1, 1939*

Winston Churchill was well aware of the power of brevity. The discipline of condensing thoughts into one side of a single sheet of A4 paper resulted in the efficient transfer of information.

A tenet of our teaching system is that every lesson is presented on *two* facing sheets of A4. We've had to double Churchill's rule as they didn't have to contend with screen grabs in 1939!

If we can't teach an essential concept in two pages of A4 we know that the subject matter needs to be broken into two smaller lessons.

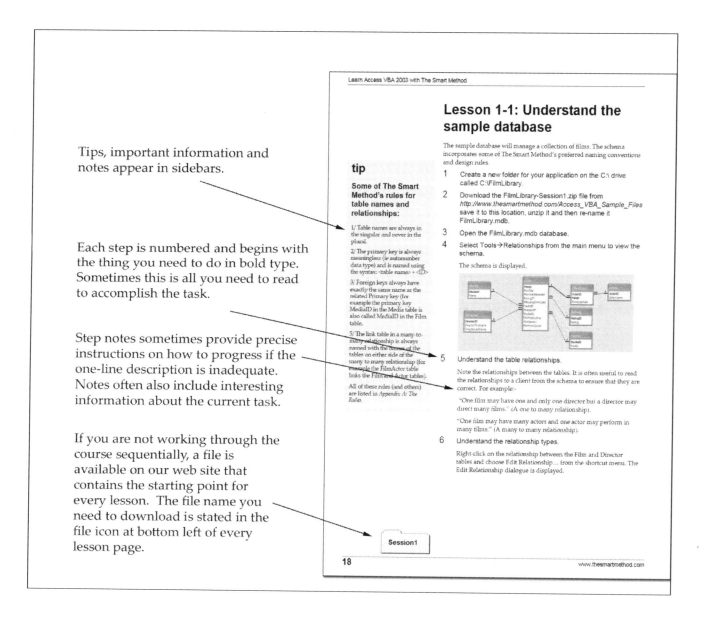

Tips, important information and notes appear in sidebars.

Each step is numbered and begins with the thing you need to do in bold type. Sometimes this is all you need to read to accomplish the task.

Step notes sometimes provide precise instructions on how to progress if the one-line description is inadequate. Notes often also include interesting information about the current task.

If you are not working through the course sequentially, a file is available on our web site that contains the starting point for every lesson. The file name you need to download is stated in the file icon at bottom left of every lesson page.

Learning by participation

> Tell me, and I will forget. Show me, and I may remember. Involve me, and I will understand.
>
> *Confucius (551-479 BC)*

Confucius would probably have agreed that the best way to teach IT skills is hands-on (actively) and not hands-off (passively). This is another of the principal tenets of the *Smart Method* teaching system. Research has backed up the assertion that you will learn more material, learn more quickly, and understand more of what you learn, if you learn using active, rather than passive methods.

For this reason pure theory pages are kept to an absolute minimum with most theory woven into the hands-on sessions either within the text or in sidebars. This echoes the teaching method in Smart Method courses, where snippets of pertinent theory are woven into the lessons themselves so that interest and attention is maintained by hands-on involvement, but all necessary theory is still covered.

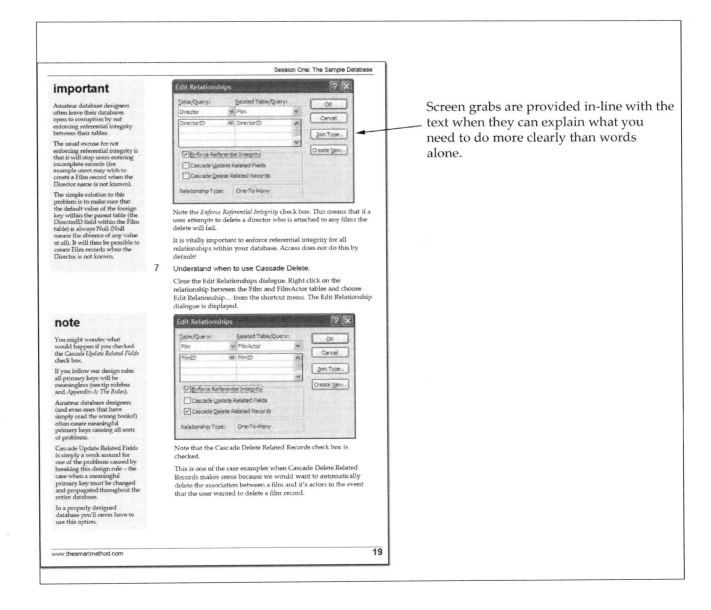

Screen grabs are provided in-line with the text when they can explain what you need to do more clearly than words alone.

Session One: Getting Started with Visual Studio

> Man is a tool-using animal. Without tools he is nothing, with tools he is all.
>
> *Thomas Carlyle, Scottish Writer (1795-1881)*

All of the tools that you need to work with ASP.NET are now available as a **free** download from Microsoft under the name Visual Studio Express. Visual Studio Express lacks some of the advanced features of the professional Visual Studio versions, but its interface is nearly identical.

Instructions for downloading and installing Visual Studio are included at the start of this session.

Visual Studio is a complex application with hundreds of features. In this session, you're going to create a very simple project and explore some of the basic functionality of Visual Studio.

Session Objectives

By the end of this session you will be able to:

- Install Visual Studio
- Check your Visual Studio and Windows version
- Set up the development environment and download the sample files
- Set up Windows for development
- Create an ASP.NET Web Application project
- Create an ASP.NET Web Site project
- Manage a project with the Solution Explorer
- Add and remove files from a project
- Run a project in debug mode
- View .aspx pages in Source and Design views
- Use automatic formatting
- Expand and collapse code regions
- Change properties in Design view
- Change properties in Source view
- Add controls to a page with the Toolbox
- Use the QuickTasks menu
- Get help

note

Other Visual Studio Express products

Along with *Express for Web*, you will find:

Express for Windows 8

This version of Visual Studio allows you to develop "apps" for Windows 8 computers and Microsoft Surface mobile devices.

Express for Windows Desktop

This version allows you to develop applications for Windows computers.

Express for Windows Phone

This version allows you to develop apps for Windows Phone devices.

Lesson 1-1: Install Visual Studio

If you are using Windows 7, the procedure is almost the same as described here for Windows 8. You should be able to figure out the differences.

Note that Visual Studio 2012 is not compatible with earlier versions of Windows. You will not be able to install it if you have Windows XP or Windows Vista.

If you have an older version of Windows and aren't able to upgrade, you can install Visual Studio 2010 and use our *ASP.NET 4.0, C# and Visual Studio 2010* course.

1   Download Visual Studio Express.

1. Open Internet Explorer and navigate to:
   http://www.microsoft.com/express

2. Click *Express 2012 Products* on the left (see sidebar if this isn't visible).

3. Click *Products* at the top of the screen.

4. Click *Express for Web* under *Express 2012 products*.

Express for Web is the version of Visual Studio Express that is used to create ASP.NET web applications. See sidebar for an explanation of the other options.

The product that you will be using in this course is *Visual Studio Express 2012 for Web*.

5. Click *Download* in the middle of the screen.

6. Click *Install Now*.

You may be taken to a screen that asks you to install the *Microsoft Web Platform Installer*. If this happens, click *Install Now* (if this does not appear, skip to the next step).

After clicking, you will be prompted to download a file. To continue, you must download and run this file.

A window appears, prompting you to install *Visual Studio Express 2012 for Web*.

7. Click *Install*.

A list of the software that will be installed is displayed, along with the appropriate license agreements.

8. Click *I Accept*.

Visual Studio downloads and installs.

Visual Studio is quite a large download, so it's recommended that you have a reasonably fast Internet connection available.

Even with a fast connection, it can take several hours to install all of the Visual Studio tools. At times nothing may seem to be happening for long periods of time, but don't switch off your computer…be patient!

See sidebar if you experience problems while installing.

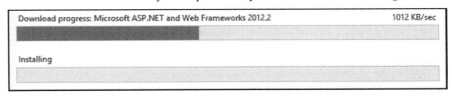

✓ The following products were successfully installed.

9. Click *Finish*.

10. Click *Exit*.

2 Start Visual Studio

After installing Visual Studio you should see *VS Express for Web* in your Start Menu.

Click on the program to start Visual Studio.

Lesson 1-2: Check your Visual Studio and Windows version

Microsoft sometimes refers to Visual Studio 2012 Express as *VS Express for Web* or *Visual Web Developer*. This book refers to it as "Visual Studio".

Visual Studio 2012 Express for Web is a freeware version of the Visual Studio IDE (Integrated Development Environment) optimized for web application development.

Microsoft provides this version free of charge for students and hobbyists so that they can learn how to use Visual Studio without having to purchase the product.

1 Open Visual Studio (if it isn't open already).

2 Check your Visual Studio version.

Click Help→About Microsoft Visual Studio Express 2012 for Web.

Microsoft Visual Studio Express 2012 for Web Version 11.0.60315.01 Update 2 © 2012 Microsoft Corporation. All rights reserved.	Microsoft .NET Framework Version 4.5.50709 © 2012 Microsoft Corporation. All rights reserved.

The two version numbers shown above are the important ones. This book was written using Microsoft Visual Studio Version *11.0.60315.01 Update 2* and Microsoft .NET Framework Version *4.5.50709*.

If you have an earlier version, please follow the steps in *Lesson 1-1: Install Visual Studio* to upgrade to the latest version. Some users have reported that they had to uninstall and re-install Visual Studio in order to upgrade.

If you have a later version it's not a problem, but some of the things described in this book might behave slightly differently.

3 Check your operating system version.

Click the *System Info* button on the dialog that you opened in the previous step.

You should see your operating system name and version in the top-right corner of the dialog that appears.

Item	Value
OS Name	Microsoft Windows 8 Pro
Version	6.2.9200 Build 9200

Microsoft Windows 8 Pro Version 6.2.9200 is the version of Windows that is used for the screenshots in this book.

You can still use this book if you have Windows 7 or a different version of Windows 8, but some of the items described in this book may behave slightly differently.

If you have a version of windows that is older than Windows 7, you may not be able to run Visual Studio 2012. You should either upgrade to a more recent version of Windows or install Visual Studio 2010 and use our other course: *Learn ASP.NET 4.0, C# and Visual Studio 2010 with The Smart Method*.

4   Close the *System Information* dialog.

5   Click *OK* to close the *About Microsoft Visual Studio Express 2012 for Web* dialog.

6   Close Visual Studio.

Lesson 1-3: Set up the development environment and download the sample files

1   Open Visual Studio (if it isn't open already).

2   Enable Expert Settings.

To access the full range of Visual Studio's features, you must enable Expert Settings.

To do this, click Tools→Settings→Expert Settings.

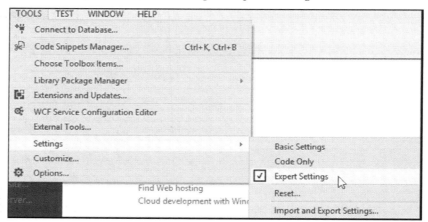

In the *Basic Settings* and *Code Only* modes you can access only a limited sub-set of Visual Studio's features. Only *Expert Settings* allows you to use every feature of Visual Studio.

3   Reset the window layout.

1.   Click Window→Reset Window Layout.

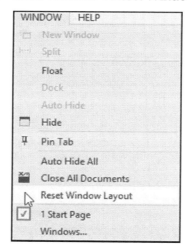

2.   When prompted to confirm, click *Yes*.

If you have never used Visual Studio before, this will probably do nothing. If you have used it before, however, it will reset the window layout so that it matches the screenshots you will see in this book.

If you ever accidentally change the layout of Visual Studio's windows by closing a toolbar or dragging a window out of its position, you can always reset the layout back to the default by using this option.

4   Download the sample files.

1.   Go to www.ASPNETCentral.com using your web browser.

2.   Click the *Sample Files* button on the top toolbar.

3.   Download the sample files.

I recommend that you extract the sample files to a folder named: *C:\Practice\ASP.NET45*. This will maintain consistency with the screen grabs and instructions in the book.

Lesson 1-4: Set up Windows for development

Microsoft go out of their way to make Windows easy to use for non IT professionals. They worry that untrained users may delete vital system files, so they hide them by default. Microsoft also feel that the concept of file extensions may confuse normal users.

While this is great for ordinary office workers, as a professional developer you don't want Windows to hide anything from you.

1 Open Windows Explorer.

Right-click in the bottom-left corner of the screen (or on the *Start* menu if you are using Windows 7) and select *File Explorer* from the shortcut menu.

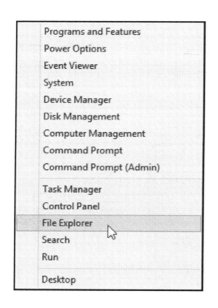

2 Browse to the C:\Practice\ASP.NET45\Images folder.

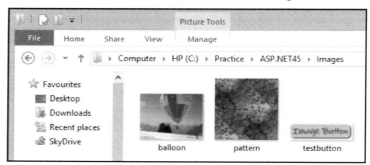

3 Stop Windows from hiding file extensions.

1. Click View→Options (see sidebar if you are using Windows 7).

2. Click the *View* tab at the top of the *Folder Options* dialog.

3. Un-tick the *Hide extensions for known file types* box if it is ticked.

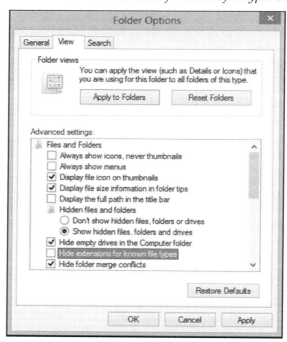

note

If you are using Windows 7

If you are using Windows 7, you will need to follow slightly different steps to change your view settings.

Instead of clicking View→Options, you will need to click:
Organize→
Folder and search options.

The *Folder Options* dialog will then appear as shown.

4. Click *OK*.

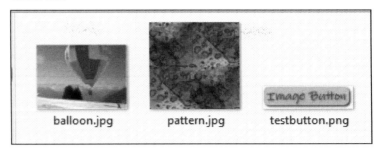

balloon.jpg   pattern.jpg   testbutton.png

You will notice that the name of the balloon image now ends in *.jpg*.

The *.jpg* was actually there all the time, but Windows was hiding it to simplify its interface.

The *.jpg* part of the file is known as its *extension* (see sidebar).

4   Stop Windows from hiding files.

Some files are *hidden* by default. Unless you change the default settings, Windows will not display these files at all.

For a normal user, hidden files wouldn't present a problem, but as a developer it's essential to be able to see all of the files that exist.

1. Re-open the *Folder Options* dialog by clicking View→Options.

2. Click the *View* tab.

3. Click *Show hidden files, folders, and drives.*

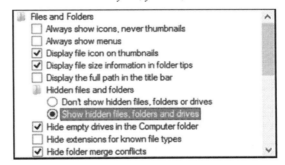

4. Click *OK*.

Windows will now display all files, even if they are hidden.

Lesson 1-5: Create an ASP.NET Web Forms Application project

An ASP.NET Web Forms Application project is the starting point in creating an ASP.NET web site. Projects contain all of the web pages, images and other files that are needed to create a web site.

In this lesson, you'll create an ASP.NET Web Forms Application project.

1 Open Visual Studio.

2 Create a new Web Forms Application project.

1. Click File→New Project...

2. Click *Visual C#* in the left-hand pane.

   This book will teach you about the C# programming language, not the Visual Basic programming language (see sidebar).

3. Click *ASP.NET Web Web Forms Application* in the central pane.

4. In the *Name* box, enter: **My Project**

   Notice that the *Solution name* box automatically copies what you enter.

5. Click the *Browse...* button and browse to *C:/Practice/ASP.NET45* (or the folder where you placed your sample files). Then click the *Select Folder* button.

6. Make sure that the *Create directory for solution* box is ticked.

7. Click *OK*.

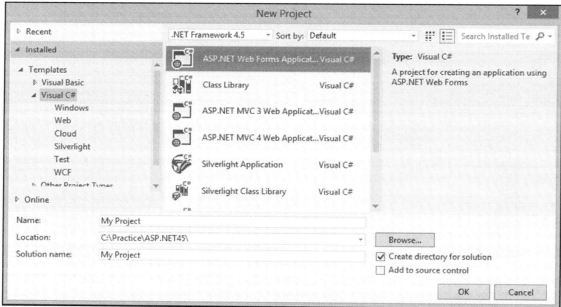

You have just created your first ASP.NET Web Forms Application project. Visual Studio will automatically open it (this may take a little time).

note

ASP.NET MVC web applications

You may have noticed the *MVC Web Application* project types when you created your project.

MVC stands for: *Model, View, Controller*. It's a programming methodology where all code is separated into those three groups.

MVC web application projects exist for programmers who want to design their web applications using the MVC methodology.

ASP.NET isn't really designed for the MVC methodology, so MVC projects tend to be harder to work with than standard web applications, especially if you're new to programming.

For this reason, you won't use MVC projects in this course.

note

My Project.suo

The *.suo* file is hidden by default, so you will only see it if you have configured Windows to display hidden files.

You should have done this in: *Lesson 1-3: Set up the development environment and download the sample files.*

The *.suo* file is used to store settings for your project, and will be automatically updated through Visual Studio.

You will never have to open it directly.

3 Close and re-open the new project.

1. Close Visual Studio, clicking *Yes* if prompted to save.

2. Navigate to your sample files folder using Windows Explorer.

3. Open the new *My Project* folder that has appeared.

Name	Date modified	Type
My Project	11/04/2013 14:26	File folder
packages	11/04/2013 14:26	File folder
My Project.sln	11/04/2013 14:26	Microsoft Visual Studio Solution
My Project.v11.suo	11/04/2013 14:30	Visual Studio Solution User Options

You will see another *My Project* folder and a file called *My Project.sln*.

My Project.sln is the *solution* file. The solution file tells Visual Studio which files are in your project. If you were to double-click on it, your project would be opened in Visual Studio.

4. Open the *My Project* folder by double-clicking on it.

Name	Date modified	Type
Account	11/04/2013 14:25	File folder
App_Data	11/04/2013 14:25	File folder
App_Start	11/04/2013 14:26	File folder
bin	11/04/2013 14:26	File folder
Content	11/04/2013 14:25	File folder
Images	11/04/2013 14:25	File folder
obj	11/04/2013 14:25	File folder
Properties	11/04/2013 14:25	File folder
Scripts	11/04/2013 14:26	File folder
About.aspx	11/04/2013 14:25	ASP.NET Server Page
About.aspx.cs	11/04/2013 14:25	Visual C# Source file
About.aspx.designer.cs	11/04/2013 14:25	Visual C# Source file
Bundle.config	11/04/2013 14:25	XML Configuration File
Contact.aspx	11/04/2013 14:25	ASP.NET Server Page
Contact.aspx.cs	11/04/2013 14:25	Visual C# Source file
Contact.aspx.designer.cs	11/04/2013 14:25	Visual C# Source file
Default.aspx	11/04/2013 14:25	ASP.NET Server Page
Default.aspx.cs	11/04/2013 14:25	Visual C# Source file
Default.aspx.designer.cs	11/04/2013 14:25	Visual C# Source file
favicon.ico	11/04/2013 14:25	Icon
Global.asax	11/04/2013 14:25	ASP.NET Server Application
Global.asax.cs	11/04/2013 14:25	Visual C# Source file
My Project.csproj	11/04/2013 14:26	Visual C# Project file
My Project.csproj.user	11/04/2013 14:26	Visual Studio Project User Options file

This folder has lots of items in it! These are the files that contain all of the code and content for your site.

You'll notice a file named *My Project.csproj*. This is the *project* file.

Projects are very similar to solutions. You can open your project by double-clicking *My Project.csproj*, just as you can open it by double-clicking *My Project.sln*. The major difference is that a solution can contain several projects.

You'll only work with one project at a time in this course, so it doesn't matter which file you use to open your projects.

5. Open the project by double-clicking the solution or project file.

Lesson 1-6: Create an ASP.NET Web Forms Site project

note

Compiling

When a project is compiled, it is changed from program code that a human can read into binary code that a web server can read.

Advantages of Web Forms Applications

1. Because a Web Forms Site project is not compiled, the web server has to compile it as the site is viewed. This makes Web Forms Sites slightly slower than Web Forms Applications.

2. Because a Web Forms Application is compiled, the code of the web site it produces will not be easy to edit.

This prevents the web site from being tampered with and allows you to protect your source code.

For these reasons you will only work with Web Forms Applications after this lesson.

note

Razor

You'll notice that options exist for *Razor v1* and *Razor v2* Web Site projects.

Razor is a new technology that allows ASP.NET web sites to be created in a different way.

Ordinary ASP.NET projects separate their page design and C# code into two separate files. Razor combines page designs and C# code into a single file – this is actually how the earliest versions of ASP worked.

You won't use Razor projects in this course, but the skills you will learn will be very relevant if you choose to use Razor in the future.

As well as Web Forms Application projects, you can also create Web Forms Site projects. A Web Forms Site is very similar to a Web Forms Application, but it is not compiled.

Compiling offers many advantages, making the Web Forms Application the preferred project type (see sidebar), but for completeness you'll also learn how to create a Web Forms Site project in this lesson.

1   Open Visual Studio (if it isn't open already).

2   Create a new Web Forms Site project.

   1.   Click File→New Web Site....

   2.   Click *Visual C#*.

   3.   Click *ASP.NET Web Forms Site*.

   4.   Click the *Browse...* button and browse to the folder where you placed your sample files, then click the *Open* button.

   5.   Append the text **\My Web Site** to the box showing the path to your Sample Files folder.

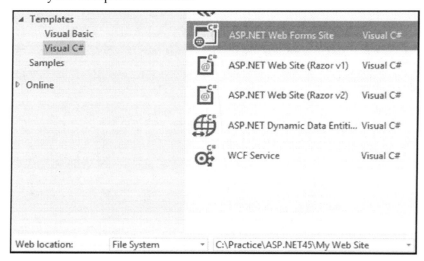

   6.   Click *OK*.

   7.   Click *Yes* to create the folder if prompted.

A new web site is automatically created and opened.

3   Close and re-open the Web Site.

   1.   Close Visual Studio.

   2.   Navigate to your sample files folder using Windows Explorer.

   3.   Open the new *My Web Site* folder that has appeared.

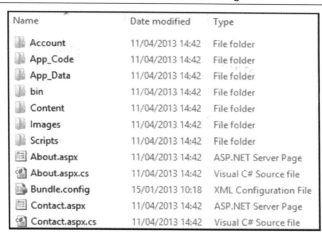

This is quite different to your Web Forms Application project!

When you created your Web Forms Application project, a *.csproj* file and a *.sln* file were created to tell Visual Studio which files are included in the project. Web Forms Site projects don't use these files; instead they assume that all of the files in the same folder are part of the project. This means that you can't open a Web Forms Site in the same way as you can open a Web Forms Application.

You'll only be using Web Forms Applications from this point on, but it's useful to know how to open a Web Forms Site.

4. Open Visual Studio.

5. Click File→Open Web Site...

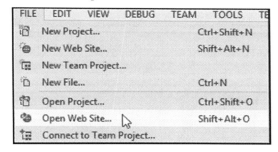

6. Browse to the *My Web Site* folder and click *Open*.

    Click *Yes* if prompted.

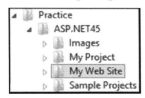

The web site project is opened in Visual Studio.

Lesson 1-7: Manage a project with the Solution Explorer

The *Solution Explorer* window can be found at the top-right of the Visual Studio screen. It displays all of the web pages and other objects that are in your current solution and allows you to edit them. It also enables you to add files to your project and remove them.

When you created *My Project* in *Lesson 1-5: Create an ASP.NET Web Forms Application project*, a lot of different files were automatically added to it. In this lesson you'll learn how to open some of those files, add new files and remove files.

1   Open Visual Studio (if it isn't open already).

2   Open *My Project* from your sample files folder.

    1.   Click File→Open Project.

    2.   Click the *My Project.sln* file in the *My Project* subfolder of your Sample Files folder.

    3.   Click *Open*.

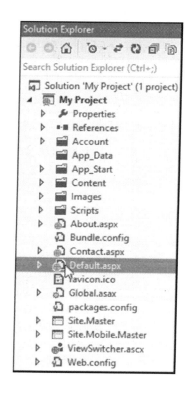

Alternatively, you can navigate to your Sample Files folder and double-click on *My Project.sln* as you did in: *Lesson 1-5: Create an ASP.NET Web Forms Application project.*

3   Double-click *Default.aspx* in the *Solution Explorer.*

This will open the HTML code of *Default.aspx* in the main window (if it wasn't visible already). You can open any file in your project by double-clicking it in this way.

Don't worry if you don't understand any of the code displayed yet. By the time you've finished this course you'll completely understand what all of it means.

An *aspx* file acts as a web page and can be understood by a web browser. You may have noticed some web addresses ending with .aspx while browsing the Internet.

Default.aspx is normally the 'home page' of a web site.

4   Open the 'code-behind' file of *Default.aspx.*

    1.   Expand *Default.aspx* by clicking the small arrow to the left of it in the *Solution Explorer.*

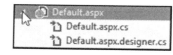

    2.   Double-click *Default.aspx.cs*

This will open the C# 'code-behind' file of *Default.aspx* in the main window.

You won't understand any of the C# code that you see in this file yet, but by the end of this course it will all make sense to you.

If you are not completing the course incrementally use the sample file: **Lesson 1-7** to begin this lesson.

Sample files with the starting point for each lesson are also provided for all of the other lessons in this session.

Every .aspx file has a code-behind file. The code-behind files are actually separate files, but they are grouped together by the Solution Explorer for clarity.

You can also open the code-behind file by right-clicking on *Default.aspx* and then clicking *View Code* from the shortcut menu.

5 Add a new page to the project.

1. Right-click on *My Project* in the *Solution Explorer* and then click Add→New Item... from the shortcut menu.

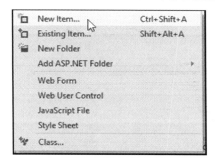

2. Click *Web* in the left pane of the dialog that appears and then click *Web Form* from the top of the center panel.

3. Enter **mypage.aspx** in the *Name* box and then click *Add*.

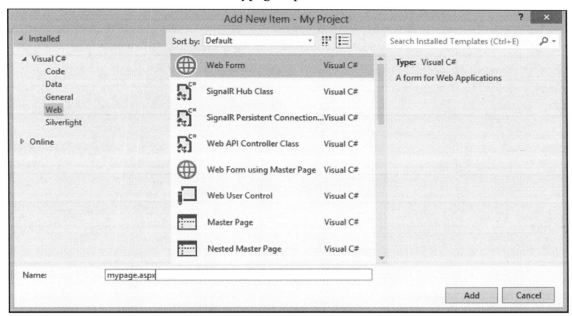

You have now added a new page to your project. Visual Studio helpfully opens its HTML code for you. You can also see that *mypage.aspx* has appeared in the *Solution Explorer*.

You'll continue learning about the *Solution Explorer* window in the next lesson: *Lesson 1-8: Add and remove files from a project*.

Lesson 1-8: Add and remove files from a project

1 Open *My Project* from your sample files folder (if it isn't open already).

2 Add a new folder to the project.

Adding a folder to a project is very similar to adding a folder in Windows.

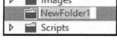

1. Right-click on *My Project* in the *Solution Explorer* and then click Add→New Folder from the shortcut menu.

   The new folder is created and its default name (*NewFolder1*) is highlighted, ready for you to type a meaningful name.

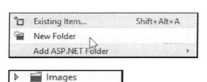

2. Type **MyFolder** as the name of your new folder and press **<Enter>**.

3 Add an image to the *Images* folder.

1. Right-click on the *Images* folder in the *Solution Explorer* and then click Add→Existing Item… from the shortcut menu.

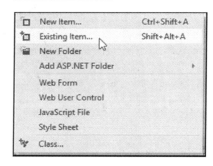

2. Navigate to your sample files folder and choose the file *balloon.jpg* in the *Images* folder, then click *Add*.

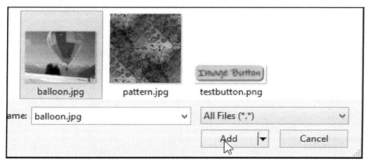

This will take a copy of *balloon.jpg* and place it in your project's *Images* folder. You can use this method to add any file to your project.

4 Remove the *About.aspx* page.

1. Right-click on the *About.aspx* page in the *Solution Explorer* and then click *Delete* from the shortcut menu.

2. Click *OK* to confirm that the file should be deleted.

If you check your Recycle Bin, you'll find that the *About.aspx* page has been moved there, along with its code-behind files.

You can also do this by pressing the **<Delete>** key.

5 Exclude *balloon.jpg* from the project.

1. Right-click on the *balloon.jpg* file that you added in step 3.

2. Click *Exclude From Project* from the shortcut menu.

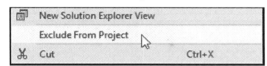

balloon.jpg disappears from your project, but if you check the *Images* folder using Windows you'll see that the file is actually still there.

By excluding *balloon.jpg*, you have stopped it from being included in the web site when it is published, but you haven't actually deleted the file from the project.

This is useful when you want to remove something from a project but aren't sure if you might need it again later.

6 Exclude the entire *Images* folder.

Right click on the *Images* folder and click *Exclude From Project* from the shortcut menu.

The *Images* folder disappears from your project, meaning that it will no longer be included when your project is published.

7 Configure the *Solution Explorer* to show files and folders that have been excluded.

Although it's useful to be able to exclude items from your project, it's also useful to be able to see the excluded items. This also makes it a lot easier to bring back items that have been excluded.

Click the *Show all files* icon at the top of the *Solution Explorer* window.

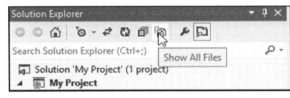

The *Images* folder re-appears, but its icon is greyed-out to indicate that it is excluded.

You can also see the *bin* and *obj* folders that are present in your project folder, but won't be published. These are a normal part of ASP.NET projects and you'll learn more about them in the Expert Skills course in this series.

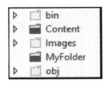

8 Include the *Images* folder.

Right-click the *Images* folder and click *Include In Project* from the shortcut menu.

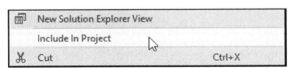

The *Images* folder's icon returns to normal. The *Images* folder will once again be included when your project is published.

9 Close your web browser and close Visual Studio.

Lesson 1-9: Run a project in debug mode

Now that you've created a project it would be useful to see it in action. Visual Studio has a virtual web server that lets you test your site without needing to upload it to the Internet.

In this lesson you'll learn how to start the virtual web server to see the pages that were automatically included in your new project.

1   Open *My Project* from your sample files folder (if it isn't already open).

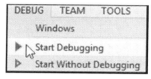
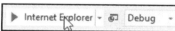

2   Start Debugging.

1.   Double-click *Default.aspx* to open it.

2.   Click Debug→Start Debugging.

You can also use the shortcut button on the top toolbar, which looks like a 'play' button next to *Internet Explorer*.

After a short delay, the *Default.aspx* page is displayed in your web browser.

The path in the address bar of your browser looks something like: *http://localhost:57931/Default.aspx*

Localhost is the web address of your own computer. When you started debugging, Visual Studio started a virtual web server on your computer at this address so that you can test your project.

Note that if you click the *About* button on this page, you will see an error. This is because you deleted the *About.aspx* file in: *Lesson 1-7: Manage a project with the Solution Explorer.*

3   Close your web browser.

Close your web browser now. This will bring you back to Visual Studio and stop debugging.

4   Change the project's start page to *mypage.aspx*.

1.   Right-click on *mypage.aspx* in the *Solution Explorer* and then click *Set As Start Page* from the shortcut menu.

2.   Start debugging.

If you can't do this, see the sidebar: *Manually stopping debugging.*

tip

Manually stopping debugging

The virtual web server doesn't always close properly when you close your browser window.

If this happens, you can stop debugging manually by clicking Debug→ Stop Debugging.

You can also use the Stop button on the debugging toolbar.

This time the path that is opened is something like: *http://localhost:57931/mypage.aspx*. You didn't add any content to *mypage.aspx*, so the page will be blank.

Because you have set *mypage.aspx* as the start page, it will always appear first when you start debugging.

5 **Select which browser is used for debugging.**

1. Close your web browser and make sure that debugging is stopped.

2. Click the drop-down arrow next to the 'play' button on the top toolbar.

   A drop-down menu appears, showing all of your installed browsers. You can change which browser is used for debugging here.

3. Click *Internet Explorer*, if it isn't selected already.

   The screenshots in this book use Internet Explorer.

Most web developers need to test that their sites work in several browsers (see sidebar).

6 **Cause a build error.**

When you start debugging, your project is 'built'. This is another word for compiling (for more on this see sidebar in: *Lesson 1-6: Create an ASP.NET Web Forms Site project*).

When your project is built, all of its code is checked for errors. If there are any major errors, the virtual web server won't be able to start and Visual Studio will try to tell you why.

1. Double-click *Default.aspx.cs* or right-click on *Default.aspx* and click *View Code* from the shortcut menu.

2. Type some nonsense in the space shown.

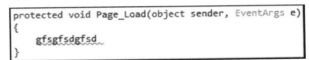

```
protected void Page_Load(object sender, EventArgs e)
{
    gfsgfsdgfsd
}
```

You'll notice that the text you typed is underlined in red. Visual Studio has already noticed that there's something wrong with this code.

3. Try to start debugging.

   A dialog appears, warning you that there are build errors and asking if you'd like to use the last successful build instead.

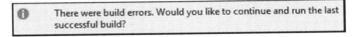

There were build errors. Would you like to continue and run the last successful build?

4. Click *No*.

5. Delete the nonsense and start debugging again.

   mypage.aspx displays properly this time (though, of course, it is still empty).

7 **Close your web browser and close Visual Studio.**

Lesson 1-10: View .aspx pages in Source and Design views

ASPX files can be viewed in two different ways. *Design* view allows you to work with the web page visually and *Source* view allows you to work with the web page's HTML code. This lesson will show you how to work with both views.

1   Open *My Project* from your sample files folder.

2   Open the HTML code of *mypage.aspx*.

To open the HTML code of *mypage.aspx*, simply double-click on it in the *Solution Explorer*. HTML stands for HyperText Markup Language (see sidebar).

3   Add some text.

In the code window you should see a gap between two lines saying *<div>* and *</div>*.

1.   Type **Welcome to My Project!** into the space between *<div>* and *</div>*.

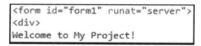

2.   Start debugging.

If you are unable to start debugging, you have probably left the web page open from the last debug session. If this is the case, click the *Stop Debugging* button on the *Debug* toolbar. The green *Start Debugging* button will then light up.

When debugging starts, the text that you added appears on the web page.

3.   Close the web browser.

4   Switch to *Design* view.

Click the *Design* button at the bottom of the code window.

The web page and its layout are displayed visually.

5   Switch to *Split* view.

Click the *Split* button at the bottom of the code window.

The *Split* view simply displays both *Design* and *Source* views simultaneously.

6   Change the text in *Design* view.

You can change text in *Design* view in the same way as you would in *Source* view.

1. Click the *Design* button.

2. Click in the white space after *Welcome to My Project!*

3. Type: **Hello world!**

7   Switch back to *Source* view.

Click the *Source* button next to the *Design* button you clicked in the previous step.

Notice how Visual Studio has automatically added the text that you typed to this page's HTML code.

8   Save changes to the file.

You may have noticed that when you made changes to *mypage.aspx*, an asterisk (*) appeared next to its name on its tab.

The asterisk indicates that changes have been made to the file. If you were to try to close the tab, you would be warned that you had unsaved changes.

Click File→Save mypage.aspx.

The asterisk disappears.

You can also press <**Ctrl**>+<**S**> to save the file that you currently have open.

9   Close Visual Studio.

Lesson 1-11: Use automatic formatting

As you saw in *Lesson 1-10: View .aspx pages in Source and Design views*, *Design* view makes it very easy to make changes to your web pages. However, when you make changes in *Design* view the code that is created is often messy and hard to understand in *Source* view.

Fortunately, Visual Studio comes with a great automatic formatting feature that will tidy up the code for you!

1   Open *My Project* from your sample files folder.

2   Open the HTML code of *mypage.aspx*.

3   Make the HTML code messy.

At the moment the HTML code isn't perfect, but it's still quite easy to read. However, HTML code can often get very messy and hard to understand.

1. Add some extra spaces before your *Welcome to My Project!* text.

```
<body>
    <form id="form1" runat="server">
    <div>
                            Welcome to My Project!
        Hello world!</div>
    </form>
</body>
```

2. Remove the line break between *<form>* and *<div>*.

```
<body>
    <form id="form1" runat="server">      <div>
                            Welcome to My Project!
        Hello world!</div>
    </form>
</body>
```

3. Remove the line breaks between the last instances of *</div>*, *</form>*, *</body>* and *</html>*.

```
<body>
    <form id="form1" runat="server">      <div>
                            Welcome to My Project!
        Hello world!</div>      </form></body></html>
```

Your code is now quite badly messed up! You could correct the formatting manually, but there is a much easier way.

4   View *mypage.aspx* in your web browser.

It's interesting to note that your web browser doesn't care how badly formatted the HTML code is, it still displays the page in exactly the same way as it did before.

5   Close your browser and return to Visual Studio.

6   Automatically fix the page formatting.

note

Use automatic formatting frequently as you work through this book

This book won't tell you to use automatic formatting again after this point, but feel free to use it if the code you add in later lessons doesn't match what is shown in the screenshots.

The screenshots in this book will always show the code correctly formatted.

1. Open *mypage.aspx* in *Source* view (if it isn't open already).

2. Click Edit→Format Document.

The code is rearranged and the formatting looks sensible again!

```
<body>
    <form id="form1" runat="server">
    <div>
        Welcome to My Project! Hello world!
    </div>
    </form>
</body>
```

This option works in all of the document types that you have opened so far. It is extremely useful when code looks messy and hard to read as it will automatically tidy everything up!

7   Open the code-behind file of *Register.aspx* in the *Account* folder.

You learned how to do this in: *Lesson 1-7: Manage a project with the Solution Explorer.*

The C# code on this page still won't make any sense to you yet, but you'll understand all of it by the end of this course.

8   Mess up the formatting of the C# code.

Automatic formatting works with C# code too.

Add different numbers of spaces before the lines of code to make them hard to read.

```
        protected void RegisterUser_CreatedUser(o
        {
FormsAuthentication.SetAuthCookie(RegisterUser.U

                string continueUrl = RegisterUs
    if (String.IsNullOrEmpty(continueUrl))
                                           {
                continueUrl = "~/";
        }
                Response.Redirect(continueU

}

        }
```

It's now confusing enough to scare even the most experienced programmers!

9   Fix the C# code automatically.

Click Edit→Format Document.

The code is automatically formatted correctly, making it a lot more readable.

```
protected void RegisterUser_CreatedUser(obj
{
    FormsAuthentication.SetAuthCookie(Regi

    string continueUrl = RegisterUser.Cont
    if (String.IsNullOrEmpty(continueUrl))
    {
        continueUrl = "~/";
    }
    Response.Redirect(continueUrl);
}
```

Lesson 1-12: Expand and collapse code regions

In Visual Studio, you often need to work with large amounts of HTML and C# code. To help you to deal with such large amounts of code, Visual Studio provides the ability to expand and collapse the code into regions. This allows you to get an overview of the code and expand only the parts you are interested in.

In this lesson you'll expand and collapse code in both a C# and an HTML file.

tip

Collapse to Definitions

Although you can expand and collapse code using the + and – icons as you do in this lesson, there are a few advanced ways to expand and collapse your code.

If you click:

Edit→Outlining→ Collapse to Definitions

…your code will be collapsed so that the biggest areas of code are hidden.

This is often the most useful way to view your code as you can then selectively expand only the code you want to see.

1 Open *My Project* from your sample files folder.

2 Expand and collapse C# code regions.

1. Open the code-behind file of *Register.aspx*, which is in the *Account* folder.

    (You learned how to do this in: *Lesson 1-7: Manage a project with the Solution Explorer*).

    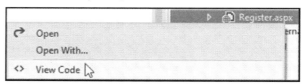

    The content of the C# code-behind file is displayed.

    ```
    namespace My_Project.Account
    {
        public partial class Register : System.Web.UI.Page
        {
            protected void Page_Load(object sender, EventArgs e)
    ```

    Code-behind files contain C# code which is used to turn a static read-only HTML web page into a dynamic ASP.NET page. Dynamic pages can execute code when users perform actions such as clicking on web page buttons.

2. Click the minus icon (⊟) next to the line:
    namespace My_Project.Account

    ```
    namespace My_Project.Account...
    ```

    The code below it seems to disappear! Don't worry though, this is a feature of Visual Studio that allows you to collapse blocks of code in order to simplify the view when a page contains a large amount of code.

3. Expand the code again by clicking the plus sign icon (⊞).

    ```
    namespace My_Project.Account
    {
        public partial class Register : System.Web.UI.Page
        {
            protected void Page_Load(object sender, EventArgs e)
    ```

    You can use any of the plus and minus icons on the page to expand and collapse different areas of code.

3   Open the HTML code of *Register.aspx*.

Simply double-click on *Register.aspx* in the *Solution Explorer*.

4   Expand and collapse HTML code regions.

1. Wait for the ⊟ buttons to appear.

Visual Studio takes some time to process an HTML file before the buttons will appear to expand and collapse its code.

Sometimes the buttons don't appear at all (even after waiting some time). If this happens, close the file and reopen it.

```
<asp:Content runat="server" ID="BodyContent" ContentPlaceHolc
    <hgroup class="title">
        <h1><%: Title %>.</h1>
        <h2>Use the form below to create a new account.</h2>
    </hgroup>

    <asp:CreateUserWizard runat="server" ID="RegisterUser" V:
        <LayoutTemplate>
            <asp:PlaceHolder runat="server" ID="wizardStepPla
            <asp:PlaceHolder runat="server" ID="navigationPla
        </LayoutTemplate>
```

2. Click the first ⊟ button, next to *<asp: Content*.

```
<%@ Page Title="Register" Language="C#" MasterPageFile
⊞ <asp:Content ID="BodyContent" ...>...</asp:Content>
```

Again, all of the page's code seems to disappear! But as before, it has just been collapsed out of sight.

3. Expand the code again by clicking the ⊞ button.

The code reappears.

```
<asp:Content runat="server" ID="BodyContent" ContentPlaceHolc
    <hgroup class="title">
        <h1><%: Title %>.</h1>
        <h2>Use the form below to create a new account.</h2>
    </hgroup>

    <asp:CreateUserWizard runat="server" ID="RegisterUser" V:
        <LayoutTemplate>
            <asp:PlaceHolder runat="server" ID="wizardStepPla
            <asp:PlaceHolder runat="server" ID="navigationPla
        </LayoutTemplate>
```

5   Close Visual Studio.

note

Web colors

On web pages, colors are usually defined using hex (short for hexadecimal) codes.

Hexadecimal is a counting system used by computers which has the numbers 0 to 9 as well as the letters A-F. This means that 1B in hexadecimal would actually be 27 in the decimal counting system that we're used to.

Hex color codes are actually 3 hexadecimal numbers put together to define a color.

The first number indicates how much red is in the color, the second how much green and the third how much blue.

This means that black would be #000000 because it has absolutely no red, green or blue.

White would be #FFFFFF, the maximum amount of every color.

The brightest possible red would be #FF0000, with 255 parts red and 0 parts blue and green.

This color coding system allows for 16,777,216 possible colors.

note

Other properties

If you switch to *Design* view and click on the properties of an object in the *Properties* window, you'll notice that a short description of the property appears at the bottom of the window.

There are so many possible properties that they won't all be covered in this book, but by using the descriptions you can quickly learn the purpose of each property.

Lesson 1-13: Change properties in Design view

You might have noticed the *Properties* window under the *Solution Explorer*. In this lesson you'll use it to change the properties of some things on web pages while in *Design* view.

1   Open the *ShiningStone* project from your sample files folder.

It can be found in the *Sample Projects* sub-folder.

2   Open the HTML code of *buy.aspx* and switch to *Design* view.

Switch to *Design* view by clicking the *Design* button at the bottom of the code window.

Please fill in the form below with your address details and p A sales representative will contact you to arrange payment.

Address 1   [   ]
Address 2   [   ]
Address 3   [   ]
Address 4   [   ]
Country   [Afghanistan   ▾]
Post Code   [   ]
Phone Number[   ]

3   View the *buy.aspx* page in your web browser.

Click the *Start Debugging* shortcut button.

OR

Right-click on *buy.aspx* in the Solution Explorer and then click *View in Browser* from the shortcut menu.

It may take some time for the web page to appear. This is normal when debugging.

Try entering text into the text boxes and selecting a country using the drop down menu.

4   Change the color of a text box.

1.   Close your web browser to stop debugging.

2.   Click the blue text box next to *Post Code*.

Post Code   asp:TextBox#TextBoxPostCode

An outline appears around the text box to indicate that it is selected. Its type and name also appear above it.

If you look at the *Properties* window, you can see that the bar at the top has also changed to indicate the name of the control that you have selected.

Properties

TextBoxPostCode System.Web.UI.WebControls.TextBox

3. Look for the *BackColor* property in the *Properties* window.

    This property controls the background color of the text box (see *Web colors* sidebar for more information).

4. Click in the box that currently says *#CCFFFF*.

    A box with three dots appears on the right-hand side of the box.

5. Click the box with the three dots and a dialog will appear prompting you to choose a color.

6. Click any color you like and then click *OK*.

7. Click on a different text box and you will see that the color of the *Post Code* text box has changed to the color that you selected.

5   Change the ID property of a control.

1. Click the *Submit Order* button.

    You should see the name *ButtonSubmitOrder* shown at the top of the *Properties* window.

    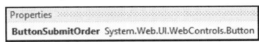

2. Scroll down to the *ID* property (it's at the end of the list if you are viewing properties in categorized view – see sidebar) and change it to: **ButtonSend**

    The name of the button changes above the *Submit Order* button and at the top of the *Properties* window.

    The *ID* property is the property that ASP.NET uses to tell controls apart. You will cover this in more depth in: *Lesson 4-1: Name controls correctly.*

3. Change the *ID* property of the button back to: **ButtonSubmitOrder**

6   Select *TextBoxAddress1* from the drop-down menu at the top of the *Properties* window.

    The *Address 1* text box is highlighted in the *Design* view in exactly the same way as it would be if you had clicked on it.

    This method of selecting objects is useful when you have a very crowded page or when there are hidden elements on the page.

7   Close Visual Studio.

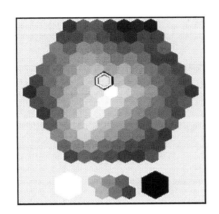

tip

Viewing properties in alphabetical order

By default, Visual Studio shows properties in categories that can be collapsed and expanded by using the small arrows to the left of each group.

You can change the properties window to show properties in alphabetical order by clicking the *alphabetical* icon at the top of the window:

The A-Z view is useful when you know a property name but cannot remember its category.

You can switch it back to grouping by categories by clicking:

The screenshots in this book use the default *Categorized* view.

Lesson 1-14: Change properties in Source view

In the last lesson you changed properties using *Design* view, but it's also possible to do the same thing in *Source* view. This is useful when your page contains hidden elements or is too complicated for *Design* view to display properly. Some developers prefer to work in *Source* view most of the time.

In this lesson, you'll use *Source* view to change the properties of controls on your page.

1   Open *ShiningStone* from your sample files folder.

   It can be found in the *Sample Projects* sub-folder.

2   Open *buy.aspx* in *Source* view.

   After opening *buy.aspx* you can switch to *Source* view by clicking the *Source* button at the bottom of the window.

3   Change the properties of controls in *Source* view using the *Properties* window.

   1.   Scroll down and click on the line that begins:

   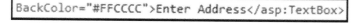

   The line should be highlighted in gray. *TextBoxAddress1* is also automatically selected in the *Properties* window.

   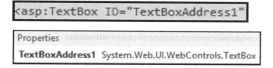

   2.   In the *Properties* window, Type **Enter Address** into the *Text* property and press <**Enter**>.

   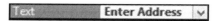

   After a brief delay, *Enter Address* appears on *TextBoxAddress1's* line in the HTML code.

   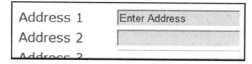

   3.   View *buy.aspx* in your web browser.

   Changing the *Text* property has placed the text *Enter Address* inside the *Address 1* text box. The *Text* property is useful when you want to display default text in a text box control.

Address 1	Enter Address
Address 2	
Address 3	

   4.   Close your web browser and return to Visual Studio.

   5.   Delete the text that you entered from the *Text* property and press <**Enter**>.

The text is removed from the code.

```
BackColor="#FFCCCC"></asp:TextBox>
```

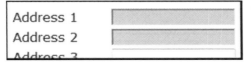

6. View *buy.aspx* in your browser again.

The text has been removed from the text box.

7. Close your browser and return to Visual Studio.

Whenever you change properties using the *Properties* window, the page's code (visible in *Source* view) is being updated. This also works the other way around: if you change properties in *Source* view, they will change in the *Properties* window.

4 Manually change properties in *Source* view.

Although you can use the *Properties* window to change properties while in *Source* view, *Source* view is really intended to be used to edit code manually.

1. Click in the space just after *<asp:TextBox* underneath *Address 2*.

```
<td>
    Address 2
</td>
<td>
    <asp:TextBox ID=
</td>
```

2. Type **Text="Enter Address"**, followed by a space.

```
<td>
    Address 2
</td>
<td>
    <asp:TextBox Text="Enter Address" ID="
</td>
```

You have just manually set the *Text* property of *TextBoxAddress2* to *Enter Address*.

3. View *buy.aspx* in your web browser.

The text has been placed in the second text box, just as you'd expect.

4. Close your web browser.

5. Remove the *Text* property by deleting the code that you added.

```
<td>
    Address 2
</td>
<td>
    <asp:TextBox ID="TextBoxAddress2"
</td>
```

Source view can be useful, as it displays all of a page's code. There are some things that *Design* view is incapable of displaying, but *Source* view will always contain everything.

5 Close Visual Studio.

Lesson 1-15: Add controls to a page with the Toolbox

You now know how to navigate through a project and make basic changes to the controls on your pages. Using the *Toolbox*, you can add controls to your pages by simply dragging and dropping them.

1   Open *My Project* from your sample files folder.

2   Open the HTML code of *mypage.aspx* and switch to *Design* view.

> You learned how to do this in: *Lesson 1-10: View .aspx pages in Source and Design views.*

3   Expand the Toolbox.

1.   Click the *Toolbox* icon in the top-left corner of the screen.

   The *Toolbox* appears.

2.   Click the *Auto Hide* icon () in the top-right corner of the *Toolbox* to 'pin' it to the window.

   This will stop the *Toolbox* from overlapping your page and will stop it from disappearing automatically (see sidebar).

4   Expand the *Standard* category in the *Toolbox* (if it isn't already expanded)

This is done the same way as in the *Solution Explorer* and *Properties Window.*

Click the [▷] icon next to the *Standard* category (unless it is already expanded).

The *Standard* category contains the most commonly-used controls.

5   Add a *Button* control to the page.

Click and drag a *Button* control from the *Toolbox* onto your page, underneath the text you added earlier.

A button is created called *Button1.*

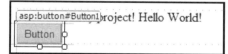

6   Switch to *Source* view.

Here you can see the code that was added to display the new *Button* control.

```
<asp:Button ID="Button1" runat="server" Text="Button" />
```

7   Add a *TextBox* control in *Source* view.

1.   In the same way as you did with the *Button*, drag a *TextBox* control from the *Toolbox* onto the page's code.

   Try to drop the *TextBox* just before the line that contains the button you added earlier (the line that begins *<asp:Button*).

tip

Auto Hide

You may have noticed that the *Solution Explorer, Properties Window* and *Toolbox* all have the same 'pin' icon in the top-right corner of their windows:

[icon]

This button switches on and off *Auto Hide.* When *Auto Hide* is switched on, the window will automatically minimize away from the screen when it is not in use. By auto-hiding your windows, you can get a large unobstructed view of the main window.

Feel free to experiment with *Auto Hide.* Remember that you can always reset your window layout to the default by clicking Window→ Reset Window Layout.

```
<asp:TextBox ID="TextBox1" runat="server"></asp:TextBox>
<asp:Button ID="Button1" runat="server" Text="Button" />
```

Some code is added to the page for your new *TextBox* control.

2. Switch back to *Design* view.

The new text box control has been inserted before the button.

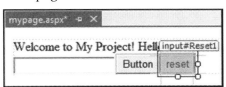

8 Add an *HTML* control.

1. Collapse the *Standard* category in the *Toolbox*.

   You can do this by clicking the ⊿ icon next to *Standard*.

2. Expand the *HTML* category in the *Toolbox*.

3. Drag an *Input (Reset)* control onto your page after your button.

Your page should now look like this:

9 Add a *Calendar* control.

You will find the *Calendar* control in the *Standard* category of the *Toolbox*.

In the same way that you added the last two controls, add a *Calendar* control to the page. Try to place it before your text box.

Your page should now look like this:

<		April 2013				>
Mon	**Tue**	**Wed**	**Thu**	**Fri**	**Sat**	**Sun**
25	26	27	28	29	30	31
1	2	3	4	5	6	7
8	9	10	11	12	13	14
15	16	17	18	19	20	21
22	23	24	25	26	27	28
29	30	1	2	3	4	5

10 Save your changes and close Visual Studio.

---

note

ASP.NET controls and HTML

If you're familiar with HTML, you have probably noticed that the objects that begin with <asp: are unfamiliar. This is because they are ASP.NET controls.

As you read earlier, HTML is the language that web browsers understand. However, these <asp: lines aren't valid HTML code so a web browser cannot understand them.

When an ASPX web page is requested by a web browser, ASP.NET controls are converted into valid HTML code by the web server before they are sent to the browser.

You will learn more about this in: *Lesson 3-1: Change properties with C#.*

Lesson 1-16: Use the QuickTasks menu

You've now learned how to add controls and change their properties, but some controls come with extra features that can only be accessed using the *QuickTasks* menu.

You'll use the *QuickTasks* menu in this lesson.

1   Open *My Project* from your sample files folder (if it isn't already open).

2   Open *mypage.aspx* and switch to *Design* view.

3   Click the Calendar control that you added in the last lesson.

4   Open the *QuickTasks* menu for the Calendar.

When a *QuickTasks* menu is available for a control, a small arrow icon will appear on the top right-hand side of the control when you select it in *Design* view.

Click the arrow icon 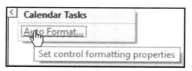 to open the *QuickTasks* menu.

5   Auto Format the calendar using *QuickTasks*.

1.   Click *Auto Format...* in the Calendar control's *QuickTasks* menu.

A dialog appears from which you can select a format for your calendar.

2.   Click the *Simple* calendar format and click *OK*.

Your calendar should now look like this:

Of course, your own calendar will show the current month and date.

6   View the code that was added by the QuickTask.

Switch to *Source* view. You can see that a lot of code was added to your page when you applied the Auto Format.

If you were very patient, you could set all of those properties yourself using the skills you've learned so far, but Auto Format makes your life a lot easier.

---

note

Other controls that use QuickTasks

Only a few of the *Standard* ASP.NET controls use *QuickTasks*, mostly the controls that display lists of items.

The more complex controls, especially those under the *Data* category have many different *QuickTasks* options.

For now it is only important that you know how to access the *QuickTasks* menu.

Any important *QuickTasks* will be covered in detail as the relevant control is introduced later in the course.

Most *QuickTasks* help to speed up tasks that would usually require you to set a lot of properties manually.

7   Add a *DropDownList* control between the *TextBox* and *Button* controls.

Using the skills you learned in *Lesson 1-15: Add controls to a page with the Toolbox*, add a *DropDownList* control to the page. You'll find it in the *Standard* category of the *ToolBox*.

8   Use *QuickTasks* to add items to your *DropDownList*.

1. Open the *QuickTasks* menu for your new *DropDownList* control and click *Edit Items....*

    A dialog appears.

2. Click the *Add* button to add a new item to your *DropDownList*.

3. Fill in the *Text* property (in the right-hand panel of the dialog) with **Yes** and press <**Enter**>.

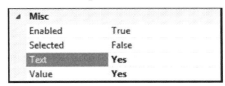

    The *Value* property is automatically set to match the *Text* property.

    You will explore the *DropDownList* control in detail in: *Lesson 4-7: Use the DropDownList control.*

4. Add another item by clicking *Add*. This time set its *Text* property to: **No**

5. Click *OK*.

6. Start debugging.

    Your *DropDownList* now offers the choices *Yes* and *No*.

    If you examine the page in *Source* view, you'll see that the following lines of code were added by the QuickTask:

    <asp:ListItem>Yes</asp:ListItem>
    <asp:ListItem>No</asp:ListItem>

9   Close your web browser.

10   Close Visual Studio.

Lesson 1-17: Get help

note

The .NET framework

The .NET framework is a huge library of controls, functions and utilities that is the foundation of ASP.NET.

The .NET framework includes all of the controls you've worked with so far and most of the C# code that you will be working with later on.

The structure and contents of the .NET framework are explored in greater depth in the Expert Skills course in this series.

Although this book will teach you all of the skills that you need to work with ASP.NET, it won't cover every single control and possible line of code.

Microsoft provides a huge library of help and reference files for ASP.NET called MSDN. This provides comprehensive documentation for every part of the .NET framework (see sidebar).

1   Open Visual Studio.

2   Click Help→View Help.

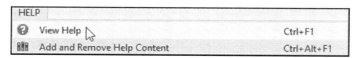

A dialog may appear asking whether you want to allow Visual Studio to display help files from the Internet.

If the dialog appears, click *Yes*.

A web browser window opens, displaying Microsoft's homepage for Visual Studio 2012.

3   Search MSDN for the DropDownList control.

Enter **dropdownlist** into the search box at the top of the page and click the magnifying glass icon to search.

4   Click on the first search result that appears.

> **System.Web.UI.WebControls.DropDownList (.NET Framework 4)**
> Represents a control that allows the user to select a single item from a drop-down list. You can control the appearance of the DropDownList control by setting the BorderColor, BorderStyle, and BorderWidth properties. The control also supports data binding.

Everything you could ever want to know about the DropDownList control is displayed.

A lot of the help file won't make much sense to you at the moment. You'll probably recognize the list of properties and their descriptions and might be able to understand some of the example code.

5   Check the .NET version of the help file.

At the time of writing there have been 6 versions of the .NET framework. This course teaches you how to use .NET 4.5, but Microsoft provides help files for all of the earlier versions.

To make sure that you're looking at the correct help file, check the text at the top of the screen just underneath the title. It should say *.NET Framework 4.5*. If it doesn't, simply click on the *Other Versions* drop-down and select *.NET Framework 4.5*.

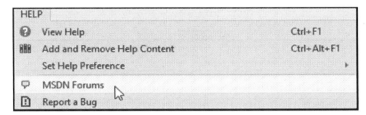

DropDownList Class

.NET Framework 4.5 | Other Versions ▾ | 2 out of 3

6   Ask for help in the MSDN forums.

As well as the reference documentation available from MSDN, Microsoft has an online forum available where you can discuss Visual Studio and ASP.NET.

HELP	
❷ View Help	Ctrl+F1
▦ Add and Remove Help Content	Ctrl+Alt+F1
Set Help Preference	▸
💬 MSDN Forums	
⚠ Report a Bug	

To access the forums, close the web browser and click: Help→MSDN Forums (from the Visual Studio menu). The web page then appears in a tab inside Visual Studio.

If you click the *Ask a Question* button, you will be prompted to register an MSDN Profile and will then be able to ask your question.

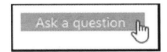

7   Search the Internet for help.

Besides Microsoft's documentation and forums, the Internet is full of other development communities and tutorials.

Sometimes the best way to find the answer to a specific problem is to use your favorite search engine.

If you search for **ASP.NET dropdownlist** using a search engine, you will probably see the MSDN page that you looked at earlier at the top of the search results, along with many other results from different places around the web.

8   Close Visual Studio.

Session 1: Exercise

1   Create a new *ASP.NET Web Forms Application* project in your sample files folder called: **Exercise1**

2   Add a new *Web Form* item to the project called: **mypage.aspx**

3   Add a *Calendar* control to the *mypage.aspx* page.

4   Use *QuickTasks* to *Auto Format* the Calendar control to the *Colorful 1* scheme.

5   Change the *ID* property of the Calendar control to: **CalendarColorful**

6   Delete the existing *Images* folder.

7   Add a new **Images** folder.

8   Add the *pattern.jpg* file from the *Images* folder in your sample files folder to your new *Images* folder.

9   Add a HTML *Image* control to the page using the *HTML* category of the *ToolBox*.

10   Set the *Src* property of the new *Image* control to: **Images/pattern.jpg**

11   Set *mypage.aspx* to be the project's start page.

12   Start the project in debug mode.

13   Save your work.

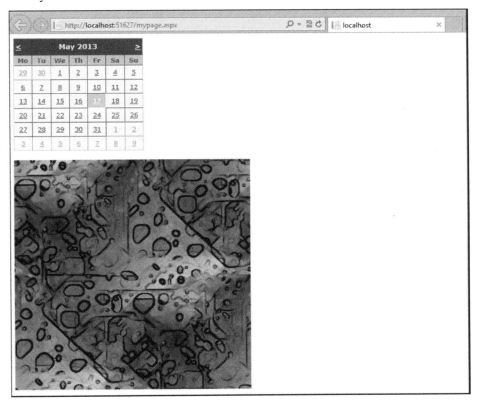

If you need help slide the page to the left

Session 1: Exercise Answers

These are the four questions that students find the most difficult to answer:

Q 8	Q 7	Q 5	Q 3
1. Right-click on the *Images* folder in the *Solution Explorer*.	1. Right-click on *Exercise1* in the *Solution Explorer*.	1. Click on the calendar in *Design* view.	1. Double-click on *mypage.aspx* in the *Solution Explorer*.
2. Click: Add→ Existing Item... from the shortcut menu.	2. Click Add→ New Folder from the shortcut menu.	2. Scroll down in the *Properties* window until you see the *ID* property.	2. Click on the *Design* button at the bottom of the main panel.
3. Browse to the *C:\Practice\ASP.NET45\Images* folder.	3. Type the name: **Images**	3. Click in the box that currently says *Calendar1* and change the text to: **CalendarColorful**	3. Drag a *Calendar* control from the *ToolBox* to the page.
4. Click on *pattern.jpg* and then click *Add*.	This was covered in: *Lesson 1-8: Add and remove files from a project.*	This was covered in: *Lesson 1-13: Change properties in Design view.*	This was covered in: *Lesson 1-15: Add controls to a page with the Toolbox.*
This was covered in: *Lesson 1-8: Add and remove files from a project.*			

If you have difficulty with the other questions, here are the lessons that cover the relevant skills:

1 Refer to: Lesson 1-5: Create an ASP.NET Web Forms Application project.

2 Refer to: Lesson 1-7: Manage a project with the Solution Explorer.

4 Refer to: Lesson 1-16: Use the QuickTasks menu.

6 Refer to: Lesson 1-8: Add and remove files from a project.

9 Refer to: Lesson 1-15: Add controls to a page with the Toolbox.

10 Refer to: Lesson 1-13: Change properties in Design view.

11 Refer to: Lesson 1-9: Run a project in debug mode.

12 Refer to: Lesson 1-9: Run a project in debug mode.

13 Refer to: Lesson 1-10: View .aspx pages in Source and Design views.

Session Two:
Understanding Web Sites

> All truths are easy to understand once they are discovered; the point is to discover them.
>
> *Galileo Galilei, Italian scientist (1564 - 1642)*

Microsoft has long realized that there are two (almost) completely different resources needed to create excellent web applications: web designers and web developers. They even provide two tools, one for each discipline (Visual Studio for web developers and Expression Web for web designers).

Web developers are mainly concerned with the functionality of a web application, which they enable using ASP.NET and C# technologies.

Web designers are mainly concerned with the appearance of web pages, which they enable using three completely different technologies: HTML, CSS and JavaScript.

In this session it is assumed that you have no existing web design skills. It is included because you'll need to understand basic web design to put your C# and ASP.NET skills into context.

Many readers of this book will already be very comfortable with web design technologies. Even if you are in this category you should still complete this session as it also includes some important background information about ASP.NET and C#.

Session Objectives

By the end of this session you will be able to:

- Understand HTML bold, italic and heading tags
- Understand HTML paragraph and break tags
- Understand the aspx page structure
- Use the title, meta, link and script tags
- Create an HTML table
- Navigate HTML with the tag navigator
- Display images and links on a page
- Work with CSS
- Use the CSS Properties window
- Use the div and span tags
- Work with JavaScript
- Work with HTML forms

Lesson 2-1: Understand HTML bold, italic and heading tags

You've already touched on HTML a few times in this book, enough to understand that it is a vital part of every web site.

This lesson covers some of the basics of writing HTML code.

1   Open *HTMLTest* from your sample files folder.

You will find this in the *Sample Projects* subfolder.

2   Open *default.aspx* in *Source* view.

3   Add some text to the file.

    1.   Type the following into the gap between *<div>* and *</div>*:

       This is paragraph 1

```
<body>
    <form id="form1" runat="server">
    <div>
        This is paragraph 1
    </div>
    </form>
</body>
```

    2.   Switch to *Design* view and you'll see the text as it will appear on the page.

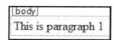

4   Make the text bold by using HTML <b> tags.

The *<b>* tag makes text bold.

    1.   Switch to *Source* view.

    2.   Change the HTML code to look like this:

       This is **<b>**paragraph 1**</b>**

```
<div>
    This is <b>paragraph 1</b>
</div>
```

    When you type the first *<b>* tag, you'll see IntelliSense at work (see sidebar).

    Everything between *<b>* and *</b>* will be made bold.

    3.   Switch back to *Design* view.

    The text *paragraph 1* is now displayed in bold.

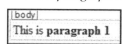

5   Make the text italic by using HTML <i> tags.

The *<i>* tag works in the same way as the *<b>* tag to make text italic.

    1.   Switch back to *Source* view again.

2. Change the HTML code to look like this:

<i>This is **<b>**paragraph 1**</b></i>**

```
<div>
    <i>This is <b>paragraph 1</b></i>
</div>
```

Everything between *<i>* and *</i>* will be made *italic*. Note that this includes the contents of the *<b>* tag.

When tags are put inside other tags like this, it is called 'nesting'.

Notice the order of the closing tags. It's important that you close HTML tags in the same order in which you opened them.

3. Switch back to *Design* view.

This time the whole paragraph is italic, with the words *paragraph 1* in bold and italic.

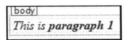

6 **Create a heading by using HTML <h1> tags.**

1. Return to *Source* view.

2. Add a new line before the existing text.

3. Add the following code on the new line:

<h1>This is the page heading</h1>

```
<div>
    <h1>This is the page heading</h1>
    <i>This is <b>paragraph 1</b></i>
</div>
```

4. Switch to *Design* view.

The contents of the *h1* tag are very big and bold!

5. Return to *Source* view.

6. Change your *<h1>* and *</h1>* tags into **<h2>** and **</h2>**tags.

```
<div>
    <h2>This is the page heading</h2>
    <i>This is <b>paragraph 1</b></i>
</div>
```

7. Switch back to *Design* view.

h2 is slightly smaller than *h1* (see sidebar for more).

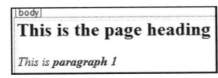

note

Other heading tags

HTML provides the heading tags: *h1, h2, h3, h4, h5* and *h6*.

The default styles for the heading tags get smaller from 1 to 6, but the default sizes can be changed using CSS, which you'll learn about in: *Lesson 2-8: Work with CSS*.

Heading tags are important because search engines often consider them to have greater weight when analyzing a site's content.

A search engine will consider *h1* headings to be the most important, then *h2*, etc.

You'll notice that the heading tags automatically insert a new line after them. This is very similar to the paragraph tag, which you'll learn about in: *Lesson 2-2: Understand HTML paragraph and break tags*.

Lesson 2-2: Understand HTML paragraph and break tags

In this lesson, you'll use the HTML paragraph and break tags to break up text on your page.

1   Open *HTMLTest* from your sample files folder.

You will find it in the *Sample Projects* subfolder.

2   Open *default.aspx* in *Source* view.

3   Add paragraph tags to the HTML code.

One of the most basic tags in HTML is the paragraph tag: <p> Paragraph tags do just what they say: they break up text into paragraphs.

1.   Add a new line after the *paragraph 1* line.

2.   Type the following on the new line:

This is paragraph 2

```
<div>
    <h2>This is the page heading</h1>
    <i>This is <b>paragraph 1</b></i>
    This is paragraph 2
</div>
```

3.   Switch to *Design* view.

Both of the pieces of text have been put on the same line, even though they're on different lines in your HTML code. This happens because web browsers ignore white space.

> *This is **paragraph 1*** This is paragraph 2

4.   Switch back to *Source* view and add *<p>* tags to contain both the text: *This is paragraph 1* and *This is paragraph 2* as shown:

<p>*<i>This is paragraph 1</i>***</p>**
<p>*This is paragraph 2***</p>**

```
<div>
    <h2>This is the page heading</h1>
    <p><i>This is <b>paragraph 1</b></i></p>
    <p>This is paragraph 2</p>
</div>
```

5.   Switch back to *Design* view.

The text has now been separated into two paragraphs.

> *This is **paragraph 1***
>
> This is paragraph 2

4   Break up a paragraph with break tags.

Although paragraph tags are useful for breaking text into paragraphs, sometimes you will want to put line breaks inside paragraphs without starting a new paragraph. For this you will use the break tag: *
*

1. Switch to *Source* view.

2. Add the following text on a new line after the two paragraphs:

   <p>Mary had a little lamb
   Its fleece was white as snow
   And everywhere that Mary went
   The lamb was sure to go</p>

   ```
   <div>
       <h2>This is the page heading</h1>
       <p><i>This is <b>paragraph 1</b></i></p>
       <p>This is paragraph 2</p>

       <p>Mary had a little lamb
       Its fleece was white as snow
       And everywhere that Mary went
       The lamb was sure to go</p>
   </div>
   ```

3. Switch to *Design* view.

   Although you've put the text in a paragraph of its own, everything is still on one line inside that paragraph.

   ```
   This is paragraph 1

   This is paragraph 2

   Mary had a little lamb Its fleece was white as snow And eve
   ```

   You might be thinking that you could fix this by putting every line inside a pair of *<p>* tags, but doing that would cause gaps to appear between the lines by default (see sidebar).

   The answer is the break tag. The break tag just inserts a single line break wherever it is placed.

4. Switch to *Source* view and change the text to the following:

   *<p>Mary had a little lamb***
**
   *Its fleece was white as snow***
**
   *And everywhere that Mary went***
**
   The lamb was sure to go</p>

   ```
   <p>Mary had a little lamb<br />
   Its fleece was white as snow<br />
   And everywhere that Mary went<br />
   The lamb was sure to go</p>
   ```

   Note that the break tag is a self-closing tag (see sidebar).

5. Start Debugging.

   Your page should now look like this:

Lesson 2-3: Understand the aspx page structure

note

<% %> Tags

In ASP.NET it is actually possible to place C# code directly onto an HTML web page by putting it between <% and %> tags.

ASP.NET's precursor (simply known as ASP), had no code-behind files, so all of the C# code was put on the aspx page inside <% %> tags.

Since ASP.NET introduced code-behind files, it is rare to see this done today.

trivia

HTML and the W3C

You've probably noticed the link to *w3.org* in the *html* tag. This is the web site of the World Wide Web Consortium or W3C.

The W3C or World Wide Web Consortium is responsible for defining international standards for the Internet.

Before the W3C began to define recognized standards, web browsers often disagreed hugely on the correct way to interpret HTML.

Since the introduction of the W3C's standards there are a lot fewer incompatibilities between browsers.

Newer versions of HTML may appear at any time as the W3C refines and improves the HTML and CSS languages.

Unfortunately, some browsers still don't fully comply with the W3C's standards, so it is still necessary to test your sites thoroughly in every type of browser that you think your users may have.

Although Visual Studio automatically creates the basic elements of an HTML page for you, it's important to understand the purpose of each element.

In this lesson you'll manually create the different parts of a structured HTML web page.

1 Open *HTMLTest* from your sample files folder.

2 Open *emptypage.aspx* in *Source* view.

This page contains only the bare bones of an *.aspx* web page.

3 Understand the *Page* tag.

The first tag is enclosed in <% tags (see sidebar). This line is never sent to web browsers and is used instead to inform ASP.NET which programming language and code-behind file should be used for this page.

```
<%@ Page Language="C#" AutoEventWireup="true" CodeBehi
```

You will never have to change this line during this course.

4 Understand the *DOCTYPE* tag.

The *DOCTYPE* tag is the first thing that a web browser reads. It tells the web browser that this is an HTML file and should be interpreted accordingly.

```
<!DOCTYPE html>
```

Again, you should never have to change this line.

5 Add a *<head>* tag.

The next tags you'll see are opening and closing *<html>* tags. These tell the browser that the code inside the tags is standard HTML code that conforms to W3C standards (see sidebar).

Between the *<html>* and *</html>* tags, add the following:

<head>

</head>

```
<html xmlns="http://www.w3.org/1999/xhtml">
    <head>

    </head>
</html>
```

The *head* tag doesn't contain any of the page's content, but instead is used to store other information about the page. You'll learn more about the *head* tag in: *Lesson 2-4: Use the title, meta, link and script tags*.

6 Add a *<body>* tag.

Everything that you actually see in a web browser is contained between two *body* tags. In the last lesson, all of the text that you added was nested inside the *body* tags.

After the *</head>* line, add the following:

<body>

</body>

```
<html xmlns="http://www.w3.org/1999/xhtml">
    <head>

    </head>
    <body>

    </body>
</html>
```

7   Add a *<form>* tag.

If you look back at *default.aspx*, you'll notice that the only thing missing from this page is the *form* tag. You'll learn more about forms in: *Lesson 2-12: Work with HTML Forms*.

For ASP.NET controls to work correctly, they need to be nested inside *form* tags. The code between the form tags runs on the server (see sidebar).

Since ASP.NET controls will be displayed on the web page, the *form* tag needs to be inside the *body* tags.

Add the following text inside the *body* tag:

<form id="form1" runat="server">

</form>

```
<html xmlns="http://www.w3.org/1999/xhtml">
    <head>

    </head>
    <body>
        <form id="form1" runat="server">

        </form>
    </body>
</html>
```

You've now created the full framework of an ASP.NET web page, capable of using ASP.NET controls and C# code.

Of course, this is normally created automatically when you add a new page to the project.

8   Save your changes and close Visual Studio.

---

note

runat="server"

When an HTML tag is marked with *runat="server"* it becomes available to ASP.NET instead of being a normal 'static' tag.

This means that you can modify its contents using C# code, which you will start doing in: *Lesson 3-1: Change properties with C#*.

For this reason, any ASP.NET controls have to be inside a form with *runat="server"* to work correctly.

Although you could place 'static' HTML content outside the *form* tag, it is best to keep all of your page's content between the *<form>* and *</form>* tags.

ASP.NET will only allow you to have one form with *runat="server"* per page.

You'll learn more about forms in: *Lesson 2-12: Work with HTML Forms*.

Lesson 2-4: Use the title, meta, link and script tags

You created a pair of *<head>* tags in: *Lesson 2-3: Understand the aspx page structure*. These define a head section which contains other tags to define information about the page that is not displayed in the web browser.

In this lesson you'll learn about four of the tags that can be added to the head section: the *title, meta, link* and *script* tags.

1 Open *HTMLTest* from your sample files folder.

2 Open *headtest.aspx* in *Source* view.

This is another empty, bare-bones aspx page.

3 Set the page's title.

1. Click between the *<title>* and *</title>* tags and type: **Head Tags**

2. View the page in your browser.

The page title is picked up by the web browser and is displayed in the page's tab.

3. Close the web browser.

4 Add a favicon using the *link* tag.

1. Add the following tag after the *title* tag:

<link rel="shortcut icon" href="/favicon.ico" />

```
<head runat="server">
    <title>Head Tags</title>
    <link rel="Shortcut Icon" href="/favicon.ico">
</head>
```

2. View the page in your browser.

A 'smiley face' icon should appear next to your page's title. This is called a *favicon*.

Note that the most up-to-date browsers will detect the favicon without needing this tag, but it is still necessary for older browsers. See sidebar if your favicon doesn't appear.

4. Close the web browser.

5 Add a page description using the *meta* tag.

Meta tags are used to provide information about your page to web browsers. They are also often read by search engines to gather information about your page to display in search results.

Add the following tag to your *<head>* tag:

<meta name="description" content="A test page" />

```
<head runat="server">
    <title>Head Tags</title>
    <link rel="Shortcut Icon" href="/favicon.ico">
    <meta name="description" content="A test page" />
</head>
```

note

If your favicon doesn't appear

Older versions of Internet Explorer don't work particularly well with favicons.

If your favicon doesn't appear, try clearing your temporary Internet files and refreshing the page.

After you have cleared your temporary Internet files, try reloading the page and your favicon should appear.

note

Meta tags and search engines

In the 1990's, meta tags were often the only thing indexed by search engines. Because of this they were extremely important to a page's search engine ranking.

In recent years, however, search engines have moved away from meta tags and towards more complex analysis of pages to determine search engine ranking.

Meta tags still shouldn't be ignored, but they no longer have the importance that they once had.

tip

Adding <link> tags by dragging and dropping

You can add a <link> tag very quickly and easily by simply dragging a CSS or JavaScript file from the *Solution Explorer* window into the <head> tag of your HTML code.

Visual Studio will automatically create a <link> tag for the file, saving you a lot of typing!

There are many other meta tags that are used for different purposes. These are usually used to provide enhanced information to search engines (see sidebar).

The contents of meta tags aren't directly visible to site visitors.

6   **Link a CSS stylesheet to the page by using the *link* tag.**

You've seen CSS mentioned briefly a few times. CSS code is used to apply a consistent appearance and layout to web pages across a site.

The *link* tag can be used to add a reference to a CSS stylesheet, allowing its styles to be applied to this page.

1.   Add the following code to your *<head>* tag:

<link rel="stylesheet" href="/styles/allred.css" />

```
<head runat="server">
    <title>Head Tags</title>
    <link rel="Shortcut Icon" href="/favicon.ico">
    <meta name="description" content="A test page" />
    <link rel="stylesheet" href="/styles/allred.css" />
</head>
```

2.   View the page in your browser.

Linking the page to the stylesheet makes the background of your page turn red! *allred.css* is a very basic stylesheet. You'll learn how to create more interesting stylesheets in: *Lesson 2-8: Work with CSS.*

3.   Close the web browser.

7   **Link a JavaScript file to the page by using the *script* tag.**

In *Lesson 1-10: View .aspx pages in Source and Design views,* you might have read the sidebar explaining that there are three main languages understood by web browsers. The first two are HTML and CSS. The only language that you haven't yet seen in action is JavaScript.

1.   Add the following text to your *<head>* tag:

<script type="text/javascript" src="/scripts/alert.js"></script>

```
<head runat="server">
    <title>Head Tags</title>
    <link rel="Shortcut Icon" href="/favicon.ico">
    <meta name="description" content="A test page" />
    <link rel="stylesheet" href="/styles/allred.css" />
    <script type="text/javascript" src="/scripts/alert.js"></script>
</head>
```

Note that *script* tags cannot be self-closing. You must have an opening *<script>* and a closing *</script>* tag for them to work.

2.   View the page in your browser.

This time a popup window appears when the page loads.

Making messages appear in popups is only one of the most basic things that JavaScript can do. You'll learn a little more about JavaScript in: *Lesson 2-11: Work with JavaScript.*

Lesson 2-5: Create an HTML table

Another important feature of HTML is the ability to create tables. If you've ever worked with Microsoft Excel, you should be familiar with tables of data laid out in a series of rows and columns.

In this lesson, you'll learn how to create an HTML table, both automatically and by manually hand-writing code.

1 Open *HTMLTest* from your sample files folder.

2 Open *tabletest.aspx* in *Design* view.

3 Automatically create a table using the design tools.

   1. Click Table→Insert Table.

   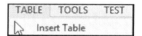

   The *Insert Table* dialog appears.

   2. Click *OK*, without changing any settings.

   A table appears, outlined in dotted lines.

   3. Click in each of the table's four cells and fill them in as shown:

   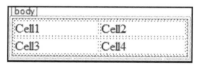

4 Add a row to the table using HTML.

   1. Switch to *Source* view.

   You can see that the table is made up of 3 different HTML tags: *<table>*, *<tr>* and *<td>*.

   The *<tr>* and *<td>* tags define table rows and table cells. They must be contained in a *table* tag to be recognized as part of a table.

```
<table class="auto-style1">
    <tr>
        <td>Cell1</td>
        <td>Cell2</td>
    </tr>
    <tr>
        <td>Cell3</td>
        <td>Cell4</td>
    </tr>
</table>
```

   As you can see, the text that you added is all contained in the *<td>* tags and is broken into rows with *<tr>* tags.

   2. Add some blank space before the *</table>* tag.

   3. Add the following code in the space:

   <tr>
       <td>Cell5</td>
       <td>Cell6</td>
   </tr>

```
        <td>Cell4</td>
    </tr>
    <tr>
        <td>Cell5</td>
        <td>Cell6</td>
    </tr>
</table>
```

note

The style tag

You probably noticed that when you created the table using *Design* view, a *style* tag was added to your page's *head* tag, setting a *width* property to 100%.

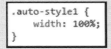

```
.auto-style1 {
    width: 100%;
}
```

This happened because the *Insert Table* dialog's *Specify width* setting was left at default.

Because you specified a width of 100%, a CSS style called *auto-style1* was created. The table's *class* property was then set to reference the *auto-style1* style.

```
<table class="auto-style1">
```

You'll learn more about CSS in: *Lesson 2-8: Work with CSS*.

Remember that you can use automatic formatting to automatically reformat the table code if it is messy. You learned how to do this in: *Lesson 1-11: Use automatic formatting*.

4. Switch back to *Design* view.

   A new row has been added containing the cells *Cell5* and *Cell6*.

   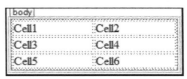

5 **Merge cells in *Design* view.**

   1. Click and drag from *Cell1* to *Cell2* so that both cells are highlighted.

      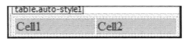

   2. Click Table→Modify→Merge Cells.

      The top two cells are merged into one big cell.

   3. Replace the text in the top cell with: **TitleCell**

   4. Switch back to *Source* view.

      You can see that the cell has been merged by changing it into a single *td* tag with a *colspan* property of 2, because it spans two table columns.

      ```
      <td colspan="2">
          TitleCell
      </td>
      ```

6 **Make *TitleCell* into a heading cell.**

   There is a special tag for table headings: the *<th>* tag.

   1. Change the *<td>* and *</td>* tags for *TitleCell* into *<th>* and *</th>* tags.

      ```
      <th colspan="2">
          TitleCell
      </th>
      ```

   2. Switch back to *Design* view.

      The *<th>* tag makes its contents bold and centered.

      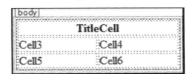

Lesson 2-6: Navigate HTML with the tag navigator

As you have learned already in this session, HTML is made up of a series of tags that are nested inside each other.

In large HTML files, it can become increasingly difficult to relate what you see in *Design* view to the code in *Source* view. Fortunately, Visual Studio provides you with the tag navigator, which shows at a glance which tag you have selected and which tags it is nested inside.

1   Open *HTMLTest* from your sample files folder.

2   Open *tabletest.aspx* in *Design* view.

3   Navigate nested tags using the tag navigator.

    1. Click in one of your table's cells.

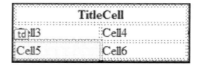

       The tag navigator should appear at the bottom of the screen.

       If the tag navigator doesn't appear, close any browser windows you have open and try closing and reopening *tabletest.aspx*.

       The navigator shows you which tag you currently have selected and the hierarchy of the tags it is nested inside.

       You can see that the *td* tag you have selected is nested inside a *tr* tag, which is inside a *table* tag, which is inside a *div* tag, which is inside a *form* tag, which is inside the *body* tag, which is inside the *html* tag.

    2. Select the entire table row using the tag navigator.

       You can select any of the tags in the navigator by clicking on them. Click on the *<tr>* button to select the whole table row.

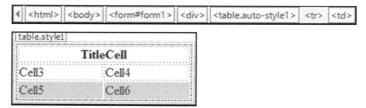

       Now the entire row is selected. If this doesn't work for you, try clicking the <td> button again followed by the <tr> button.

       Notice as well that the *<tr>* tag is now selected in the *Properties* window (if your properties window has disappeared you need to reset your window layout to default as described in: *Lesson 1-3: Set up the development environment*).

3. Select the entire table using the tag navigator.

Click the *<table.auto-style1>* tag in the tag navigator to select the entire table.

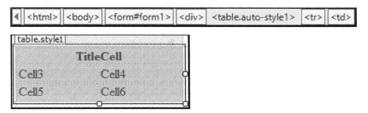

Again, you can see that the *table* tag is selected in the *Properties* window, ready for you to change its properties.

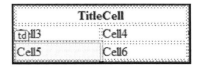

4 Select only a tag's content using the tag navigator.

1. Click on *Cell5*.

2. Hover your mouse cursor over the *<tr>* button in the tag navigator.

You'll notice that a black down arrow appears to the right of the button. This indicates that there is a drop-down menu.

3. Click the down arrow next to *<tr>* and then click *Select Tag Content* from the drop-down menu.

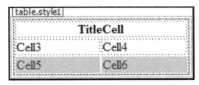

Now only the text inside the *<tr>* tag is selected.

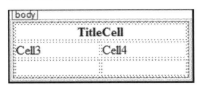

4. Press *<Delete>*.

The contents of the cells are deleted, but the cells themselves are left intact.

75

---

note

Deleting

A lot of Visual Studio's interface is standardized across the application. Deleting is a good example.

Pressing the *<Delete>* key will delete whatever you currently have selected, whether it is a control in *Design* view or a file in the *Solution Explorer*.

The same is true if you right-click and then click *Delete* from the shortcut menu.

Lesson 2-7: Display images and links on a page

With the skills you've learned so far in this session, you're close to being able to create useful HTML pages.

This lesson will show you how to add hyperlinks and images to a page.

1   Open *HTMLTest* from your sample files folder.

2   Open *linktest.aspx* in *Design* view.

3   Create a link in *Design* view.

   1.   Type the following text onto the page:

        The Smart Method

   2.   Select the text either by clicking and dragging or by using the tag navigator to select the *div* tag's content (you learned how to do this in: *Lesson 2-6: Navigate HTML with the tag navigator*).

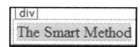

   3.   Click Format→Convert to Hyperlink....

        A dialog appears.

   4.   Type **http://www.aspnetcentral.com** into the dialog and click *OK*.

   5.   View *linktest.aspx* in your browser and try clicking on the link.

        The ASPNETCentral.com web site home page appears.

   6.   Close the browser and return to *Design* view.

4   Change the link's properties using *Design* view.

   1.   Click on your link in *Design* view.

        The *Properties* window should display *<A>* as its selected object. The *<a>* tag is used to define an HTML hyperlink.

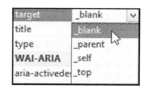

   2.   Change the *target* property of the link to **_blank** using the *Properties* window.

        You'll notice that the *target* property has a drop-down menu. It is quicker to choose *_blank* from the drop-down list than to type it in manually

   3.   View the page in your browser and click on the link.

        This time the link opens in a new browser tab (or a new window if you are using an older browser).

5   Add a link in *Source* view.

   1.   Close your browser and switch to *Source* view.

2. After the pair of <a></a> tags that define the hyperlink to *The Smart Method,* add the following hyperlink code:

<a href="http://www.excelcentral.com">
Learn Excel</a>

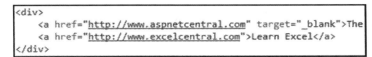

3. Switch back to *Design* view.

The HTML tag that you added has created a new link.

6 Add an image in *Design* view.

In the same way as you did in *Lesson 1-15: Add controls to a page with the Toolbox,* drag an *Image* control from the *HTML* category of the *Toolbox* onto the page, below the two links.

7 Set the image path in *Design* view.

1. Select the I*mage* control and find the *src* property in the *Properties* window.

   If the *src* property is not visible, it is because you have either added a standard image control instead of an HTML image control or because you have placed the image control inside the hyperlink *<a>* tags.

2. Click the *browse* icon next to the *src* property (⋯) and select *balloon.jpg* from the *images* folder.

3. Click *OK.*

The image now appears on the page. Notice that the *src* property has been set to *images/balloon.jpg.* This is the *path* to the image (see sidebar).

8 Change the image path in *Source* view.

1. Switch to *Source* view.

2. Change the *src* property of the *img* tag to: **images/pattern.jpg**

   ```
   <img alt="" src="images/pattern.jpg" />
   ```

3. Switch back to *Design* view.

   The image has changed to display *pattern.jpg.*

You should now have a good idea of how to change properties using both the *Design* and *Source* views.

9 Save your changes and close Visual Studio.

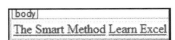

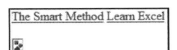

note

Paths

If you're a seasoned Windows and Internet user, you probably understand that paths are used to tell computers which folder a file is in.

In this lesson, the images that you need to display are in the *images* folder, so the path begins with *images.*

If an image called *image.jpg* was in a sub-folder of *images* called *photos,* the path would be:

images/photos/image.jpg

HTML paths are always relative to the current location of the page. If your page was in a folder called *pages,* you'd need to use the following path to get to the *images* folder:

../images/image.jpg

../ in a path means to go up one level (ie to the folder that this folder is in).

If paths are getting confusing, using the browse feature, as you do in this lesson, will always return the correct path.

Lesson 2-8: Work with CSS

note

Most developers are not CSS experts

As only very basic CSS will be covered in this book, you might not feel entirely confident that you understand it fully.

The important thing to take from the CSS lessons is an appreciation of how a professional web designer uses CSS to design attractive and consistent web pages. You do not need an in-depth understanding of CSS in order to work through the rest of this course.

Journalists do not get involved with the page layouts of newspapers. This is left to typesetters and page layout artists. But the journalist still needs to know what is possible.

In the same way it isn't essential for a web developer to cultivate extensive web design skills. A reasonable knowledge of how the technologies work will suffice.

note

CSS can also be used to create page layouts

You've already discovered HTML tables. Before the advent of CSS most web designers used HTML tables (usually with invisible borders) to arrange their pages neatly into columns.

There is now a new way of arranging page elements that relies entirely upon CSS properties.

Most web designers have now abandoned the earlier table-based layouts and create their layouts entirely with CSS.

CSS is the language that is used to define the styles of elements on modern web pages. CSS has over a hundred different properties that you can use to define styles and many different CSS techniques are used to create the pages that you see on the Internet.

Covering every CSS property and technique would be the subject matter for an entire book in itself, but you will briefly cover some of the most important ones in this lesson.

1   Open *HTMLTest* from your sample files folder.

2   Open *csstest.aspx* in *Source* view.

3   Link the *csstest.css* stylesheet from the *styles* folder.

Add the following tag to the page's head section (anywhere in the area between the *<head>* and *</head>* tags):

<link rel="Stylesheet" href="/styles/csstest.css" />

4   Create a CSS class.

CSS classes are ways of grouping style properties together in CSS and giving them a name. Elements on your page can then be referenced to the name of the class in order to use its styles.

1.   Double-click on *csstest.css* in the *styles* folder to open it for editing. Note that the file is currently empty.

2.   Add the following code to the CSS file:

```
.BigText
{
    font-size: xx-large;
}
```

You have just created a CSS class called *BigText* that makes the text of any HTML tag that references it extra, extra large.

5   Assign the BigText class to an HTML tag.

You've created a CSS class, but you need to assign it to an element on the page before it will affect anything.

1.   Open *csstest.aspx* in *Source* view.

2.   Change the line that says *<div id="Div1">* to the following:

<div id="Div1" class="BigText">

```
<div id="Div1" class="BigText">
    <p>Paragraph 1</p>
    <p>Paragraph 2</p>
    <p>Paragraph 3</p>
</div>
```

Note that CSS class names are case sensitive, so *bigtext* will not work.

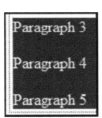

3. Switch to *Design* view.

    The text of all of the elements nested inside *Div1* has been made extra, extra large by your CSS class.

6   **Create a CSS identifier.**

    Identifiers are similar to classes, but instead of using the *class* property they automatically attach themselves to any element with the same *ID* property. It is easier to understand identifiers by seeing them in action:

    1. Open *csstest.css*.

    2. Add the following CSS code:

        #Div2
        {
            color: White;
            background-color: Blue;
        }

        ```
        .BigText
        {
            font-size: xx-large;
        }

        #Div2
        {
            color: White;
            background-color: Blue;
        }
        ```

    3. Switch back to *csstest.aspx* in *Design* view.

        The *#Div2* identifier has set the text color to white and the background color to blue for all elements within the div tag that has its ID property set to *Div2*.

7   **Use inline CSS.**

    Although it's best practice to keep all of your CSS styles in separate CSS files, you can also place CSS code directly into the *style* property of an HTML tag.

    1. Switch back to the *Source* view of *csstest.aspx*.

    2. Change the code of *<p>Paragraph 1</p>* to the following:

        <p style="font-size: xx-small">Paragraph 1</p>

        ```
        <div id="Div1" class="BigText">
            <p style="font-size: xx-small">Paragraph 1</p>
            <p>Paragraph 2</p>
            <p>Paragraph 3</p>
        </div>
        ```

    3. Switch back to *Design* view.

        Paragraph 1 now has smaller text than the other paragraphs.

        Inline CSS always overrides any styles that are set by the *class* property.

    ASP.NET often automatically generates inline CSS styles when converting ASP.NET controls into HTML code.

Lesson 2-9: Use the CSS Properties window

To make it easier to work with CSS, Visual Studio provides the *CSS Properties* window.

By using it in *Design* view, you can very easily create and modify CSS styles.

1 Open *HTMLTest* from your sample files folder.

2 Open *csstest.aspx* in *Design* view.

3 Display the *CSS Properties* window.

Click View→CSS Properties.

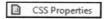

4 Modify the *BigText* style using the CSS Properties window.

1. Select *Div1* using the drop-down menu in the *Properties* window (the normal *Properties* window, not the *CSS Properties* window).

The *.BigText* style that you created in *Lesson 2-8: Work with CSS* is shown in the *Applied Rules* box at the top of the *CSS Properties* window. It also shows that *BigText* comes from the *csstest.css* file.

Towards the top of the *CSS Properties* list, you can see the *font-size* property, which is part of the *.BigText* CSS class.

Beneath *font-size*, you can see a complete list of the CSS properties that are available. You can use the *CSS Properties* window to set them just like you set properties in the *Properties* window.

2. Using the drop-down menu in *CSS Properties*, change the *font-size* from **xx-large** to **xx-small**.

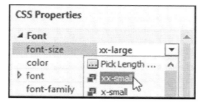

The change appears immediately in the *Design* panel.

note

CSS 3

At the time of writing, there are three versions of CSS, with CSS3 being the latest version.

Visual Studio 2012 is the first version of Visual Studio to support CSS3 properties.

CSS3 enables some new properties, such as the *opacity* property.

While CSS3 is now well supported by the most up-to-date browsers, older browsers may be unable to deal with CSS3.

All of the properties that you will work with in this book are compliant with CSS2, meaning that they should be supported by just about any web browser.

3. Open *csstest.css* from the *styles* folder.

   Here you can see that the *.BigText* class has been automatically changed.

5 **Add a new style using the CSS Properties window.**

1. Open *csstest.aspx* in Design view.

2. Select *Div1* using the drop-down menu in the *Properties* window (if it isn't selected already).

3. **Either**

   Clear the *Class* property in the *Properties* window.

   Or

   Right-click on *.BigText* in the *Applied Rules* section of the *CSS Properties* window and then click *Remove Class* from the shortcut menu.

   This removes the reference to *.BigText* from *Div1*. The text returns to its normal size except for the first line.

4. Right-click in the *Applied Rules* box in the *CSS Properties* window and then click *New Style...* from the shortcut menu.

   The *New Style* dialog appears.

5. Enter **.RedText** into the *Selector* box (be careful not to enter two dots by mistake as the dialog doesn't select the existing dot).

   This is the name of your new CSS class, which will work in exactly the same way as the *BigText* class you created in: *Lesson 2-8: Work with CSS.*

6. Choose *Existing style sheet* from the *Define in* drop-down.

   This tells the dialog that you want to create your style in an existing *.css* file instead of creating another one or creating an inline style.

7. Choose *styles/csstest.css* from the *URL* drop-down.

8. Choose *Red* from the *color* drop-down.

9. Click *OK*.

   The text in *Div1* is now displayed in red.

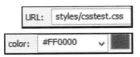

10. Open *csstest.css*.

    A new *.RedText* class has been automatically created with the color property that you selected.

Lesson 2-10: Use the div and span tags

In *Lesson 2-8: Work with CSS* you applied a CSS style to *div* tags, but you might be wondering exactly what a *div* is.

Div and *span* tags (which will be covered in this lesson) are used as containers for your page's content in order to apply a CSS style to multiple elements. In this lesson, you'll work with the *div* tag and its partner the *span* tag.

1   Open *HTMLTest* from your sample files folder.

2   Open *divspantest.aspx* in *Source* view.

3   Add two *div* tags containing some text.

    1.   Add the following HTML in the space between the *form* tags:

      \<div id="Div1">Div1\</div>
      \<div id="Div2">Div2\</div>

```
<form id="form1" runat="server">
    <div id="Div1">Div1</div>
    <div id="Div2">Div2</div>
</form>
```

    2.   Switch to *Design* view.

      The two *div* tags are displayed, but they are on separate lines despite the fact that you didn't use any *p* or *br* tags. This is because the *div* tag automatically starts a new line after its closing tag.

      You'll also notice that both of the *div* tags have picked up a background color. This is because there is a CSS stylesheet linked to this page (*divspantest.css*) that defines styles for any tag with the ID property *Div1* or *Div2*. Later in this lesson you will edit the *divspantest.css* stylesheet.

4   Add two *span* tags with text.

    1.   Switch back to *Source* view and add the following HTML after the two *div* tags:

      \Span1
      \Span2

```
<form id="form1" runat="server">
    <div id="Div1">Div1</div>
    <div id="Div2">Div2</div>
    <span>Span1</span>
    <span>Span2</span>
</form>
```

    2.   Switch to *Design* view.

      The pieces of text held in the *span* tags are shown side by side. Unlike *div*, the *span* tag doesn't add any line breaks automatically.

note

Measurements in pixels (px)

You might be wondering what the *px* means at the end of some CSS properties. *px* is short for *pixels*.

As you might be aware, your computer screen is made up of thousands of tiny dots called *pixels*. These measurements tell the user's web browser how to display your page using pixels as a measurement unit.

This can cause problems however, as different users might have more or fewer pixels displayed on their screen. A user with more pixels would see everything appear smaller.

To stretch a site to the size of the user's screen, you can use percentage measurements by using % in place of *px*.

There are also two other measurements called *em* and *pt* which are used to set sizes relative to the font in use.

5   Use CSS to set the size of the *Div2* element.

1.   Open *divspantest.css* from the *styles* folder.

Here you can see the CSS identifiers that have already been created for *Div1* and *Div2*.

```
#Div1
{
     background-color: Yellow;
}

#Div2
{
     background-color: Orange;
}
```

2.   Add the following CSS code to the #*Div2* identifier:

width: 300px;
height: 300px;

```
#Div1
{
     background-color: Yellow;
}

#Div2
{
     background-color: Orange;
     width: 300px;
     height: 300px;
}
```

Switch back to *divspantest.aspx* and you'll see that the *Div2* box has increased in size thanks to your CSS.

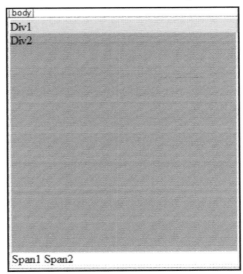

Most modern web sites use a combination of *div* and *span* tags with CSS to create their layouts and style their content.

Some ASP.NET controls automatically create *div* and *span* tags. You'll see this in action in: *Lesson 3-1: Change properties with C#.*

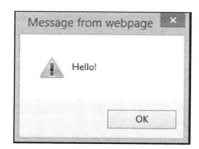

Lesson 2-11: Work with JavaScript

As well as HTML and CSS, the remaining language recognized by a web browser is JavaScript. JavaScript is code that can be used to add interactive features to web pages without having to obtain information from the server. For this reason it is called client-side code (in IT terminology a browser is referred to as a "client").

Although you won't need to write any JavaScript code in order to create basic ASP.NET sites, it's important that you can recognize it when you see it as ASP.NET can automatically add JavaScript code to *aspx* pages.

1 Open *HTMLTest* from your sample files folder.

2 Open *scripttest.aspx* in *Source* view.

You can see that a link to *scripttest.js* has already been added to this page.

```
<script type="text/javascript" src="/scripts/scripttest.js"></script>
```

3 Add some inline JavaScript code.

In the same way as CSS, you can add JavaScript directly to the page instead of keeping it in a separate file. But just like with CSS, it is best practice to keep your JavaScript code in separate files.

1. Add the following code to the *head* tag, under the existing *script* tag pair:

    <script type="text/javascript">
    alert("Hello!");
    </script>

    ```
    <head runat="server">
        <title></title>
        <link rel="Stylesheet" href="/s
        <script type="text/javascript"
        <script type="text/javascript">
            alert("Hello!");
        </script>
    </head>
    ```

2. View *scripttest.aspx* in your browser (*Design* view isn't capable of executing JavaScript).

    You should see your message pop up on the screen. This is one of the most basic JavaScript functions.

3. Close your browser and remove the JavaScript code that you just added.

4 Assign a JavaScript function to an HTML tag's onclick event.

1. Return to *scripttest.aspx* in *Source* view.

2. Change the code of *<div id="Button">* to:

    <div id="Button" **onclick="ClickMessage()">**

    ```
    <div id="Button" onclick="ClickMessage()">
        Click Me!
    </div>
    ```

note

ASP.NET and JavaScript

Many of ASP.NET's special functions are accomplished using JavaScript, but you might never know this as it's all generated automatically behind the scenes.

Although there's a lot more to know about JavaScript, the basic understanding provided by this lesson will enable you to complete and understand all of the lessons in this book.

note

Client-Side and Server-Side

JavaScript is *Client-Side* code. This means that it runs on the computer of the person visiting your web site, not on the web server that is hosting your web site.

Because JavaScript is client-side, you can never rely on it running: the visitor might have disabled JavaScript in their browser settings.

The C# code that you'll be learning later on is *Server-Side* and can't be directly interfered with by visitors to your site.

3. View the page in your browser.

4. Click the *Click Me!* Button.

> ⚠ Clicked!

A message pops up as before. This message was displayed by the *ClickMessage* function in the *scripttest.js* file. You'll examine the *ClickMessage* function in a moment.

By adding the function's name to the div's *onclick* property, you've made it run when the div is clicked.

5 Change colors with JavaScript.

1. Close your browser and open the *scripttest.js* file from the *scripts* folder.

Here you can see the *ClickMessage* JavaScript function.

```
function ClickMessage() {
    alert("Clicked!");
}
```

2. Replace the line *alert("Clicked!");* with:

**document.getElementById("Button")
.setAttribute("style", "background-color: red;");**

```
function ClickMessage() {
    document.getElementById("Button")
    .setAttribute("style", "background-color: red;");
}
```

This might seem like a complicated piece of code, but if you break it down into its components it's not so difficult.

document.getElementById("Button")
This tells JavaScript to search the page for an element with an ID of *Button*. The blue *div* on the page is called *Button*, so it will find that.

setAttribute("style", "background-color: red;");
This tells JavaScript to set the *style* property of the tag to *background-color: red;*. You used the *style* property in *Lesson 2-8: Work with CSS*.

You've already set the *ClickMessage()* function to run when the *div* is clicked. When the user clicks on the *div*, the JavaScript will change the div's HTML code to the following:

*<div id="Button" **style="background-color: red;"** onclick="ClickMessage()">Click Me!</div>*

3. View *scripttest.aspx* in your browser.

4. Click on the *Click Me!* div.

The color of the div changes when it is clicked.

> Click Me!

6 Save your changes and close Visual Studio.

Lesson 2-12: Work with HTML Forms

HTML forms are the only mechanism available in HTML that is able to send information to the web server. All of the buttons and text boxes you've added in previous lessons have been *form controls*.

HTML forms are relatively simple, but they are the backbone of ASP.NET.

1   Open *HTMLTest* from your sample files folder.

2   Open *formstest.html* in *Design* view.

A *.html* file is a pure HTML file that doesn't contain any of ASP.NET's special features. Browsers will recognize HTML files with both the *.htm* and *.html* file extensions but *.html* is the file extension favored by Visual Studio 2012.

You should recognize the design as an HTML table with some text in the cells. This is going to be your form.

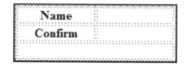

3   Add an HTML Text input control.

1.   Add an *Input (Text)* control from the *HTML* category of the *Toolbox* to the cell to the right of *Name*.

The *Input (Text)* control is the HTML equivalent of the ASP.NET *TextBox* control, which you'll learn about in: *Lesson 4-4: Use the TextBox control.*

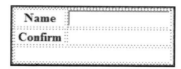

2.   Set the *name* property of the new control to: **Name**

The *name* property is used to identify the data that will be sent by the form (see sidebar).

4   Add an HTML Checkbox input control.

1.   In the same way as you did in the last step, add an *Input (Checkbox)* control in the cell next to *Confirm*.

The *Input (Checkbox)* control is the HTML equivalent of the ASP.NET *CheckBox* control, which you'll learn about in: *Lesson 4-5: Use the CheckBox control.*

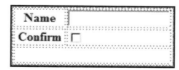

2.   Set the *Name* property of the new checkbox to: **Confirm**

5   Add an HTML Submit input control.

Add an *Input (Submit)* control from the *HTML* category of the *Toolbox* to the bottom cell of the table.

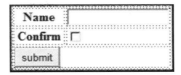

The *Input (Submit)* HTML control is used to send the contents of the form to the server. It's the equivalent of the ASP.NET *Button* control, which you'll learn more about in: *Lesson 4-2: Use the Button control.*

6   Set the *action* property of the form.

1.   Switch to *Source* view.

   As you can see, there are no *asp* elements on this page at all. This is a pure HTML page that could be served by any web server to any web browser (see sidebar).

2.   Set the *action* property of the *form* tag to: **formsubmit.aspx**

   You can do this by adding the property to the tag using the code **action="formsubmit.aspx"** or by clicking on the *form* tag and using the *Properties* window to set the *action* property.

The *action* property tells the form where to send the data that the user has entered when the submit button is clicked.

formsubmit.aspx is an ASP.NET page that will process the data and display it.

When using aspx pages, you'll never need to manually set the *action* property. You'll learn more about how ASP.NET sends and receives data in: *Lesson 3-11: Send data between pages.*

7   Submit the form.

1.   View *formstest.html* in your browser.

2.   Complete the form and click *submit*.

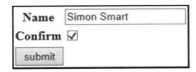

   You are redirected to *formsubmit.aspx*, which receives the data that you entered and displays it.

   Your name is: *Simon Smart*
   You ticked *confirm*.

Almost everything that ASP.NET does revolves around this system of HTML forms sending data to the web server. Visual Studio generates most of the HTML code that makes this work automatically, but with the knowledge you've gained from this lesson you should be able to understand what it is doing behind the scenes.

Session 2: Exercise

1   Open *exercise.aspx* within the *HTMLTest* sample project in *Source* view.

2   Set the page title in the head section to: **Session 2 Exercise**

3   Add a link to the CSS file called *layout.css*. It can be found in the *styles* folder.

4   Add a pair of *div* tags to the page (between the *form* tags).

5   Type the text **Site Name** between the *div* tags.

6   Set the *class* property of the *div* tag to the CSS class: **header**

7   Switch to *Design* view and add an HTML table to bottom of the page using the default settings.

8   Remaining in *Design* view, merge the bottom two cells of the HTML table.

9   In the first cell of the HTML table, type the text: **Site**

10   Switch to *Source* view and make the *Site* text bold using HTML tags.

11   Switch to *Design* view and type the text: **ASPNETCentral Website** into the top-right table cell.

12   Make the text you have just typed into a hyperlink to: **http://www.ASPNETCentral.com**

13   Add an HTML Image control to the bottom row of the table and configure it to display the *pattern.jpg* image from the *images* folder.

14   Using the *CSS Properties* window, set the *color* CSS property of the *Site Name* text to: **White**

15   Add a link to the JavaScript file *exercise.js*. It can be found in the *scripts* folder.

16   Add JavaScript code to *exercise.js* to display a pop-up message.

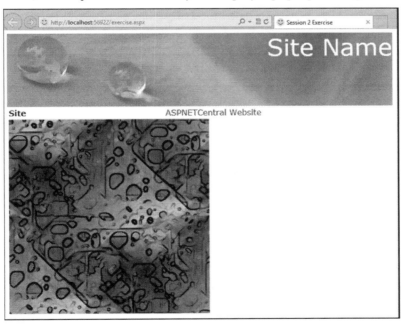

HTMLTest - start   HTMLTest - end

If you need help slide the page to the left

Session 2: Exercise Answers

These are the four questions that students find the most difficult to answer:

Q 14	Q 8	Q 7	Q 6
1. Switch to *Design* view. 2. Click on the *header* div so it is highlighted. *<DIV>* should appear as the selected item in the *Properties* window. 3. Click View→ CSS Properties. 4. Open the drop-down menu next to *color* in the *CSS Properties* window and click the white box. This was covered in: *Lesson 2-9: Use the CSS Properties window.*	1. Switch to *Design* view. 2. Click and drag from the bottom-left cell of the table to the bottom right, so they are both highlighted. 3. Click Table→Modify→ Merge Cells. This was covered in: *Lesson 2-5: Create an HTML table.*	1. Switch to *Design* view. 2. Click below the *header* div. 3. Click Table→ Insert Table. 4. Click OK on the dialog that appears. This was covered in: *Lesson 2-5: Create an HTML table.*	1. Switch to *Source* view. 2. Modify the *div* tag to: **<div class="header">** **Site Name** **</div>** This was covered in: *Lesson 2-10: Use the div and span tags.*

If you have difficulty with the other questions, here are the lessons that cover the relevant skills:

1   Refer to: Lesson 1-7: Manage a project with the Solution Explorer.

2   Refer to: Lesson 2-4: Use the title, meta, link and script tags.

3   Refer to: Lesson 2-4: Use the title, meta, link and script tags.

4   Refer to: Lesson 2-10: Use the div and span tags.

5   Refer to: Lesson 2-10: Use the div and span tags.

9   Refer to: Lesson 2-5: Create an HTML table.

10   Refer to: Lesson 2-1: Understand HTML bold, italic and heading tags.

11   Refer to: Lesson 2-5: Create an HTML table.

12   Refer to: Lesson 2-7: Display images and links on a page.

13   Refer to: Lesson 2-7: Display images and links on a page.

15   Refer to: Lesson 2-4: Use the title, meta, link and script tags.

16   Refer to: Lesson 2-11: Work with JavaScript.

Session Three: ASP.NET Web Pages

> You cannot open a book without learning something.
>
> *Confucius, Chinese philosopher (551BC – 479BC)*

At this point you have a good grounding in how HTML, CSS and JavaScript are all interpreted by a web browser in order to display a web page.

In this session you'll see how ASP.NET integrates with HTML, CSS and JavaScript to create exciting interactive web sites.

You'll also write your first C# code in this session.

Session Objectives

By the end of this session you will be able to:

- Change properties with C#
- Add event handlers to Controls
- Use Breakpoints
- Use Watches and Locals
- Understand the Exception object
- Understand the Page object
- Understand Request and Response
- Understand PostBack
- Work with ViewState
- Move between pages using C#
- Send data between pages
- Use Session
- Edit the Web.config file

note

default.aspx .designer.cs

You've probably noticed that when you expand an .aspx file, there's a file called *[filename].aspx.designer.cs* as well as *[filename].aspx.cs*.

This file is used by the *Design* view of the Visual Studio interface. All of the code inside it is automatically generated and you will never have to edit it.

important

C# and semicolons (;)

You'll notice that the line of code you add in this example ends in a semi-colon.

Semi-colons are required by C# to indicate the end of a line of code. You might have noticed in *Lesson 2-11: Work with JavaScript* that JavaScript uses the same convention.

You'll notice, however, that the code that defines the method doesn't have a semi-colon at the end of it.

Lines that 'contain' other code using *{* and *}* don't need semi-colons because the *{* and *}* define the area they affect.

Because C# doesn't consider a line of code to be finished until it sees a semi-colon, you can split a long line of code onto multiple lines without causing any problems.

If you are not completing the course incrementally use the sample file: **Lesson 3-1** to begin this lesson.

Sample files with the starting point for each lesson are also provided for all of the other lessons in this session.

Lesson 3-1: Change properties with C#

You've already worked with HTML controls and briefly viewed ASP.NET's code-behind files.

In this lesson, you'll use some very basic C# code to change the properties of controls on a web page.

1 Open *CSharpTest* from your sample files folder.

2 Open *default.aspx* in *Design* view.

3 Add a *Label* control from the *Standard* category of the *Toolbox*.

4 Set the *ID* property of the new *Label* control to: **LabelOutput**

5 Open the code-behind file of *default.aspx*

You learned how to do this in: *Lesson 1-7: Manage a project with the Solution Explorer.*

6 Add some code to set the *Text* property of the new label.

You can see the C# code that goes with *default.aspx* on this page. At the moment, the important part is:

protected void Page_Load(object sender, EventArgs e)
{
}

```
protected void Page_Load(object sender, EventArgs e)
{

}
```

This is a *method*. Methods are the way that C# code is organized into pieces that can be run individually.

The *Page_Load* method is an *event handler*. An event handler is a special type of method that runs in response to something happening. In this case the event that triggers the event handler is the page loading. You'll learn more about event handlers in: *Lesson 3-2: Add event handlers to controls.*

The *{* and *}* symbols show where the method begins and ends. Everything between the *{* and *}* is part of the method. As you can see, at the moment the method is empty.

1. Add the following line of C# code in the gap between the *{* and *}*.

   LabelOutput.Text = "Hello world!";

```
protected void Page_Load(object sender, EventArgs e)
{
    LabelOutput.Text = "Hello world!";
}
```

Hello world!

2. View the page in your browser.

The *Text* property of the *Label* control is changed by your C# code when the page loads, and *Hello world!* is displayed.

7 Examine what ASP.NET has done.

1. View *default.aspx* in your browser, if it isn't visible already.

2. View the source of the page.

   To do this in *Internet Explorer*, right-click on the page and then click *View Source* from the shortcut menu.

   You should see a line of code that says:

   <span id="LabelOutput">Hello world!</span>

   ```
   <div>

       <span id="LabelOutput">Hello world!</span>

   </div>
   ```

3. Close your browser and return to *default.aspx* in *Source* view.

   Compare the *Label* code here. It should say:

   <asp:Label ID="LabelOutput" runat="server" Text="Label">
   </asp:Label>

   ```
   <asp:Label ID="LabelOutput" runat="server" Text="Label"></asp:Label>
   ```

When a user requests your page, the web server converts the *asp:* controls into HTML code that their web browser can understand. In this case, the *<asp:Label>* control is converted into a set of HTML *<span>* tags.

The real power of ASP.NET is in the use of event handlers and C# code to change the properties of elements on the page in response to user interaction, making pages interactive.

8 Add some code to make the Label control's text bold.

1. Switch back to *default.aspx.cs* (the code-behind file).

2. Add the following line of code on the next line of the *Page_Load* event handler:

   LabelOutput.Font.Bold = true;

   ```
   protected void Page_Load(object sender, EventArgs e)
   {
       LabelOutput.Text = "Hello world!";
       LabelOutput.Font.Bold = true;
   }
   ```

   This piece of code is a little different to the last one (see sidebar).

3. View the page in your browser.

   Your C# code makes the text bold.

   Hello world!

Lesson 3-2: Add event handlers to controls

An *event handler* is a piece of code that is triggered by something happening. In the last lesson you worked with the *Page_Load* event, which runs whenever a page loads.

In this lesson you'll add some more event handlers to the page.

tip

Creating event handlers by double-clicking

You can create an event handler very quickly by simply double-clicking a control. This will automatically create an event handler for the control's default event.

All controls have a default event, representing the event that is most often used by that control.

In the case of the *Button* control, the default event is *Click*. This means you can easily add a *Click* event handler to a *Button* control by simply double-clicking it.

1   Open *CSharpTest* from your sample files folder.

2   Open *default.aspx* in *Design* view.

3   Add a *Button* control from the *Standard* category of the *Toolbox*.

Place it after the *Label* control that you added in: *Lesson 3-1: Change properties with C#.*

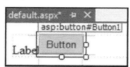

4   Set the *ID* property of the new button to: **ButtonChangeText**

5   Add a *Click* event handler to the button.

   1.   Make sure that you are in *Design* view.

   2.   Select the *Button* control so that *ButtonChangeText* appears in the *Properties* window.

   3.   Click the *events* button 🗲 in the *Properties* window.

      It can be found just below the drop-down menu.

      You will see a list of the possible events for the *Button* control.

   4.   Double-click in the empty box next to *Click*.

      You are taken to the code-behind file of *default.aspx,* where some code has been automatically added:

```
protected void ButtonChangeText_Click(object sender, EventArgs e)
{

}
```

      This is the *event handler* for the button's *click* event. When the button is clicked, any code between the { and } will run.

   5.   Add the following line of code to the new event handler:

      LabelOutput.Text = "Text changed!";

```
protected void ButtonChangeText_Click(obje
{
    LabelOutput.Text = "Text changed!";
}
```

   6.   View the page in your browser and click the button.

note

The order of events

In this lesson you have two events both trying to set the *Text* property of a Label control, but the *Click* event 'wins'. This is because the events are always processed in a certain order.

When the button is clicked, the page reloads and the *Page_Load* event sets the Label control's text to *Hello World!* At a later point in time the *Click* event occurs and sets the Label control's text property to *Text Changed!*

On a real web site you'd probably try to avoid this and make sure that only one piece of code affects the Label control at a time.

The text in the *Label* control changes. This works because the *Click* event comes after the *Page_Load* event (see sidebar: *The order of events*).

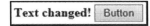

7. Close your web browser.

6 Add a *Calendar* control to the page from the *Standard* category of the *Toolbox*.

7 Change the *ID* property of the *Calendar* control to: **CalendarSelect**

If your *Properties* window is still displaying *Events* you will have to switch back to *Properties* by clicking the *Properties* icon.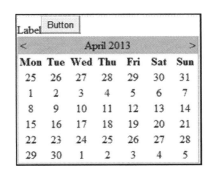

8 Add an event handler to the *Selection Changed* event of the *Calendar* control.

1. In the same way as you did for the *Button* control, select the *Calendar* control in *Design* view and then click the *events* button in the *Properties* window.

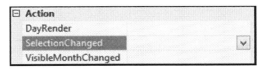

As you can see, the *Calendar* control has a different set of events to the *Button* control. You'll learn more about the events of different controls in: *Session Four: ASP.NET Controls.*

2. Double-click in the empty box next to *SelectionChanged* in the *Properties* window.

The *SelectionChanged* event happens when the user selects a date from the calendar.

3. Add the following code to the new event handler that is automatically generated:

LabelOutput.Text = CalendarSelect.SelectedDate.ToString();

```
protected void CalendarSelect_SelectionChanged(object sender,
{
    LabelOutput.Text = CalendarSelect.SelectedDate.ToString();
}
```

This code will set the *Text* property of your *Label* control to the date that was selected in the calendar.

You will learn about *ToString* in: *Lesson 5-9: Convert variables using cast and ToString.*

4. View the page in your browser.

5. Click on a date in the calendar.

The event handler code runs and the *Label* control displays the date that was selected.

9 Close your web browser and close Visual Studio.

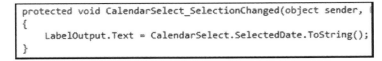

note

'Hidden' events

Although the vast majority of ASP.NET events can be accessed through *Design* view, you might be wondering where you can click to set page events like *Page_Load*.

Unfortunately, it's not possible to access those events through the designer so you have to type them in manually if you want to use them.

The important 'missing' events are:

Page_Init
Happens before *Page_Load*.

Page_PreRender
Happens after *Page_Load*, just before the page's controls are converted into HTML code.

Page_Unload
The last event in the page life cycle. Happens after the page has been sent to the user.

You won't be using any of these events in this course, but it is good to be aware of their existence.

Lesson 3-3: Use Breakpoints

So far, you've been able to tell that your code is working properly by running it and seeing the results. When things don't work the way you expect them to, it is helpful to be able to get a closer look at what is going wrong.

Breakpoints let you pause your code and examine the current state of the application.

1   Open *CSharpTest* from your sample files folder.

2   Open *default.aspx.cs* (The code-behind file of *default.aspx*).

3   Add a breakpoint to the *CalendarSelect_SelectionChanged* event handler.

tip

Setting breakpoints by clicking the left bar

As well as right-clicking and clicking *Insert Breakpoint*, you can quickly add and remove breakpoints by clicking in the gray bar on the left where the breakpoint indicator circles appear.

If you click the breakpoint indicator circle the breakpoint will be removed.

important

The difference between Debug mode and View in Browser

So far you've been able to view your pages either by starting debugging or right-clicking on them in the *Solution Explorer* and clicking *View in Browser* from the shortcut menu.

At this point, an important difference between the two emerges.

If you choose *View in Browser* from the *Solution Explorer*, Visual Studio won't process your break points.

For breakpoints to work properly, you must always use Debug mode by clicking Debug→Start Debugging or by clicking the 'play' button on the toolbar:

1. Click on the line of code that sets *LabelOutput*'s *Text* property in the *CalendarSelect_SelectionChanged* event handler.

    ```
    protected void CalendarSelect_SelectionChanged(object sender,
    {
        LabelOutput.Text = CalendarSelect.SelectedDate.ToString();
    }
    ```

2. Right-click on the code and then click Breakpoint→Insert Breakpoint from the shortcut menu.

    The line is highlighted in red, and a red circle appears in the bar to the left. This indicates that a breakpoint is present.

    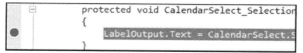

4   Inspect properties while code is running.

1. Run *default.aspx* in Debug mode (see sidebar).

2. Click on a date in the calendar.

    You should be automatically brought back to Visual Studio with the line you added a breakpoint to highlighted in yellow.

    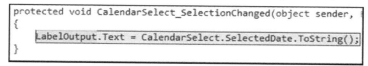

    Your web application is now paused at the point where you placed the breakpoint.

3. Examine the current *Text* property of the *LabelOutput* control.

You can quickly check the current values of properties by hovering your mouse cursor over them. Hover your cursor over the *.Text* part of *LabelOutput.Text*.

You can see that the current value of *LabelOutput.Text* is: *Hello world!*

4. View the rest of the properties of the *LabelOutput* control.

By hovering your mouse cursor over *LabelOutput* itself and expanding the categories by clicking the + symbol, you can see the rest of the *LabelOutput's* control's properties.

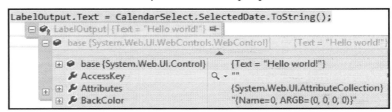

note

The Debug Toolbar

As well as using the *Debug* menu, you can use the icons on the Debug toolbar.

▶ Continue ⌄

‖ ■ ↻

These allow you to continue, pause, stop and restart debugging.

↳. ↳ ↪

These correspond to *Step Into*, *Step Over* and *Step Out*.

The difference between these isn't obvious at the moment, but will make more sense in: *Session Six: C# Classes, Namespaces and Methods*.

For now you only need to use *Step Over*.

5 Step through code using the *Debug* tools.

Although it's useful to see the values of properties at your breakpoint, it's even more useful to be able to step through your code line by line and see what is affected.

1. Click Debug→Step Over.

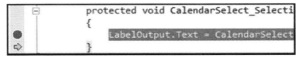

The next line of code is highlighted in yellow and has a small yellow arrow in the bar to the left. You have now stepped through the last line and onto this one.

Because you stepped through the last line, it will have updated the *LabelOutput* control's *Text* property.

2. Check the *Text* property of the *LabelOutput* control.

As you did before, move your mouse cursor over *.Text* in the *LabelOuput.Text* code.

The property has been updated by the previous line of code.

3. Click Debug→Continue.

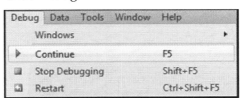

You are returned to your web browser and the site continues running as normal.

You can also continue running by clicking the 'play' button on the toolbar (see sidebar).

Lesson 3-4: Use Watches and Locals

In *Lesson 3-3: Use Breakpoints,* you learned how to pause your application at certain points in order to inspect the current state of controls and values. However, using that technique only allows you to inspect the values of objects that your code directly refers to.

Using the *Watch* and *Locals* windows, you can inspect any values that are available, regardless of whether or not your code makes reference to them.

1   Open *CSharpTest* from your sample files folder.

2   Open *default.aspx.cs* (The code-behind file of *default.aspx*).

3   Start debugging.

4   Click on a date in the calendar.

> The breakpoint that you added in *Lesson 3-3: Use Breakpoints* should pause the code inside the *CalendarSelect_SelectionChanged* event handler.

5   View properties using the *Locals* window.

> 1.   Click the *Locals* button at the bottom-left of the screen.
>
>
>
> The *Locals* window will appear (if it wasn't visible already).
>
>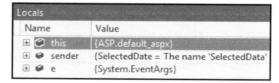
>
> *Locals* contains all of the properties that are currently available to your code in a tree structure. It's not always the easiest way to find what you're looking for, but it always contains every value that is available to your application.
>
> 2.   Expand *this* by clicking the plus-sign icon next to it.
>
> The *this* object is the object that contains the code that is running. In this case, *this* is the *default.aspx* page.
>
>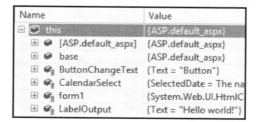
>
> 3.   Expand *LabelOutput* in the *Locals* window.
>
> The properties of the *LabelOutput* control are displayed.

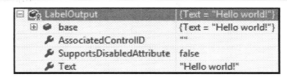

Note that these are only properties that have a value. You could view a complete list of the control's properties by expanding *base*.

4. Return to your web browser by clicking Debug→Continue.

6   View properties using the *Watch* window.

The *Watch* window works very similarly to the *Locals* window, but you can choose the values that you want to appear in it. It's usually a much more convenient way of inspecting values in your application.

1. Click on a date on the calendar again.

Your code should pause at the breakpoint once more.

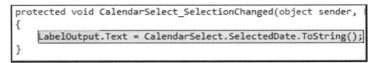

2. Display the *Watch* window by clicking the *Watch* button at the bottom-left of the screen.

3. Select *LabelOutput.Text* by clicking and dragging your mouse cursor over it.

4. Right-click on the highlighted text and then click *Add Watch* from the shortcut menu.

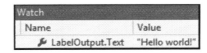

LabelOutput.Text and its current value appear in the *Watch* window.

Watch	
Name	Value
LabelOutput.Text	"Hello world!"

5. Use *Step Over* to step to the next line.

The value of *LabelOutput.Text* is updated in the *Watch* window. The *Watch* window is very useful for keeping an eye on the current values of important properties.

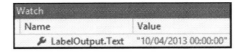

You'll be using the *Watch* window more in the coming lessons.

7   Stop debugging and close Visual Studio.

Lesson 3-5: Understand the Exception object

So far all of your code may have run without any problems, but unfortunately that won't always be so. When things do go wrong, Visual Studio will do its best to tell you what the problem is.

You've already seen a build error in *Lesson 1-9: Run a project in debug mode*, but those only appear when Visual Studio is able to detect a problem before the code runs.

Exceptions appear when something goes wrong while the code is running. By looking at the exception, you will hopefully be able to work out what the problem is.

1   Open *CSharpTest* from your sample files folder.

2   Open *debugme.aspx.cs* (The code-behind file of *debugme.aspx*).

There is some code in here that you won't recognize, but the important thing is that it's going to cause an error by trying to divide by zero.

You will understand everything that this code is doing after: *Lesson 5-10: Perform basic mathematical operations.*

3   Cause an exception.

1.   Start debugging to view *debugme.aspx* in Debug mode.

2.   Click the *Crash Me* button.

You should be brought back to Visual Studio. If not, switch back to it manually without closing the browser window.

The line that caused the exception is highlighted in yellow and a box has appeared showing the details of the exception.

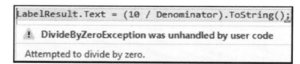

This exception is very obvious. The error message at the top tells you that it was caused by attempting to divide by zero.

Unfortunately not all error messages are as easy to understand.

4   Use troubleshooting tips.

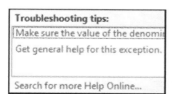

You'll notice that the *Exception* window shows a list of *Troubleshooting tips*. You can click on them to read articles relevant to the problem, which might help you to fix it.

You can also click *Search for more Help Online...* to be redirected to a search page which will allow you to search Microsoft's articles for anything relevant.

5   View the details of the exception.

An exception isn't just an error message; it has properties, just like the controls on your page.

Actions:
View Detail...
Enable editing
Copy exception detail to the clipboard

note

null

You can see two *null* values for properties in the screenshots of the *Exception* object and you might have noticed them in a few other properties you saw earlier.

null is a value that literally means 'nothing'. A property with a value of *null* is considered not to have a value.

It's important to note that there's a difference between 0 and *null*, since 0 is a number and *null* is the absence of a number.

You'll learn more about *null* in: *Lesson 5-12: Understand null.*

1. Click the *View Detail...* link in the *Exception* box.

2. Expand *System.DivideByZeroException* by clicking the arrow.

System.DivideByZeroException	{"Attempted to divide by zero."}
[System.DivideByZeroException]	{"Attempted to divide by zero."}
▷ Data	{System.Collections.ListDictiona
HelpLink	null
HResult	-2147352558
▷ InnerException	null
Message	Attempted to divide by zero.
Source	CSharpTest
StackTrace	at CSharpTest.debugme.Butto
▷ TargetSite	{Void ButtonCrash_Click(System

The most important properties of the exception are *InnerException*, *Message*, *Source* and *StackTrace*.

InnerException will contain another exception if this one had a deeper cause. Essentially, the Inner Exception is the exception that caused this one. Since this exception didn't have a deeper cause, the Inner Exception is *null* (see sidebar).

Message is the error message that you've already seen displayed on the main exception box.

Source is the *namespace* that caused the error. You'll learn about namespaces in: *Lesson 6-4: Work with namespaces.*

StackTrace shows the operation that caused the error. If you read it you'll see that the first line tells you that the error originated in *debugme.ButtonCrash_Click.*

6 **Fix the problem.**

This error happened because the number that the code divided by was zero. You can fix this by changing the number.

1. Click *OK* and stop debugging.

   Either close your web browser or click Debug→Stop Debugging.

2. Change the line *int Denominator = 0;* to:

   int Denominator = 2;

   ```
   protected void ButtonCrash_Click(object sender, Event/
   {
       int Denominator = 2;
       LabelResult.Text = (10 / Denominator).ToString();
   }
   ```

3. View the page in Debug mode and click the button.

   This time there are no errors. Instead the result of 10 divided by 2 is displayed.

7 **Close your browser and close Visual Studio.**

Lesson 3-6: Understand the Page object

Every *.aspx* page has an object behind it called the *Page* object which contains a lot of useful properties about the status of the page.

In this lesson you'll inspect the *Page* object and view some of the more important parts of it.

1   Open *CSharpTest* from your sample files folder.

2   Open *default.aspx.cs* (the code-behind file of *default.aspx*).

3   Add a breakpoint to the *ButtonChangeText_Click* event.

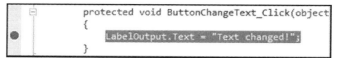

Right click on the line that begins *LabelOutput.Text* and click Breakpoint→Insert Breakpoint or click in the gray bar to the left of the line.

4   Run *default.aspx* in Debug mode and click the button.

Your code should pause at the breakpoint.

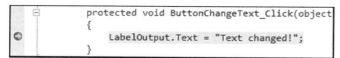

5   Display the Watch window.

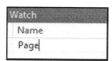

Click the *Watch* tab, at the bottom left hand side of the screen, to display the *Watch* window if it's not visible already.

6   Clear all current watches.

Right-click in the *Watch* window and then click *Clear All* from the shortcut menu.

This will clear any existing watches from the window.

7   Manually add a watch for the *Page* object.

1.   Click in the empty box under *Name* in the *Watch* window.

2.   Type **Page** into the box and press <**Enter**>.

A watch is created for the *Page* object.

8   Expand *Page* in the *Watch* window.

Expand the *Page* object to view its properties by clicking the + sign next to it in the *Watch* window.

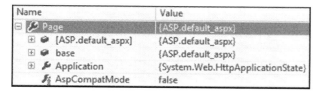

9   Add a watch for *Page.Controls*.

As you can see, the *Page* object has an overwhelming number of properties, most of which won't make much sense to you at the moment.

The *Page* object can be thought of as a container for absolutely everything on an ASP.NET page.

1. Collapse the *Page* object by clicking the minus sign next to *Page*.

2. In the same way as you did for *Page*, add a watch for:
   Page.Controls

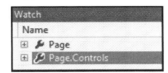

3. Expand *Page.Controls*.

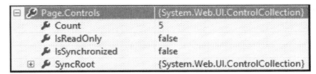

You can see that the *Count* property is 5. This is because *Page.Controls* is a collection containing 5 controls. You'll learn all about collections in: *Lesson 8-2: Create a collection*.

note

The Page.Controls collection

Page.FindControl is a short-cut to enable easier access to the controls that are stored in the *Page.Controls* collection.

You could have retrieved *LabelOutput* using the more confusing syntax:

Page.Controls[3].Controls[1]

This is the 'real' location of the *LabelOutput* control. This type of syntax will make more sense to you after: *Lesson 8-1: Create an array*.

10   View the properties of the *LabelOutput* control through the *Page* object.

The *Page* object has a *FindControl* method that allows you to easily find a control on the page.

Add the following watch to the *Watch* window:

Page.FindControl("LabelOutput")

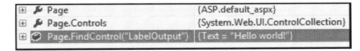

The *LabelOutput* control is found within the *Page* object and its *Text* property is displayed. The controls in the *Page* object are contained in the *Page.Controls* collection, but *FindControl* makes it easy to locate a specific control (see sidebar).

As you've seen already, you don't need to use *Page.FindControl* under normal circumstances. You've only done this to illustrate that everything you add to a page becomes part of the *Page* object.

You'll examine some other important parts of the *Page* object in the rest of this session.

11   Stop debugging and close Visual Studio.

Lesson 3-7: Understand Request and Response

On 'plain' HTML web pages, a web browser sends a request to a web server and the web server responds by sending back the page's HTML code.

ASP.NET works in-between receiving the request from the browser and sending the response back to them, and you can see this in action by inspecting the *Page.Request* and *Page.Response* objects.

1 Open *CSharpTest* from your sample files folder.

2 Open *requestresponse.aspx.cs* (the code-behind file of *requestresponse.aspx*).

3 Add a breakpoint to the *Page_Load* event handler.

You might be wondering how to add a breakpoint to an event handler that doesn't have any code in it; Visual Studio won't allow you to add a breakpoint to a blank line.

Instead, set the breakpoint on the line with the } sign on it.

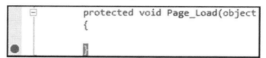

4 Run *requestresponse.aspx* in Debug mode.

Your code should be paused almost immediately, as the breakpoint is reached as soon as the page loads.

5 Clear any existing watches and add a watch for *Page.Request*.

This was covered in: *Lesson 3-6: Understand the Page object*.

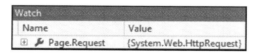

6 Inspect *Page.Request*.

The *Page.Request* object contains all of the information that was sent to the web server by the visitor to the page.

1. Expand *Page.Request* and find *UserAgent* in the properties list.

   The *UserAgent* property tells you which browser the visitor is using.

In a slightly cryptic way the text informs me that I am using Microsoft Internet Explorer 10 (MSIE 10.0). This will be different if you are using a different browser.

2. Examine the other properties of *Page.Request*.

UserHostAddress shows the IP address of the visitor (127.0.0.1 or ::1 means it is your own machine).

Url shows the web address that the visitor entered to get to this page.

7   Manipulate *Page.Response*.

1. Stop debugging and remove the breakpoint.

2. Run *requestresponse.aspx* in Debug mode.

   You can see that it is filled with 'Lorem Ipsum' dummy text.

   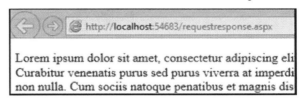

   ```
   http://localhost:54683/requestresponse.aspx

   Lorem ipsum dolor sit amet, consectetur adipiscing eli
   Curabitur venenatis purus sed purus viverra at imperdi
   non nulla. Cum sociis natoque penatibus et magnis dis
   ```

3. Stop debugging and return to the code-behind file of *requestresponse.aspx*.

4. Add the following code to the *Page_Load* event handler:

   Page.Response.Write("Hello world!");
   Page.Response.End();

   ```
   protected void Page_Load(object sender, EventArgs e)
   {
       Page.Response.Write("Hello world!");
       Page.Response.End();
   }
   ```

5. Run *requestresponse.aspx* in Debug mode.

   The big block of text that was on the page has disappeared and has been replaced by *Hello World!*.

   ```
   http://localhost:50085/requestresponse.aspx

   Hello world!
   ```

   This happened because you ended the page's response to the visitor early by using *Page.Response.End*. If you hadn't ended the response, the web server would have gone on to add the page's content to the response (see sidebar for more on this).

By using *Page.Response.Write*, as you did in this example, you can add content directly to the web server's response without it being on the *.aspx* page at all. This is useful for testing and debugging purposes, but it is better practice to use controls on the page to display content.

ASP.NET allows you to 'listen' to the user's *Request* and modify the web server's *Response* appropriately. In practice you will rarely need to access the *Page.Request* and *Page.Response* objects directly as ASP.NET does most of the work for you.

For example, when the user clicks a *Button* control, it is reflected in the user's *Request* to the web server. The web server then automatically runs the *Button* control's *Click* event handler which may modify the *Response* by changing the properties of controls.

---

note

The page lifecycle

You might still be a little confused about why there's no content on the page because you stopped the response during *Page_Load*.

This is because ASP.NET doesn't add the page's content until it *Renders* the page (converts the ASP.NET controls into HTML).

Page rendering happens after *Page_Load*. Because you ended the response before the page had a chance to render, the remainder of the page remained blank.

Microsoft's documentation contains a full list of the order in which events are executed when a page is requested (the page lifecycle).

Lesson 3-8: Understand PostBack

In *Lesson 2-12: Work with HTML Forms*, you created an HTML form that sent (or *posted*) data to another page. ASP.NET normally uses a form to *post* data back to the same page; this is called *PostBack*.

By using *PostBack*, the user sends data to your web site without moving between pages. ASP.NET's controls expect this, and you can use it to your advantage.

1 Open *CSharpTest* from your sample files folder.

2 Open the code-behind file of *postbacktest.aspx.*

3 See PostBack in action.

1. View *postbacktest.aspx* in your browser.

2. Click the button that says *Click Me*.

You might notice a brief 'flicker' as the page reloads, although this has been mostly eliminated in the latest web browsers. This happens because the page's form was submitted and the data 'posted back'.

3. Choose an item from the drop-down list.

This time the page does not reload and the form is not submitted. By default, changing the value of a drop-down menu doesn't cause the form to be submitted.

4. Click the check-box.

You'll notice that this doesn't cause a post-back either.

5. Close your web browser and return to Visual Studio.

4 Use C# code to check whether the page has posted back.

1. Add the following code to the *Page_Load* event handler:

LabelIsPostBack.Text = Page.IsPostBack.ToString();

```
protected void Page_Load(object sender, EventArgs e)
{
    LabelIsPostBack.Text = Page.IsPostBack.ToString();
}
```

Page.IsPostBack is a value that tells you whether the page has been posted back. *ToString* converts the value into text.

2. View *postbacktest.aspx* in your browser.

The *Label* at the top of the page says *False*. This tells you that the page has not yet been posted back. The user has just loaded the page for the first time and hasn't clicked on any controls yet.

3. Click the button.

The label changes to say *True*. This means that the user has submitted the form and posted back some data.

This is useful because it allows you to make some of your code run only when the page first loads, rather than running every time the page is posted back. You'll see how this can be done in: *Lesson 7-1: Use the if statement*.

4. Close your web browser.

note

How ASP.NET posts back without a button

In the HTML form you created in *Lesson 2-12: Work with HTML Forms*, the only way to submit the form was to click a button.

In this lesson you've seen that ASP.NET can submit its form when other things happen. It does this by automatically generating JavaScript code to submit the form.

If you open the page in your browser and view the source (right-click and *View Source* in Internet Explorer), you'll see that ASP.NET has added lines with *javascript:__doPostBack*. This JavaScript code causes the form to be submitted.

Because JavaScript is client-side code, you should always be aware that someone browsing your site might have disabled JavaScript, in which case the post-back will not work.

5 **Make a non-PostBack control post back when it is clicked.**

Earlier you saw that the *DropDownList* and *CheckBox* controls don't automatically post back when you click on them. If your page needs to be updated when the user changes one of these controls, you might want them to post back. This can be achieved by setting the *AutoPostBack* property.

1. Open *postbacktest.aspx* in *Design* view.

2. Select the *DropDownListPostBack* control.

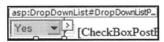

3. Set the control's *AutoPostBack* property to: **True**

You learned how to do this in: *Lesson 1-13: Change properties in Design view*.

4. View the page in your browser.

5. Try changing the value of the drop-down list.

This time the page posts back and the label at the top of the page confirms this.

The *AutoPostBack* property is available on most controls that don't automatically post back.

6 **Close Visual Studio.**

Lesson 3-9: Work with ViewState

Have you ever used an online form and become really annoyed when all of the contents of the controls disappeared after a post-back? This is the problem that *ViewState* elegantly solves.

In this lesson you'll see *ViewState* in action and discover how you can also use *ViewState* to store values of your own

1 Open *CSharpTest* from your sample files folder.

2 Open *viewstatetest.aspx* in *Design* view.

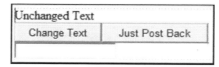

You can see that there is a *Label* control, two *Button* controls and a *TextBox* control on this page.

3 See ViewState in action.

1. View *viewstatetest.aspx* in your browser.

2. Click the *Change Text* button.

The Label at the top of the screen changes to say: *Text Changed!*

3. Click the *Just Post Back* button.

The Label continues to say *Text Changed!* even after the page is posted back; the *state* of the Label control has been maintained thanks to *ViewState*.

4. Examine the hidden *ViewState* data.

As you've done before, view the source of the page by right-clicking (in Internet Explorer) and then clicking *View Source* from the shortcut menu.

5. Look for the *aspNetHidden* div near the top of the page.

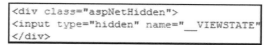

The middle line contains all of the *ViewState* data. It looks like nonsense because it's encrypted, but it is easy to decrypt using tools available on the Internet so don't rely on it to be secure.

4 Disable ViewState and see the difference.

1. Close your browser and return to *viewstatetest.aspx*.

2. Change the *EnableViewState* property of the *LabelText* control to: **False**

3. View *viewstatetest.aspx* in your browser.

4. Click the *Change Text* button.

The text changes just as it did before.

5. Click the *Just Post Back* button.

This time the state of the Label control isn't maintained by *ViewState*, so the text reverts back to its original value.

5   **Store a value in *ViewState*.**

As well as letting ASP.NET automatically store the values of your controls in *ViewState*, you can also use *ViewState* to store values of your own.

1. Close your web browser and open the code-behind file of *viewstatetest.aspx*.

2. Put the following code in the *Page_Load* event handler:

ViewState["MyText"] = "Hello World!";

```
protected void Page_Load(object sender, EventArgs e)
{
    ViewState["MyText"] = "Hello World!";
}
```

This code will store the text *Hello World!* in *ViewState*, next to a *key* of *MyText*. The key will be used to retrieve the text from *ViewState*.

3. Replace the code in the *ButtonChangeText_Click* event handler with:

LabelText.Text = ViewState["MyText"].ToString();

```
protected void ButtonChangeText_Click(object sender, EventArgs e)
{
    LabelText.Text = ViewState["MyText"].ToString();
}
```

This code sets the *Text* property of the *LabelText* control to the value that you stored under *MyText* in *ViewState*.

4. View the page in your browser.

5. Try clicking the *Change Text* button.

The text *Hello World!* is retrieved from *ViewState* and displayed in the *Label* control.

Storing values in ViewState is useful when you have a value that you need to keep after a post-back but don't want to put in a visible control on the page.

---

anecdote

ViewState troubles

I was once called upon to urgently solve a problem while another developer was away on holiday. His web application had suddenly stopped working and nobody knew why.

The page in question had a large table that was populated with data from a database and *ViewState* had been left on.

Because *ViewState* makes the browser send back the state of the control, the browsers were sending back a huge amount of data every time the page posted back. This made the page run very slowly, but didn't actually stop it from working.

Over time, as the database grew, more and more data was being sent back until, on that day, it exceeded the request limit of 4 megabytes and ASP.NET stopped it from working.

After simply disabling *ViewState* on the table, everything worked perfectly again.

Lesson 3-10: Move between pages using C#

note

Advantages and disadvantages of Response.Redirect

The *Page.Response.Redirect* method is the most often-used method of moving between pages using C# code.

When you use *Response.Redirect* the new page is loaded exactly as if the user had clicked on a link or typed the address into their address bar. The page that they are taken to has no ties to the page they came from. This can be an advantage or a disadvantage, depending on what you are trying to do.

One disadvantage of using *Response.Redirect* or any method of transferring between pages in C# is that you cannot open the new page in a new window.

Links that open in new windows can only be made with HTML or JavaScript.

You should now have a pretty good idea of how ASP.NET works on a single page. You know how to change the properties of elements on the page and capture the data that the user has entered.

Although you learned how to create HTML hyperlinks in *Lesson 2-7: Display images and links on a page*, it's also possible to move between pages using C# code.

1 Open *CSharpTest* from your sample files folder.

2 Open the code-behind file of *movepage1.aspx*.

3 Add code to move to *movepage2.aspx* using *Page.Response.Redirect*.

> You learned about the *Page.Response* object in *Lesson 3-7: Understand Request and Response.* By using its *Redirect* method, you can send the browser to a different page.
>
> 1. Add the following code to the *ButtonMove_Click* event handler:
>
> **Page.Response.Redirect("movepage2.aspx");**
>
> ```
> protected void ButtonMove_Click(object sender, EventArgs e)
> {
>     Page.Response.Redirect("movepage2.aspx");
> }
> ```
>
> 2. View *movepage1.aspx* in your browser.
>
>
>
> 3. Click the button.
>
> You are redirected to *movepage2.aspx*.
>
>
>
> Notice that the web browser's address bar shows that you are now on *movepage2.aspx*.

note

How Page.Response. Redirect works

When you move between pages using *Response.Redirect*, ASP.NET sends a response to the web browser with the special code number: 302.

The 302 code tells the web browser that the page it is looking for has temporarily moved to the location you specified.

When the web browser sees the 302 code and the new location, it automatically sends a new request to the new location, effectively redirecting the user.

4 Move to *movepage2.aspx* with a hyperlink.

> 1. Close your browser and open *movepage1.aspx* in *Source* view.
>
> 2. Add an HTML link after the button using the code:
>
> **<a href="movepage2.aspx">Next Page</a>**
>
> ```
> 
>     <asp:Button ID="ButtonMove" runat="server"
>     <a href="movepage2.aspx">Next Page</a>
> 
> ```
>
> 3. View *movepage1.aspx* in your browser.

4.   Click the *Next Page* link.

This has exactly the same result as *Response.Redirect*.

5   Move to *movepage2.aspx* with *Page.Server.Transfer*.

This is the first time that you've seen the *Server* object. The *Server* object contains methods that tell the web server to carry out certain operations. For now you're interested in its *Transfer* method.

1.   Close your browser and return to the code-behind file of *movepage1.aspx*.

2.   Replace your *Page.Response.Redirect* line of code with:

Page.Server.Transfer("movepage2.aspx");

```
protected void ButtonMove_Click(object sender, EventArgs e)
{
    Page.Server.Transfer("movepage2.aspx");
}
```

3.   View *movepage1.aspx* in your browser.

4.   Click the button.

Once again you are redirected to *movepage2.aspx*, but look at the address bar:

The browser still thinks that you're on *movepage1.aspx*! This is the major difference with *Server.Transfer*.

Server.Transfer switches to the new page internally, but doesn't tell the browser. From the perspective of the person viewing your site, they haven't changed pages at all.

Using *Server.Transfer* also keeps a reference to the previous page, as you'll see in: *Lesson 3-11: Send data between pages*.

6   Close your browser and close Visual Studio.

note

Advantages and disadvantages of Server.Transfer

Page.Server.Transfer is useful if you don't want site visitors to know that they are changing pages. You might want to do this if you have a multi-step process split into several pages.

In *Lesson 3-11: Send data between pages*, you'll see that *Server.Transfer* can also be used to pass data between pages.

The disadvantage of *Server.Transfer* is that without knowing the address of the actual page they are on, your visitors won't be able to bookmark the page.

As with *Response.Redirect*, you can't use *Server.Transfer* to open a new window.

note

Page.Server. TransferRequest

If you try *Server.TransferRequest*, it will seem to work in exactly the same way as *Server.Transfer*. The difference is in how *ASP.NET* is working in the background.

With *Server.Transfer*, ASP.NET doesn't create a completely new *Request*, which means it doesn't re-check things like authentication. You'll learn about authentication in: *Session Nine: Authentication*.

TransferRequest creates an entirely new request for the page. Although this is more complete and secure, it is also slower.

Lesson 3-11: Send data between pages

You now know how to retrieve data from a page, access the properties of controls and transfer between pages, but you'll often want the site to remember something that the user has entered on a previous page after they move to a new page.

In this lesson you'll learn a few of the ways to send data from one page to another.

1   Open *CSharpTest* from your sample files folder.

2   Open *passdata1.aspx* in *Design* view.

You can see that there is a text box and a button on this page. You're going to write code that will send the contents of the text box to another page, which will display it.

3   Send data using *PreviousPage*.

If you use *Server.Transfer* to move between pages, you can actually access the *Page* object of the previous page.

1. Open the code-behind file of *passdata1.aspx*.

2. Add the following code to the *ButtonSend_Click* event handler:

   Page.Server.Transfer("passdata2.aspx");

   As mentioned in *Lesson 3-10: Move between pages using C#*, *Server.Transfer* will keep a link open to the previous page.

3. View *passdata1.aspx* in your browser.

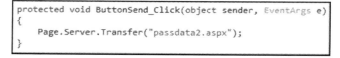

4. Change the text in the text box if you wish and then click the *Send to Next Page* button.

   passdata2.aspx picks up the data and displays it, but because you used *Server.Transfer*, you still appear to be on *passdata1.aspx*.

5. Close your browser and open the code-behind file of *passdata2.aspx*. You will see the following code:

   LabelReceivedData.Text = ((TextBox)Page.PreviousPage.FindControl("TextBoxText")).Text;

note

Advantages and disadvantages of Page.PreviousPage

The *Page.PreviousPage* method isn't widely used for passing data between pages. Most developers prefer the QueryString method.

The main disadvantage of the *Page.PreviousPage* method is that it only works if you use *Server.Transfer* to move to the target page.

Using the *Server.Transfer* method means that the person using your site won't be aware that they've moved between pages.

Sometimes that is exactly what you want, but most of the time you will need to use another method of passing data.

note

Other ways of passing data

There are other ways of moving data between pages besides the ones mentioned in this lesson.

You could store values in cookies or a database, or even use plain HTML forms as you did in: *Lesson 2-12: Work with HTML Forms.*

This code retrieves the *TextBoxText* control from the previous page and displays its *Text* property in the *Label* control on this page. It probably looks a little confusing at the moment. You won't be able to fully understand this code until you've completed: *Lesson 5-9: Convert variables using cast and ToString.*

Page.PreviousPage is a link to the *Page* object you came from.

FindControl("TextBoxText") looks for the *TextBoxText* control on the previous page.

4 Send data using *QueryString*.

The QueryString method is the most widely used method of sending data between pages.

While browsing the Internet, you might have noticed that sometimes web addresses look something like:

www.[site].com/[page].aspx?page=10&product=13

The values after the question mark are *QueryString* values, and you can use them to send data between pages.

1. Open the code-behind file of *passdata1.aspx.*

2. Replace the *Page.Server.Transfer* line of code with:

   **Page.Response.Redirect
   ("passdata3.aspx?text=" + TextBoxText.Text);**

   ```
   protected void ButtonSend_Click(object sender, EventArgs e)
   {
       Page.Response.Redirect("passdata3.aspx?text=" + TextBoxText.Text);
   }
   ```

3. View *passdata1.aspx* in your browser.

4. Change the text in the text-box if you wish and then click the *Send to Next Page* button.

   passdata3.aspx retrieves the text you entered and displays it.

   If you look at the address bar, you can see how the text was sent to *passdata3.aspx.*

   http://**localhost**:54683/passdata3.aspx?text=excelcentral.com

5. Close your browser and view the code-behind file of *passdata3.aspx.*

   Here you can see that the text was retrieved using *Page.Request.QueryString.*

   ```
   if (Page.Request.QueryString["text"] != null)
   {
       LabelReceivedData.Text = Page.Request.QueryString["text"];
   }
   ```

   You'll fully understand this code later in the course, after completing: *Lesson 7-1: Use the if statement.*

Lesson 3-12: Use Session

In *Lesson 3-11: Send data between pages,* you saw how you can use *Server.Transfer* and *Response.Redirect* to send values between pages.

Session is another way of transferring values between pages, but session values don't just travel between pages, they remain in place for as long as a user's session lasts.

When a user first sends a *Request* to the web server, they are assigned a *Session* which keeps track of them until it has been 20 minutes (by default) since their last *Request.* The session is then said to have "timed out".

1 Open *CSharpTest* from your sample files folder.

2 Store a value using *Session*.

   1. Open the code-behind file of *passdata1.aspx.*

```
protected void ButtonSend_Click(object sender, EventArgs e)
{
    Page.Response.Redirect("passdata3.aspx?text=" + TextBoxText.Text);
}
```

   2. Replace the line beginning with *Page.Response.Redirect* with the following code:

Session["Text"] = TextBoxText.Text;

```
protected void ButtonSend_Click(object sender, EventArgs e)
{
    Session["Text"] = TextBoxText.Text;
}
```

This code stores the contents of *TextBoxText.Text* (ie the text the user types into the text box) in *Session* under the key of *Text.*

Session keys work in exactly the same way as the *ViewState* key that you used in: *Lesson 3-9: Work with ViewState.*

3 Retrieve a value from *Session*.

   1. Open the code-behind file of *passdata4.aspx.*

```
public partial class passdata4 : System.Web.UI.Page
{
    protected void Page_Load(object sender, EventArgs e)
    {

    }
}
```

   2. Add the following code to the *Page_Load* event handler:

LabelReceivedData.Text = Session["Text"].ToString();

```
protected void Page_Load(object sender, EventArgs e)
{
    LabelReceivedData.Text = Session["Text"].ToString();
}
```

This code will retrieve the value stored under the *Text* key from *Session* and display it in a *Label* control on the page.

4 Transfer the value from *passdata1.aspx* to *passdata4.aspx.*

note

Session variables and web farms

Some large-scale web applications spread their traffic over multiple web servers. This is known as a 'web farm'.

Session variables that are stored on one web server in the 'farm' will not be automatically shared with the other servers. This means that users can lose all of their session variables if the web farm sends their request to a different server.

This problem can be fixed by running something called "state server", which maintains session variables across all of the servers in the web farm.

1. Open the code-behind file of *passdata1.aspx*.

```
protected void ButtonSend_Click(object sender, EventArgs e)
{
    Session["Text"] = TextBoxText.Text;
}
```

2. Add the following line of code to the *ButtonSend_Click* event handler:

   Page.Response.Redirect("passdata4.aspx");

```
protected void ButtonSend_Click(object sender, EventArgs e)
{
    Session["Text"] = TextBoxText.Text;
    Page.Response.Redirect("passdata4.aspx");
}
```

As you learned in *Lesson 3-10: Move between pages using C#*, this will send the user to the *passdata4.aspx* page after placing the contents of the *TextBox* in *Session["Text"]*.

passdata4.aspx will then retrieve the value from *Session* and display it.

3. View *passdata1.aspx* in your browser.

4. Change the text in the text box if you wish and then click the *Send to Next Page* button.

passdata4.aspx retrieves the text that you typed from the *Session* object and displays it on the page.

5 Close Visual Studio.

Lesson 3-13: Edit the Web.config file

You might have been wondering what the *Web.config* file does, as you've seen it in every project that you've worked with so far.

Web.config is an XML file (see sidebar) which contains settings to tell the web server how to handle your web site. By changing the settings in *Web.config* you can modify many important settings.

Changing settings in Visual Studio often automatically makes changes to your *Web.config* file.

note

XML

XML isn't actually a specific programming language; it's really a standard for storing information. The HTML code that you wrote earlier was a form of XML.

XML always works as a series of nested tags enclosed in < and > symbols, which open and close in the same way that HTML tags do.

The *Web.config* file recognizes different tags to HTML, but basically works the same way.

Because XML can be used to store any kind of value in a hierarchy it's an extremely versatile way to store data.

1   Open *CSharpTest* from your sample files folder.

2   Open *Web.config.*

There is actually very little code inside the *Web.config* file. This is because you are using ASP.NET 4.5. ASP.NET 4.5 automatically manages a lot of settings that had to be specified in the *Web.config* file in previous versions.

```xml
<?xml version="1.0"?>

<!--
  For more information on how to configure your ASP.NET a
  http://go.microsoft.com/fwlink/?LinkId=169433
  -->

<configuration>
    <system.web>
      <compilation debug="true" targetFramework="4.5" />
      <httpRuntime targetFramework="4.5" />
    </system.web>
</configuration>
```

3   Use *Web.config* to switch *customErrors* on.

customErrors is a setting that determines whether ASP.NET displays the details of error messages to visitors to the site.

On a live site, the details of errors should be hidden from visitors as they contain glimpses into the site's code which may be a security risk.

1.   Add the following line of code to *Web.config* inside the *system.web* tag:

\<customErrors mode="On"\>\</customErrors\>

```xml
<system.web>
  <compilation debug="true" targetFramework="4.5" />
  <httpRuntime targetFramework="4.5" />
  <customErrors mode="On"></customErrors>
</system.web>
```

2.   View *crashme.aspx* in your browser.

Do this either by right-clicking on *crashme.aspx* and clicking *View in Browser* from the shortcut menu or by opening it and clicking Debug→Start Without Debugging.

You need to view the page without debugging, as otherwise Visual Studio will stop execution before the error is shown.

A *Runtime Error* dialog is displayed, but it offers no further details of the error itself. In fact, it shows instructions of how to modify your *Web.config* file to show the error details.

> ### Runtime Error
>
> **Description:** An application error occurred on the server. The current cu
>
> **Details:** To enable the details of this specific error message to be viewab the details to be viewable on remote machines, please set "mode" to "Off".

4 Switch *customErrors* off.

1. Close your browser and return to *Web.config*.

2. Change the *customErrors* line to:

    <customErrors mode="Off"></customErrors>

3. View *crashme.aspx* in your browser.

    This time the full details of the error message are displayed, as you have switched off *customErrors*.

    > ### Attempted to divide by zero.
    >
    > **Description:** An unhandled exception occurred during the execution of the
    >
    > **Exception Details:** System.DivideByZeroException: Attempted to divide by

    You can also see a snippet of code that shows which line caused the error. This is the reason that *customErrors* shouldn't be switched off on a live web server, as it might show code that could help someone break into your system.

    ```
    Line 13:          {
    Line 14:              int Zero = 0;
    Line 15:              int Crash = 1 / Zero;
    Line 16:          }
    Line 17:      }
    ```

    There is a third setting for *customErrors* called *RemoteOnly* (see sidebar).

5 Extend the length of sessions.

In *Lesson 3-11: Send data between pages*, you learned that a user's session on an ASP.NET site lasts for 20 minutes after their last request, but that is only the default. Using *Web.config*, you can make sessions last longer.

1. Close your browser and open *Web.config*.

2. Add the following line inside the *system.web* tag:

    <sessionState timeout="60"></sessionState>

    ```
    <system.web>
      <compilation debug="true" targetFramework="4.5" />
      <httpRuntime targetFramework="4.5" />
      <customErrors mode="Off"></customErrors>
      <sessionState timeout="60"></sessionState>
    </system.web>
    ```

    This will make sessions last for 60 minutes instead of 20.

There are many, many other settings that can be changed in *Web.config*, but for now it is just important that you understand what *Web.config* does and how you can edit its settings.

Session 3: Exercise

1   Open the *CSharpTest* sample project and open *exercise.aspx*.

2   Disable *ViewState* on the *TextBoxText* control by setting its *EnableViewState* property to: **False**

3   Add a *Click* event handler to the *ButtonChangeText* control.

4   Add code to the new *Click* event handler to set the *Text* property of the *TextBoxText* control to: **The Smart Method**

5   Add a *Click* event handler to the *ButtonSendData* control.

6   Add code to the *ButtonSendData* control's *Click* event to move to *passdata2.aspx* using *Server.Transfer*.

7   Set a breakpoint in the *Click* event of *ButtonSendData*.

8   Run *exercise.aspx* in Debug mode and type some text into the text box.

9   Click *Send Data* and then use the *Watch* window to get the value of *TextBoxText.Text*.

10   Stop debugging and add code to the *ButtonSendData* control's *Click* event handler to store the *Text* of the *TextBoxText* control in *Session* under the key of *Text*.

11   Change the *ButtonSendData* control's *Click* event handler to redirect the user to *passdata4.aspx* using *Response.Redirect* instead of *Server.Transfer*.

CSharpTest - start

CSharpTest - end

If you need help slide the page to the left

Session 3: Exercise Answers

These are the four questions that students find the most difficult to answer:

Q 9	Q 7	Q 6	Q 3
1. Run *exercise.aspx* in Debug mode by clicking: Debug→Start Debugging. 2. Click on the *Send Data* button. Your code will be paused. 3. Return to the code-behind file of *exercise.aspx* if you aren't automatically sent there. 4. Click on the *Watch* button at the bottom of the screen. 5. Click in an empty box in the *Watch* window and type: **TextBoxText.Text** 6. Press <**Enter**>. This was covered in: *Lesson 3-3: Use Breakpoints.*	1. Open the code-behind file of *exercise.aspx*. 2. Right-click on the *Page.Server.Transfer* line in the *ButtonSendData_Click* event handler. 3. Click: Breakpoint→ Insert Breakpoint from the shortcut menu. This was covered in: *Lesson 3-3: Use Breakpoints.*	1. Open the code-behind file of *exercise.aspx*. 2. Add the following code to the *ButtonSendData_Click* event handler: **Page.Server. Transfer("passdata2.aspx");** This was covered in: *Lesson 3-10: Move between pages using C#.*	1. Open *exercise.aspx* in *Design* view. 2. Select the *ButtonChangeText* control by clicking on it. 3. Click on the *Events* button in the *Properties* window. ⚡ 4. Double-click in the empty box next to *Click*. This was covered in: *Lesson 3-2: Add event handlers to controls.*

If you have difficulty with the other questions, here are the lessons that cover the relevant skills:

1　　Refer to: Lesson 1-7: Manage a project with the Solution Explorer.

2　　Refer to: Lesson 3-9: Work with ViewState.

4　　Refer to: Lesson 3-1: Change properties with C#.

5　　Refer to: Lesson 3-2: Add event handlers to controls.

8　　Refer to: Lesson 1-9: Run a project in debug mode.

10　　Refer to: Lesson 3-11: Send data between pages.

11　　Refer to: Lesson 3-10: Move between pages using C#.

Session Four: ASP.NET Controls

> A designer knows he has achieved perfection not when there is nothing left to add, but when there is nothing left to take away.
>
> *Antoine de Saint-Exupéry, French writer and aviator (1900 – 1944)*

In this session you'll work with the different controls that ASP.NET has to offer in greater depth and gain an understanding of what they can do.

You'll also learn some of the best practices for naming controls and structuring your pages.

Session Objectives

By the end of this session you will be able to:

- Name controls correctly
- Use the Button control
- Use the Label and Literal controls
- Use the TextBox control
- Use the CheckBox control
- Use the RadioButton control
- Use the DropDownList control
- Use the RequiredFieldValidator control
- Use the RangeValidator and ValidationSummary controls
- Use common properties

Lesson 4-1: Name controls correctly

Almost every time you've added a control in this book, you've changed its ID property instead of leaving it at the default value. Using consistent names for your controls is one of the most important things to do when working with C# or ASP.NET.

Whenever you create a control, you should always set its ID property to something meaningful before doing anything else with it.

In this lesson, you'll create a number of controls and set their ID properties according to the naming convention used by this course.

1   Open *My Project* from your sample files folder.

2   Add a new Web Form called: **namingtest.aspx**

You learned how to do this in: *Lesson 1-7: Manage a project with the Solution Explorer.*

3   Switch to *Design* view.

4   Add an ASP.NET *Label* control to the page.

You learned how to do this in *Lesson 1-15: Add controls to a page with the Toolbox.*

5   Add three ASP.NET *Button* controls to the page.

Your page should now look like this:

6   Set the *Text* properties of the *Button* controls.

1.   Set the *Text* property of the first *Button* to: **Monday**

2.   Set the *Text* property of the second *Button* to: **Tuesday**

3.   Set the *Text* property of the third *Button* to: **Wednesday**

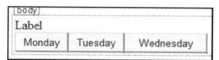

7   Name the *Button* controls correctly.

At the moment you have *Button* controls that say *Monday, Tuesday* and *Wednesday* on them, but their ID properties still say *Button1, Button2* and *Button3*.

Although you could work with them this way, it would be very confusing when you looked at the code as you'd have no idea which button was which without checking the page.

1.   Set the *ID* property of *Button1* to: **ButtonMonday**

2.   Set the *ID* property of *Button2* to: **ButtonTuesday**

3.   Set the *ID* property of *Button3* to: **ButtonWednesday**

8   Name the *Label* control correctly.

This book always uses the convention [Control Type][Name], which is always in Mixed Case.

Using this convention, it's always easy to understand which type of control the code is working with and what the control does.

Set the *ID* property of the *Label1* control to: **LabelDay**

9   See IntelliSense at work.

1. Add a *Click* event handler to the *ButtonMonday* control.

   You learned how to do this in: *Lesson 3-2: Add event handlers to controls*.

2. Type **Button** into the code window (inside the new event handler).

   The *IntelliSense* menu appears.

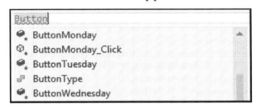

   Because you named all of your buttons properly, you can see all of them listed together in the *IntelliSense* menu at a glance.

3. Delete the *Button* text that you just added.

4. Type **Label** into the *Code* window.

   The *IntelliSense* menu appears again.

5. Choose *LabelDay* by double-clicking on it in the *IntelliSense* menu.

   Alternatively, scroll down to it using the arrow keys and press **<Enter>**.

   You'll learn more about *IntelliSense* in: *Lesson 5-1: Use IntelliSense*.

6. Add **.Text = "Monday";** to the end of the line.

```
protected void ButtonMonday_Click(object
{
    LabelDay.Text = "Monday";
}
```

With this code, you can see at a glance that the *ButtonMonday* control will set the *LabelDay* control's *Text* property to *Monday* when clicked.

If you hadn't named your controls, here is how the code would have looked:

```
protected void Button1_Click(object
{
    Label1.Text = "Monday";
}
```

As you can see, by naming your controls you have made your code a lot easier to understand and work with.

Lesson 4-2: Use the Button control

note

Button events

If you look at the available events for each of the button controls, you'll see that there are a few other events in addition to *Click*.

Using any event other than *Click* for a button is extremely rare.

You've already worked with the *Button* control quite a bit at this point, but there are a few different types of button control that act in a similar way.

You'll learn about the different types of button controls in this lesson.

1   Open *My Project* from your sample files folder.

2   Add a new Web Form called: **controlstest.aspx**

3   Open *controlstest.aspx* in *Design* view.

4   Add a *Button* control to the page.

5   Set the properties of the *Button* control.

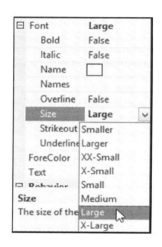

1.   Set the *ID* property of the *Button* to: **ButtonTest**

2.   Set the *Text* property of the *Button* to: **Standard Button**

3.   Set the *BackColor* property of the *Button* to: **Black**

   You learned how to set the *BackColor* property in *Lesson 1-13: Change properties in Design view.*

4.   Set the *ForeColor* property of the *Button* to: **White**

5.   Set the *Font Size* property of the *Button* to: **Large**

   To do this, you will need to expand the *Font* property in the *Properties* window. You can then select the size from a drop-down menu.

Your *Button* control should now look like this:

As you can see, you have quite a lot of control over the appearance and style of your buttons.

6   Add a *LinkButton* control to the page, below the *Button*.

The *LinkButton* control behaves in exactly the same way as a *Button* control, but the server will convert it into an HTML <a> tag rather than an HTML *Input (Submit)* control.

This control appears to be a hyperlink but acts like a button. Unlike a hyperlink, it uses JavaScript code to 'post back' the page.

tip

The LinkButton control and HTML

It is possible to put any valid HTML code into a *LinkButton's Text* property. This code will appear inside a pair of HTML <a> </a> tags when sent to the browser.

This allows advanced developers to make any part of an HTML page into a button.

7   Set the properties of the *LinkButton* control.

1.   Set the *ID* property of the *LinkButton* to: **LinkButtonTest**

2. Set the *Text* property of the *LinkButton* to: **Link Button**

3. Set the *ForeColor* property of the *LinkButton* to: **Red**

4. Set the *Font Bold* property of the *LinkButton* to: **True**

8   Add an *ImageButton* to the page, below the *LinkButton*.

It will actually appear just after the *LinkButton*. This is because of the way the page is structured at the moment, and isn't something to worry about.

The *ImageButton* control, as you might expect, is a button that uses an image. Note that unlike the *LinkButton* control, the *ImageButton* doesn't need to use any JavaScript code to submit the form.

9   Add *testbutton.png* to the *Images* folder.

You will find *testbutton.png* in the *C:\Practice\ASP.NET45\Images* folder.

You learned how to add files to a project in: *Lesson 1-7: Manage a project with the Solution Explorer*.

10 Set the properties of the *ImageButton* control.

1. Set the *ID* property of the *ImageButton* to: **ImageButtonTest**

2. Set the *ImageURL* property of the *ImageButton* to:
    ~/Images/testbutton.png

    You can either type this in or use the browse button next to the property to find the image (see sidebar for explanation of the tilde).

3. Set the *AlternateText* property of the image button to **Test Image Button** (see sidebar).

The *Button*, *LinkButton* and *ImageButton* controls provide a choice of three different appearances for your buttons.

11 Remove the controls from the page.

You're going to be using *controlstest.aspx* to test controls through the rest of this session, so you need to remove the buttons before continuing.

To do this, select them in *Design* view and either press <**Delete**> or right-click and then click *Delete* from the shortcut menu.

---

note

Tilde (~) paths

In this lesson, you use a tilde (~) symbol in the *ImageURL* property of the *ImageButton*.

The tilde indicates the 'top level' of your site, ie the root folder where your *Web.config* file is stored.

You can use the tilde in this way on any control that has the *runat="Server"* property. Controls that don't run on the server cannot use the tilde.

---

note

Alternate text

The *AlternateText* property is exclusive to images. In HTML, it will add: *alt="[Text]"* ...to the image.

Alternate text was originally intended for the users of text-only browsers: where their browser couldn't display an image, the text was displayed instead.

Although every major web browser is able to display images today, alternate text is still useful for two reasons:

1. Search engines use alternate text to identify which keywords to attach to an image.

2. Visually impaired users can use alternate text in conjunction with text to speech software.

---

note

Labels and Literals without text

Label and Literal controls normally display their *Text* property on the page.

Visual Studio adds placeholder text when the *Text* property is empty, as otherwise you wouldn't be able to see the control in *Design* view.

A *Label* control has its *Text* property set to *Label* when it is first created. If you clear the *Text* property of a *Label* control, it will still appear in *Design* view as *[LabelID]*.

A *Literal* control's *Text* property is blank when it is first created. It appears in *Design* view as: *[Literal "LiteralID"]* until the *Text* property has been set.

When the *Text* property is blank the control won't actually display any text in the user's browser.

note

Viewing controlstest.aspx in your browser

You changed the *Start Page* of this project to *mypage.aspx* in: *Lesson 1-9: Run a project in debug mode*. This means that *mypage.aspx* will always appear first when you start debugging.

To view *controlstest.aspx* in your web browser, you can either:

1. Right-click *controlstest.aspx* in the *Solution Explorer* window and click *View in Browser* from the shortcut menu.

OR

2. Start debugging normally and then navigate to *controlstest.aspx* using your browser's address bar.

OR

3. Change the *Start Page* to *controlstest.aspx*.

Lesson 4-3: Use the Label and Literal controls

You've already worked with the *Label* control several times. Using a *Label* control is probably the easiest and best way to make a piece of text on a page accessible to your C# code.

In this lesson you'll learn a little bit more about the capabilities of *Label* controls and about the similar *Literal* control.

1 Open *My Project* from your sample files folder.

2 Open *controlstest.aspx* in *Design* view.

3 Add a *Label* control to the page.

4 Set the properties of the *Label* control.

   1. Set the *ID* property to: **LabelTest**

   2. Change the *Text* property to: **Test Label**

   3. Set the *Font Bold* property to: **True**

      Most controls that contain text have the same text formatting properties as *Label* controls.

5 Add a *Literal* control to the page, next to the *Label* control.

The *Literal* control looks a little strange. This is because it doesn't have any *Text*, so a placeholder is shown instead (see sidebar).

6 Set the properties of the *Literal* control.

   1. Set the *ID* property of the *Literal* control to: **LiteralTest**

   2. Set the *Text* property of the *Literal* control to: **Test Literal**

You'll notice there are a lot fewer properties for a *Literal* control than there are for a *Label* control. You'll see why in a moment.

7 See the difference between *Label* and *Literal* controls.

   1. View *controlstest.aspx* in your browser (see sidebar).

   2. View the source of the page.

      As you've done before, right-click in Internet Explorer and then click *View Source* from the shortcut menu.

```
<span id="LabelTest" style="font-weight:bold;">Test Label</span>
Test Literal
```

You can see that the *Label* control has been converted into a *span* tag by the server. The server has converted the *Font Bold* property into inline CSS code.

The *Literal* control only sends exactly what you put into its *Text* property to the browser. This is the reason it has so few properties.

The server will never change it in any way. This is useful when you want to use C# to place HTML code directly onto the page.

The *Label* control is the best choice when you simply want to display text in the user's browser.

note

The other events of Label and Literal controls

As well as the *Load* event, you'll notice the *Init, PreRender* and *Unload* events. These correspond to *Page_Init, Page_PreRender* and *Page_Unload* in the same way as *Load* corresponds to *Page_Load*.

You'll also see *DataBinding* and *Disposed*.

Disposed happens when the control is removed from the web server's memory, which will happen after the control has been converted to HTML and sent to the user's web browser.

DataBinding is a special event that only happens if the control is attached to a data source, such as a SQL database. You'll learn more about binding data to controls in: *Lesson 11-8: Bind data to a control using C# code.*

It isn't just the *Label* and *Literal* controls that have these events; they're available on every ASP.NET control. In practice, however, it is very rare to have to use them. You won't need to use any of these events throughout the rest of this course.

8   Use the *Load* event.

1.   Close your browser and return to *controlstest.aspx* in *Design* view.

2.   Select *LabelTest* and add a *Load* event handler to it.

Do this in the same way as you added the *Click* event handler to your buttons earlier: Select the control, click the *Events* button (in the *Properties* window) and double-click in the empty box next to *Load*.

3.   Add the following code to the *Load* event handler of *LabelTest*:

LabelTest.Text = "Label Load Event Fired!";

```
protected void LabelTest_Load(object sender, Ev
{
    LabelTest.Text = "Label Load Event Fired!";
}
```

4.   View *controlstest.aspx* in your browser.

The *Text* property of the *Label* is updated when the page loads.

The *Load* events (for each control on the page) happen immediately after the *Page_Load* event. You'd see the same effect if you put the code into the *Page_Load* event handler instead.

In general, it's better to use the *Page_Load* event handler rather than the *Load* event handlers of each individual control. This keeps all of the code that runs when the page loads in the same place.

The person viewing your site can't interact directly with *Label* or *Literal* controls, so there are no other important events.

9   Close your browser and remove the controls.

Remove both the *Label* and *Literal* controls.

10   Remove the *LabelTest_Load* event handler.

1.   Try running the project in *Debug* mode.

You'll find that it is unable to run. This is because you left the event handler code for the *Label* control behind after you deleted it, and it no longer makes sense to ASP.NET.

2.   Remove the *LabelTest_Load* event handler.

Simply open the code-behind file and delete the event handler.

3.   Try running the project again.

This time the project will be able to start.

11   Close Visual Studio.

Lesson 4-4: Use the TextBox control

You've already worked with the *TextBox* control a few times. It's one of the most common controls in ASP.NET. The *TextBox* control provides the easiest way to allow users of your site to input text.

1   Open *My Project* from your sample files folder.

2   Open *controlstest.aspx* in *Design* view.

3   Add a *TextBox* control to the page.

4   Set the ID property of the *TextBox* control to: **TextBoxTest**

You now have a *TextBox* control with the default properties.

5   Make *TextBoxTest* bigger.

1.   Set the *Width* property of the *TextBoxTest* control to: **300px**

2.   Set the *Height* property of the *TextBoxTest* control to: **75px**

3.   View the page in your browser.

4.   Type some text into the text box.

Although the text box has lots of room, the text all stays on one line.

5.   Close the browser.

6   Make *TextBoxTest* work with multiple lines.

1.   Set the *TextMode* property of *TextBoxTest* to: **MultiLine**

2.   View the page in your browser.

3.   Try typing in some text.

This time the text is spread across multiple lines.

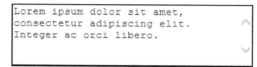

4.   Close the browser.

7   Set the width of the *TextBox* in columns.

As well as setting the width of a text box in pixels, you can also set it using columns. A column is a single letter.

1.   Clear the *Width* property of *TextBoxTest*.

Simply remove the text from the property.

2.   Set the *Columns* property of *TextBoxTest* to: **50**

Note that you can set the height of a *TextBox* control using the *Rows* property in the same way as you set the width using the *Columns* property.

It's up to you how you prefer to specify the height and width of a *TextBox* control.

8   Use the *TextChanged* event.

1.   Add a *TextChanged* event handler to *TextBoxTest*.

You learned how to do this in: *Lesson 3-2: Add event handlers to controls.*

2.   Put the following code in the new event handler:

Response.Write(TextBoxTest.Text);

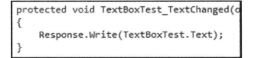

```
protected void TextBoxTest_TextChanged(o
{
    Response.Write(TextBoxTest.Text);
}
```

3.   View the page in your browser.

4.   Type some text into the text box.

Nothing actually happens as the *TextChanged* event isn't fired. This is because the page hasn't been posted back, so the server doesn't know that the text has been changed.

5.   Close your browser and return to *controlstest.aspx*.

6.   Add a *Button* control to the page, and set its ID property to: **ButtonSubmit**

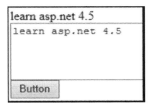

7.   View the page in your browser.

8.   Type some text into the text box and click the button.

The page posts back when you click the button. The server sees that the text has been changed, so the *TextChanged* event fires and your C# code adds the text to the top of the *Response*.

9.   Click the button again without changing the text.

The text hasn't changed since the last time the page was posted back, so the *TextChanged* event handler doesn't fire when the page posts back this time.

10. Close your browser and return to Visual Studio.

9   Set the maximum length of the text box.

1.   Set the *MaxLength* property of the *TextBoxTest* control to: **10**

2.   View the page in your browser.

3.   Type some text into the text box.

Unfortunately, the *MaxLength* property has no effect. The user can still enter as much text as they like.

4.   Close the browser and set the *TextMode* property of the *TextBoxTest* control back to: **SingleLine**

5.   View the page in your browser.

6.   Type some text into the text box.

This time the text is limited correctly. Unfortunately, *MaxLength* does not work with *MultiLine* text boxes.

10   Close the browser and remove the controls and code.

note

AutoPostBack

When a *TextBox* control has its *AutoPostBack* property set to *True*, it will submit the form as soon as the user clicks away from the text after editing it.

This property is rarely used for *TextBox* controls.

Lesson 4-5: Use the CheckBox control

note

The CheckBox control and HTML

In the same way as all ASP.NET controls, the *CheckBox* control is converted into HTML code when the page is sent to a web browser.

The *CheckBox* control is based on the HTML *Input (Checkbox)* control, but adds more features.

Although it is possible to use the controls from the *HTML* category in ASP.NET, it's almost always better to use ASP.NET's equivalent from the *Standard* category of the *Toolbox*.

note

Groups of check boxes

If you want to create a page with lots of check-box choices, you should be aware of the *CheckBoxList* control.

CheckBoxList controls work very similarly to *DropDownList* controls, except the items are shown as check boxes instead of in a drop-down menu.

You'll learn more about *DropDownList* controls and other list-based controls later in this session.

In this lesson you'll learn more about the *CheckBox* control, which you've only seen very briefly at this point.

A check box is simply a box that the user can check or un-check. You have probably seen them while browsing the Internet.

1   Open *My Project* from your sample files folder.

2   Open *controlstest.aspx* in *Design* view.

3   Add a *CheckBox* control to the page.

4   Set the ID property of the *CheckBox* control to: **CheckBoxTest**

Much like the *Literal* control, the *CheckBox* control displays a placeholder containing its *ID* unless you set its *Text* property.

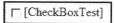

5   Make the *CheckBoxTest* control checked by default.

Set the *Checked* property of the *CheckBoxTest* control to: **True**

The control is now checked by default.

6   Set the *Text* property of the *CheckBox* control to: **Confirm**

The text appears to the right of the *CheckBox* control.

7   Set the *TextAlign* property of the *CheckBox* control to: **Left**

This makes the text appear to the left of the *CheckBox* control instead of to the right.

8   Add a *CheckedChanged* event handler to the control.

1. In the same way as you've done before, add a *CheckedChanged* event handler to the *CheckBoxTest* control.

    You learned how to do this in: *Lesson 3-2: Add event handlers to controls.*

    The *CheckedChanged* event happens when the user ticks or unticks the *CheckBox*.

2. Add the following code to the *CheckedChanged* event handler:

    Response.Write(CheckBoxTest.Checked.ToString());

```
protected void CheckBoxTest_CheckedChanged(object se
{
    Response.Write(CheckBoxTest.Checked.ToString());
}
```

This code will display the *Checked* property of your *CheckBox* control on the page.

3. View *controlstest.aspx* in your browser.

4. Un-check *CheckBoxTest*.

Nothing happens despite the *CheckedChanged* event handler being in place.

This is because the form hasn't been posted back.

9   Make the *CheckBoxTest* control post back when it is clicked.

1. Close the browser and return to *controlstest.aspx* in *Design* view.

2. Set the *AutoPostBack* property of the *CheckBoxTest* control to: **True**

3. View *controlstest.aspx* in your browser.

4. Un-check *CheckBoxTest*.

This time the page posts back when you click the check box and the event handler code writes the current status of the *CheckBox* onto the screen. *True* means that the box is checked, *False* means that the box is un-checked.

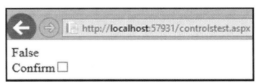

5. Check the *CheckBox* again.

The page posts back again and the event handler displays *True*, since the box is now checked.

Instead of setting the *AutoPostBack* property, you could also have added a *Button* control to the page as you did in: *Lesson 4-4: Use the TextBox control*.

10   Close the browser and remove the controls and code.

Remove the *CheckBoxTest* control from the page.

Don't forget to remove the *CheckBoxTest_CheckedChanged* event handler from the code-behind file.

11   Close Visual Studio.

Lesson 4-6: Use the RadioButton control

You haven't used the *RadioButton* control yet in this course, but it's likely that you've seen radio buttons while browsing the Internet.

Radio buttons are very similar to check boxes, but only allow the user to choose one option at a time. You'll learn more about the *RadioButton* control in this lesson.

1 Open *My Project* from your sample files folder.

2 Open *controlstest.aspx* in *Design* view.

3 Add a *RadioButton* control to the page.

A placeholder containing the *ID* property is shown in exactly the same way as with the *CheckBox* control.

4 Set properties of the new *RadioButton* control.

1. Set the *ID* property to: **RadioButtonChoice1**

2. Set the *Text* property to: **Choice 1**

5 Add another *RadioButton* control to the page.

Try to place it below the first one.

6 Set the properties of the new *RadioButton* control.

1. Set the *ID* property to: **RadioButtonChoice2**

2. Set the *Text* property to: **Choice 2**

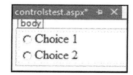

7 See the *RadioButton* control in action.

1. View *controlstest.aspx* in your browser.

2. Click on each of the radio buttons.

Both options become selected with no way to de-select them. This isn't the way that you want things to work.

This happened because you haven't told the two *RadioButton* controls that they belong to the same group yet.

8 Assign the two *RadioButton* controls to a group.

1. Close the browser and return to *controlstest.aspx* in *Design* view.

2. Set the *GroupName* property of both of the radio buttons to: **Choices.** Be careful not to add any trailing spaces.

3. View *controlstest.aspx* in your browser.

4. Click on each of the radio buttons.

This time you're only able to select one choice at a time, which is how radio buttons are supposed to work.

Note that if you had used a *RadioButtonList* control instead (see sidebar), the *GroupName* properties would have been set automatically.

5. Close your browser.

9 **Make *RadioButtonChoice1* selected by default.**

Set the *Checked* property of the *RadioButtonChoice1* control to: **True**

The first choice is now selected by default.

10 **Add a *CheckedChanged* event handler to your control.**

1. Add a *CheckedChanged* event handler to the *RadioButtonChoice1* control.

This event handler will fire when the first *RadioButton* control is checked or unchecked.

2. Add the following code to the new event handler:

Response.Write(RadioButtonChoice1.Checked.ToString());

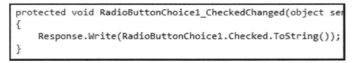

```
protected void RadioButtonChoice1_CheckedChanged(object se
{
    Response.Write(RadioButtonChoice1.Checked.ToString());
}
```

This code will write either *True* or *False* onto the screen depending on whether *RadioButtonChoice1* is selected or not.

3. View *controlstest.aspx* in your browser.

4. Try clicking on each of the *RadioButton* controls.

As with the *CheckBox* control, the *RadioButton* control doesn't automatically post back by default, so nothing happens.

5. Close the browser and set the *AutoPostBack* properties of the *RadioButtonChoice1* and *RadioButtonChoice2* controls to: **True**

6. View *controlstest.aspx* in your browser again.

7. Try clicking on each of the *RadioButton* controls.

The event handler works when you click on *Choice 1*, but nothing happens when you click on *Choice 2*. This is because although *Choice 2* is causing a post-back, it doesn't have an event handler.

This could easily be fixed by giving the *RadioButtonChoice2* control a *CheckedChanged* event handler as well.

8. Close the browser.

11 **Remove the controls and event handler code.**

Lesson 4-7: Use the DropDownList control

note

Other list-based controls

In previous lessons, the *CheckBoxList* and *RadioButtonList* controls were mentioned, both of which work in a similar way to *DropDownList* controls.

BulletedList and *ListBox* controls are also based on lists and are also very similar.

Everything that you learn about the *DropDownList* control in this lesson can be applied to the other list-based controls as well.

You learned a little about the *DropDownList* control in: *Lesson 1-16: Use the QuickTasks menu.*

The *DropDownList* control is a little different to the controls that you've worked with so far in this session. List-based controls like the *DropDownList* contain multiple items, each with their own set of properties. They also have properties and events that affect every item in the list.

1   Open *My Project* from your sample files folder.

2   Open *controlstest.aspx* in *Design* view.

3   Add a *DropDownList* control to the page.

4   Set the *ID* of the new *DropDownList* to: **DropDownListTest**

5   Add items to the *DropDownList*.

You might remember doing this in: *Lesson 1-16: Use the QuickTasks menu.*

1.   Click *Edit Items…* from the *QuickTasks* menu of *DropDownListTest*.

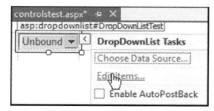

2.   Click *Add* to add a new item to the list.

3.   Set the new item's *Text* property to: **Product 1**

4.   Set the new item's *Value* property to: **1**

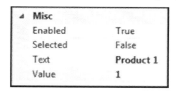

5.   In the same way, create a **Product 2** item with a *Value* of: **2**

6.   Create a **Product 3** item with a *Value* of: **3**

7.   Click *OK*.

You might be wondering what the *Value* property is for. Items in *DropDownLists* are allowed to have both a *Text* property that is shown to the user and a *Value* property that is hidden from the user but is visible to your C# code.

The *Value* property is especially useful when your *DropDownList* control is linked to items in a database (see sidebar).

6   Add a *SelectedIndexChanged* event handler to your control.

note

List-based controls and databases

List-based controls can be made to retrieve their lists from a database instead of typing them in manually.

You'll learn how to do this in: *Lesson 11-2: Attach a data source to a control.*

note

The SelectedIndex property

As well as the *Text* and *Value* properties, each item in a *DropDownList* control has an automatically-generated *Index* property.

These index numbers are always unique and are used to identify a specific item.

The *SelectedIndex* property contains the index number of the currently selected item in the drop-down list.

Index numbers are zero-based (see sidebar below).

note

Zero-based indexing

All lists in ASP.NET are zero-based. This means that the first item in the list is numbered 0 instead of 1 as you might expect.

When you run the example code, you'll see that the *Index* number of the first item is 0.

As well as the *Text* and *Value* properties, each item in a *DropDownList* control is automatically assigned a unique *Index* number (see sidebar).

1. Add a *SelectedIndexChanged* event handler to the *DropDownListTest* control.

2. Add the following code to the new event handler:

   Response.Write(DropDownListTest.SelectedValue);

   This code will display the *Value* property of the item that the user has selected at the top of the page.

3. Add a new line inside the event handler (after the previous line) with the following code:

   Response.Write("<br />");

   This code will simply add an HTML break tag after the *Value*.

4. Add a new line inside the event handler (after the previous line) with the following code:

   Response.Write(DropDownListTest.SelectedItem.Text);

   This code will display the contents of the *Text* property of the selected item.

5. Add another line to place a <br /> tag after the previous line:

   Response.Write("<br />");

6. Add one more line to the event handler:

   Response.Write(DropDownListTest.SelectedIndex);

   This code will display the *Index* property of the selected item (see sidebar for an explanation of index numbers).

```
protected void DropDownListTest_SelectedIndexChanged(ob
{
    Response.Write(DropDownListTest.SelectedValue);
    Response.Write("<br />");
    Response.Write(DropDownListTest.SelectedItem.Text);
    Response.Write("<br />");
    Response.Write(DropDownListTest.SelectedIndex);
}
```

7. View *controlstest.aspx* in your browser.

8. Change the value in the *DropDownList*.

   Nothing happens because the page isn't posted back. You've seen the same behavior with the *CheckBox* and *RadioButton* controls.

9. Close the browser, return to *Design* view and then set the *AutoPostBack* property of *DropDownListTest* to: **True**

10. View *controlstest.aspx* in your browser again.

11. Change the value in the *DropDownList*.

    This time the *SelectedIndexChanged* event handler runs and each of the relevant properties are displayed.

7 Remove the controls and event handler code.

Lesson 4-8: Use the RequiredFieldValidator control

You now know how to work with the controls needed to create almost any online form. One thing that you'll often want to do with online forms is to validate the user's input to make sure that they are entering everything correctly.

Although you could validate user input using a combination of C# and JavaScript code, ASP.NET provides a series of controls that will automatically generate the validation code for you. The *RequiredFieldValidator* control is one of these controls.

1   Open *ShiningStone* from your sample files folder.

2   Open *buy.aspx* in *Design* view.

This is the form that a visitor to the site would use to buy a product. It isn't finished yet, and one thing it needs is validation.

3   Add a *RequiredFieldValidator* control to the page.

Drag a *RequiredFieldValidator* control from the *Validation* category of the *Toolbox* and drop it just after the *TextBox* following *Address 1*.

Address 1		RequiredFieldValidator

A *RequiredFieldValidator* control simply makes sure that the user has entered something into the control that it validates. In this case you're going to make it validate that some text has been entered into the *TextBoxAddress1* control.

4   Set the properties of the new *RequiredFieldValidator* control.

1. Set the *ID* property to: **RequiredFieldValidatorAddress1**

2. Set the *Text* property to: *****

   This is the message that will appear if the control fails to validate, ie if the user doesn't fill in the field.

3. Set the *ControlToValidate* property to: **TextBoxAddress1**

   The *ControlToValidate* property tells the validator which control it is going to check.

5   See the *RequiredFieldValidator* control in action.

1. View *buy.aspx* in your browser.

2. Click *Submit Order* without entering anything into any of the text boxes.

   The page doesn't post back and your * text appears where you placed the *RequiredFieldValidator* control.

Address 1		*

3. Type something into the *Address 1* text box.

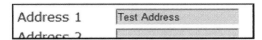

4. Click *Submit Order.*

    This time the page posts back without problems.

5. Close the web browser.

6 **Double-check your validation using C# code.**

Although the messages that you've seen displayed so far are very fast and helpful, the web server implements them by using JavaScript code. A malicious user could bypass your validation by simply disabling JavaScript.

Fortunately, you can use C# code to very easily check that the user hasn't somehow bypassed your validation rules.

1. Open the code-behind file of *buy.aspx.*

2. Add the following code to the *ButtonSubmitOrder_Click* event handler:

    if (Page.IsValid)
    {
       Response.Write("OK!");
    }

    ```
    protected void ButtonSubmitOrder_Click(object sender, EventArgs e)
    {
        if (Page.IsValid)
        {
            Response.Write("OK!");
        }
    }
    ```

    This code will re-check the user input against all of the validation controls on the page and will only write *OK!* if all validation rules succeed. This is a very useful security enhancement.

    This code uses an *if* statement. You'll learn all about them in: *Lesson 7-1: Use the if statement.*

3. View the page in your browser.

4. Enter some text into the *Address1* text box.

5. Click *Submit Order.*

    ![http://localhost:49753/buy.aspx]
    OK!

    The form is submitted and the C# test succeeds. If you'd disabled JavaScript to try to bypass the validation, the C# test wouldn't succeed and you wouldn't see *OK!*.

7 **Close Visual Studio.**

Lesson 4-9: Use the RangeValidator and ValidationSummary controls

The *RequiredFieldValidator* control is very useful, but Visual Studio comes with other validation controls to help you make sure that your users have entered the right values into your forms.

The *RangeValidator* control allows you to check that the user has entered the correct type of value and allows you to restrict the value to a range.

The *ValiationSummary* control lets you easily display a list of validation error messages to let the user know what they have entered incorrectly.

1   Open *ShiningStone* from your sample files folder.

2   Open *buy.aspx* in *Design* view.

3   Add a *RangeValidator* control next to *Phone Number*.

The *RangeValidator* control allows you to restrict a value to a specific type and range.

Add a *RangeValidator* control to the right of the *Phone Number* text box control.

Phone Number | RangeValidator

4   Set the properties of the new *RangeValidator* control.

1. Set the *ID* property to: **RangeValidatorPhoneNumber**

2. Set the *Text* property to: *

3. Set the *ControlToValidate* property to: **TextBoxPhoneNumber**

4. Set the *Type* property to: **Integer**

The *Type* property makes sure that the contents of the validated control are of a certain type. Setting it to *Integer* will make sure that the user enters a whole number into the *TextBoxPhoneNumber* control.

5. Set the *MinimumValue* property to: **0**

6. Set the *MaximumValue* property to: **999999**

The *MinimumValue* and *MaximumValue* properties control which numbers the *RangeValidator* will accept as valid. In this case, if the number is below 0 or above 999999, it will be considered invalid. This will restrict users to phone numbers with six digits or less.

5   See the *RangeValidator* control in action.

1. View *buy.aspx* in your browser.

2. Enter some text into the *Address 1* text box.

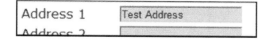
Address 1 | Test Address
Address 2 |

3. Enter **999999** into the *Phone Number* text box.

note

Advanced validation controls

Along with the *RequiredFieldValidator* and *RangeValidator* controls you'll see the *CompareValidator*, *CustomValidator* and *RegularExpressionValidator* controls.

The *CompareValidator* control is used when you want to validate by comparing one control with another.

The *CustomValidator* control allows you to enter your own JavaScript code to be used for validation.

The *RegularExpressionValidator* control allows you to validate using a Regular Expression. Regular Expressions aren't covered in this course, but you can learn all about them in the Expert Skills course in this series.

Phone Number 999999

4. Click: *Submit Order*.

http://localhost:49753/buy.aspx

OK!

The form submits successfully because *999999* is within the range that is allowed by your *RangeValidator* control.

5. Enter **9999999** into the *Phone Number* text box.

Phone Number 9999999

6. Click *Submit Order*.

Phone Number 9999999   *

This time the validator's error message appears because *9999999* is higher than the *MaximumValue* property.

In a real project you would probably use a *RegularExpressionValidator* control to make sure that the user enters a valid phone number (see sidebar).

7. Close the web browser.

6 Add a *ValidationSummary* control.

As well as displaying error messages next to the controls themselves, you can use a *ValidationSummary* control to show a list of validation problems.

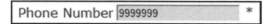

Submit Order

• Error message 1.
• Error message 2.

1. Add a *ValidationSummary* control just after the *Submit Order* button.

2. Set the *ID* property of the new *ValidationSummary* control to: **ValidationSummaryBuy**

The *ValidationSummary* control will automatically display the *ErrorMessage* properties from any other validation controls on the page.

7 Set error messages for your validation controls.

1. Set the *ErrorMessage* property of the *RequiredFieldValidatorAddress1* control to: **Address 1 Required**

2. Set the *ErrorMessage* property of the *RangeValidatorPhoneNumber* control to: **Invalid Phone Number**

8 Test the *ValidationSummary* control.

1. View *buy.aspx* in your browser.

2. Enter **abc** in the *Phone Number* text box.

3. Click the *Submit Order* button.

The validation summary appears, showing the *ErrorMessage* properties, along with the asterisks from the *Text* properties.

• Address 1 Required
• Invalid Phone Number

Lesson 4-10: Use common properties

note

Other common control properties

Enabled
Determines whether the control is disabled or not. If you set the *Enabled* property to *False*, the control will still be visible but grayed out to tell the user that the control will not work. The user will not be able to interact with the control.

ToolTip
Controls the text that will appear when a user hovers their mouse cursor over the control.

EnableViewState
You learned about this in *Lesson 3-9: Work with ViewState.*

EnableTheming
Determines whether theming is enabled for the control. You can learn more about themes in the Expert Skills course in this series.

CausesValidation
Enables and disables the validation features that you learned about in: *Lesson 4-8: Use the RequiredFieldValidator control.*

BackColor and *ForeColor*
Controls the background color and text color of a control.

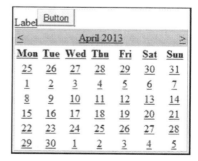

You've become familiar with the properties of the most common controls in this session, but you've probably noticed that there are a few properties that are common to all controls.

In this lesson you'll look at some of the most common properties and learn what they do.

1   Open *My Project* from your sample files folder.

2   Open *controlstest.aspx* in *Design* view.

3   Add some controls to the page.

   1.   Add a *Label* control and name it: **LabelTest**

   2.   Add a *Button* control and name it: **ButtonTest**

   3.   Add a *Calendar* control and name it: **CalendarTest**

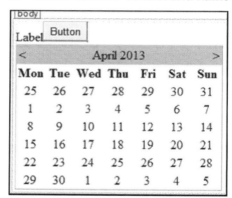

4   Change the *Font* properties.

   1.   Set the *Font Underline* property of the *LabelTest* control to: **True**

   2.   Set the *Font Underline* property of the *ButtonTest* control to: **True**

   3.   Set the *Font Underline* property of the *CalendarTest* control to: **True**

The property has the same effect on each control. The *Font* properties are available on all controls that contain text.

5   Use the *Visible* property.

All ASP.NET controls have a *Visible* property. If *Visible* is set to *False*, the HTML from the control is never sent to the user's browser.

   1.   Set the *Visible* property of the *CalendarTest* control to: **False**

   2.   View *controlstest.aspx* in your browser.

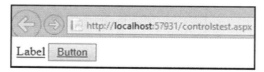

The *CalendarTest* control doesn't appear on the page. If you view the source of the page in Internet Explorer, you'll see that the calendar isn't just hidden, it is completely omitted from the page.

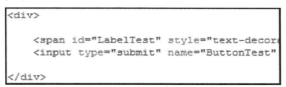

```
<div>

    <span id="LabelTest" style="text-decor
    <input type="submit" name="ButtonTest"

</div>
```

3. Close the browser.

6 **Use the *Height* and *Width* properties.**

Almost every control has *Height* and *Width* properties that can be used to control their size.

1. Set the *Width* property of the *ButtonTest* control to: **150px**

2. Set the *Width* property of the *CalendarTest* control to: **10px**

   The *Calendar* control only shrinks slightly. This is because it can't shrink smaller than the content inside it.

   If you were to reduce the *Font Size* property of the *CalendarTest* control it would shrink to a smaller size.

7 **Use the *CSSClass* property.**

When you set a control's styles using its properties, the web server automatically creates CSS code to display them on the page.

It's more efficient and organized to keep your CSS in a different file and assign CSS classes to your controls. You can do this on almost every control by using the *CSSClass* property.

1. Add a link to the *Site.css* file in the *Content* folder.

   Switch to *Source* view and add the following line of code to the *<head>* tag:

   <link href="Content/Site.css" rel="stylesheet" type="text/css" />

2. Switch back to *Design* view.

   The CSS file has taken effect and the page's colors and layout have changed.

3. Set the *CSSClass* property of the *LabelTest* control to: **message-error**

4. Set the *CSSClass* property of the *ButtonTest* control to: **message-error**

5. Set the *CSSClass* property of the *CalendarTest* control to: **message-error**

The font becomes red and slightly larger when you apply the *message-error* CSS class. You'll notice, however, that the text remains underlined. This is because any properties that you set on the controls themselves will override the styles set by CSS classes.

8 **Remove the controls and code.**

Remember to remove the reference to the CSS file.

Session 4: Exercise

1   Open the *ShiningStone* sample project and open *buy.aspx* in *Design* view.

2   Set the maximum length of each of the address text box controls to 50.

3   Make each of the address text boxes 50 columns wide.

4   Add a *CheckBox* control in the space before the *Submit Order* button.

5   Set the *Text* property of the *CheckBox* control to: **I accept the terms and conditions**

6   Set the *CheckBox* control's ID property to: **CheckBoxAcceptTerms**

7   Add a *RequiredFieldValidator* control next to the *Address 2* text box and configure it appropriately.

8   Add a *RequiredFieldValidator* next to the *Post Code* text box and configure it appropriately.

9   Make the background color of the *Post Code* text box match the background color of the *Address 1* text box.

10   Make the font of the *Submit Order* button bold.

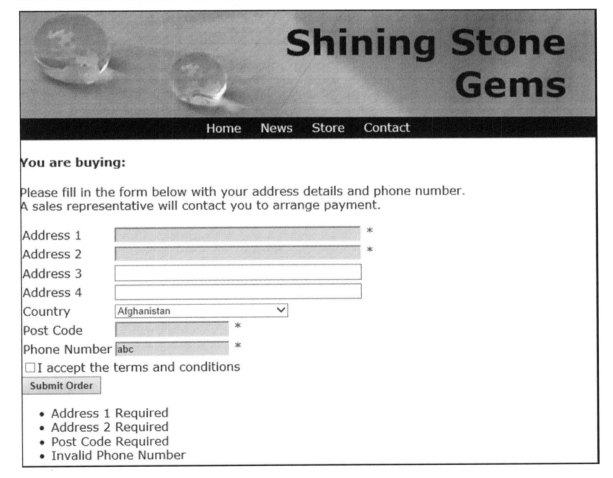

Session 4: Exercise Answers

These are the four questions that students find the most difficult to answer:

Q 9	Q 7	Q 6	Q 2
1. Open *buy*.aspx in *Design* view. 2. Click one of the pink text boxes. 3. Examine the *BackColor* property. You will see that it is set to: *#FFCCCC* 4. Click the *Post Code* text box. 5. Set the *BackColor* property to: **#FFCCCC** This was covered in: *Lesson 1-13: Change properties in Design view.*	1. Open *buy*.aspx in *Design* view. 2. Drag a *RequiredFieldValidator* from the *Validation* category of the *Toolbox* to the space after *TextBoxAddress2*. 3. Select the *RequiredFieldValidator*. 4. Set the *ID* property to: **RequiredFieldValidatorAddress2** 5. Set the *Text* property to: * 6. Set the *ErrorMessage* property to: **Address 2 Required** 7. Set the *ControlToValidate* property to: **TextBoxAddress2** This was covered in: *Lesson 4-8: Use the RequiredFieldValidator control.*	1. Open *buy*.aspx in *Design* view. 2. Select *CheckBox1* and set its *ID* property to: **CheckBoxAcceptTerms** This was covered in: *Lesson 4-1: Name controls correctly.*	1. Open *buy*.aspx in *Design* view. 2. Select each of the address text box controls by clicking on them. 3. Set the *MaxLength* property of each text box control to: **50** This was covered in: *Lesson 4-4: Use the TextBox control.*

If you have difficulty with the other questions, here are the lessons that cover the relevant skills:

1   Refer to: Lesson 1-7: Manage a project with the Solution Explorer.

3   Refer to: Lesson 4-4: Use the TextBox control.

4   Refer to: Lesson 4-5: Use the CheckBox control.

5   Refer to: Lesson 4-5: Use the CheckBox control.

8   Refer to: Lesson 4-8: Use the RequiredFieldValidator control.

10   Refer to: Lesson 4-10: Use common properties.

Session Five: C# Variables

Numbers constitute the only universal language.

Nathanael West, American author and screenwriter (1903 – 1940)

So far you've mostly worked with Visual Studio's visual features and haven't written a lot of C# code.

From this point on you'll start to learn a lot more about C# and how it fits in with the pages you design, starting with variables.

A variable is a container for a value. The value could be a number, a piece of text, a date or any one of the large number of variable types that C# understands.

In this session you'll learn about the different types of variable that C# can understand and how they can interact with each other.

Session Objectives

By the end of this session you will be able to:

- Use IntelliSense
- Create a variable
- Use string variable properties and methods
- Use integer variables
- Use floating point variables
- Use Boolean variables
- Use DateTime variables
- Convert variables using Convert and Parse
- Convert variables using cast and ToString
- Perform mathematical operations
- Use the Math library for advanced mathematics
- Understand null
- Use object and var variables

Lesson 5-1: Use IntelliSense

You've already seen IntelliSense quite a few times in the previous sessions but have mostly ignored it. The IntelliSense menu is the menu that appears as you're typing code, providing suggestions for what you might mean.

IntelliSense is one of Visual Studio's most useful features, and you'll learn more about how to use it in this lesson.

1   Open *ShiningStone* from your sample files folder.

2   Open the code-behind file of *buy.aspx*.

3   Examine the IntelliSense Menu.

1. Add a new line to end of the *ButtonSubmitOrder_Click* event handler.

2. Type **textbox** on the new line.

    The IntelliSense menu appears, showing all available objects that contain the word *textbox*.

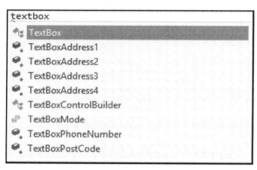

4   Select *TextBoxAddress1* from the IntelliSense menu.

1. Highlight *TextBoxAddress1*.

    You can do this either by clicking on it or by scrolling down to it with the arrow keys.

    A box appears on the right giving you some information about the selected item.

    TextBox buy.TextBoxAddress1
    TextBoxAddress1 control.

    It's not particularly useful in this case, but it can help you when you're not sure exactly what you're looking for.

2. Choose *TextBoxAddress1*.

    You can decide that *TextBoxAddress1* is what you were looking for by either double-clicking on it or pressing <**Enter**>.

    IntelliSense automatically completes the name.

5   Examine the properties of the *TextBoxAddress1* control using IntelliSense.

    Press: <.>

note

IntelliSense and other languages

IntelliSense works best with C#, but you've probably noticed that it will also appear when you are working with HTML, CSS and JavaScript.

Although IntelliSense is useful when working with other languages, it isn't as reliable as it is with C#. There can be a long delay before IntelliSense appears and it doesn't always present a complete list of possible choices.

If you are not completing the course incrementally use the sample file: **Lesson 5-1** to begin this lesson.

Sample files with the starting point for each lesson are also provided for all of the other lessons in this session.

This makes IntelliSense list the properties of the *TextBoxAddress1* control.

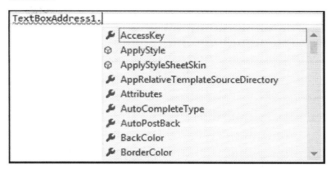

note

IntelliSense icons

You will have noticed that IntelliSense contains various different icons. These indicate the type of the item.

There are a lot of different icons in IntelliSense, but here are a few of the most common.

 : Class

A class is a type of object. *TextBox*, for example, is a class. You'll learn more about classes in: *Lesson 6-1: Create a class.*

 : Control

You will have noticed that this is the icon used for the controls on your page.

🔧 : Property

A property such as the ones that you can change in *Design* view.

⊚ : Method

A method is an action (something that an object is able to do) that might make changes or return some kind of value. Methods can have many different uses. You'll learn more about methods in: *Lesson 6-5: Create and use methods.*

⚡ : Event

An event is a method that runs in response to something happening. It is rare to refer directly to events using C# code.

{ } : Namespace

A namespace is a container for classes, controls, etc. You will learn about namespaces in: *Lesson 6-4: Work with namespaces.*

You can scroll up and down the large list of properties either by clicking the scrollbar with the mouse or by using the arrow keys.

You can see all of the text box's properties in this list, plus a few items with different icons, such as *ApplyStyle*, as seen in the screenshot. *ApplyStyle* is a method (see sidebar).

6 Select the *Text* property using IntelliSense.

1. Scroll down to the *Text* property either using the arrow keys or the scrollbar.

2. Refine the search by typing: **te**

Your search is narrowed to only show items that contain *te*. This allows you to very quickly find an item if you have some idea of its name.

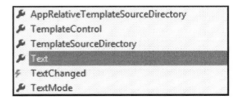

3. Make sure that *Text* is selected.

If you used the mouse to scroll down to *Text*, you will need to click on it.

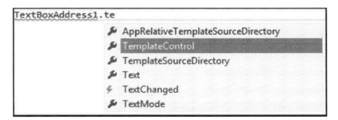

4. Press <**Enter**> or double-click on *Text*.

Once again, the text is automatically filled in.

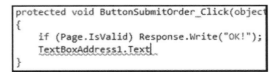

7 Remove the line of code that you added.

8 Close Visual Studio.

Lesson 5-2: Create a variable

note

Visual Studio warnings

In *Lesson 1-9: Run a project in debug mode*, you saw that code with errors is underlined in red. In this lesson, you can see some code underlined in green.

Green underlining indicates a warning rather than an error. If you hover your mouse cursor over the marked line, you will see the warning that Visual Studio is giving you.

In this case, Visual Studio is just warning you that the *TestString* variable isn't being used for anything. As soon as you add some code to make use of the variable, the green underline will disappear.

Warnings won't stop you from running a project. They are there only for information purposes.

1   Open *ShiningStone* from your sample files folder.

2   Open the code-behind file of *buy.aspx*.

3   Add a string variable to the *Page_Load* event handler.

Add the following code to the *Page_Load* event handler:

string TestString = "Hello World!";

```
protected void Page_Load(object sender, EventArgs e)
{
    string TestString = "Hello World!";
}
```

A variable can be thought of as a container for data. You have just created a new *string* variable called *TestString* which contains the text *Hello World!* You'll notice that *TestString* is underlined in green. This is a warning message (see sidebar).

A *string* variable always contains text. You'll learn more about strings in: *Lesson 5-3: Use string variable properties and methods.*

4   Set the *Text* property of the *TextBoxAddress1* control to match the value of the *TestString* variable.

1.   Add a new line to the *Page_Load* event handler.

2.   Type: **TextBoxAddress1.Text**

3.   Look to the side of the IntelliSense menu.

The first word (*string*) tells you that the *Text* property of a *TextBox* control can be manipulated in the same way as a *string* variable. You could have guessed that by the fact that it can contain a piece of text.

4.   Complete the line of code so that it appears as follows:

TextBoxAddress1.Text = TestString;

```
protected void Page_Load(object sender,
{
    string TestString = "Hello World!";
    TextBoxAddress1.Text = TestString;
}
```

You may notice that *TestString* appears in the IntelliSense menu as you type.

5.   View *buy.aspx* in your browser.

The *Address 1* text box displays *Hello World!* This happened because your code copied the text stored in the *TestString* variable to the *Text* property of the *TextBoxAddress1* control.

6.   Close your browser and return to Visual Studio.

5   Change the value of the *TestString* variable.

The reason variables are called variables is that their values can vary. *TestString* doesn't have to stay at the value you defined when you created it. In fact it is very easy to change its value.

1. Add a new line after the one where you created *TestString*.

2. Put the following code on your new line:

TestString = "Please enter address";

This code will change the value of the *TestString* variable from *Hello World!* to *Please enter address*. This technique works with any kind of variable.

```
protected void Page_Load(object sender,
{
    string TestString = "Hello World!";
    TestString = "Please enter address";
    TextBoxAddress1.Text = TestString;
}
```

3. View *buy.aspx* in your browser.

Because the value of the *TestString* variable was changed, the new value is used in the text box.

| Address 1 | Please enter address |

4. Close the web browser.

6 Remove all code from the *Page_Load* event handler.

7 Create a variable using the text from a control.

As well as setting a control's properties from a variable, you can set the value of a variable from a control's properties.

1. Add the following line of code to the end of the *ButtonSubmitOrder_Click* event handler:

string Address1 = TextBoxAddress1.Text;

This code creates a new *string* variable called *Address1*. It also copies the *Text* property of the *TextBoxAddress1* property into the new *Address1* variable.

2. Add the following code on the next line:

Response.Write(Address1);

This code will display the contents of the *Address1* string variable on the page.

```
if (Page.IsValid)
{
    Response.Write("OK!");
}
string Address1 = TextBoxAddress1.Text;
Response.Write(Address1);
```

3. View *buy.aspx* in your browser.

4. Fill in the highlighted text boxes (the text boxes have been highlighted to indicate that they are required fields).

You may remember that in: *Lesson 4-9: Use the RangeValidator and ValidationSummary controls* you set a rule that the *Phone Number* had to be a number between 0 and 999999 so make sure that your phone number is within this range.

5. Click *Submit Order*.

The text that you entered appears at the top of the page, just after the validation message that you added earlier.

note

String means exactly the same as string

If you look carefully in the IntelliSense menu when typing *string*, you'll notice that there's also an entry called *String* (where the first letter is capitalized).

In code, *String* means exactly the same thing as *string*.

So which is the better writing style?

All of Microsoft's examples use the lower-case version and, for that reason, I've used the same in the code examples in this book.

There's also a very good argument to suggest that the upper-case version represents better coding practice because *String* is the 'real' name of the string type in the .NET framework.

There are similar alternative names for some other variable types, as you will see later in this session.

Lesson 5-3: Use string variable properties and methods

1 Open *ShiningStone* from your sample files folder.

2 Open the code-behind file of *buy.aspx*.

3 Attach two strings together.

As well as setting the value of a string, as you did in *Lesson 5-2: Create a variable*, you can join two strings together using a + sign. Joining two strings together is also called *concatenating*.

1. Add a new line after: *string Address1 = TextBoxAddress1.Text;*

2. Put the following code on the new line:

   Address1 = "<br />" + Address1;

   ```
   if (Page.IsValid) Response.Write("OK!");
   string Address1 = TextBoxAddress1.Text;
   Address1 = "<br />" + Address1;
   Response.Write(Address1);
   ```

   This code will add an HTML break tag (*
*) to the beginning of the *Address1* string variable.

   You learned about the HTML break tag in: *Lesson 2-2: Understand HTML paragraph and break tags.*

3. View *buy.aspx* in your browser.

4. Fill in the required fields appropriately and click *Submit Order*.

   This time the *Address1* string is displayed on its own line because of the HTML *
* tag that you added to it.

   ```
   OK!
   Address 1
   ```

5. Close your web browser.

4 Find out the length of a string variable.

C#'s string variables offer a number of useful properties and methods. One of the most useful properties is *Length*.

1. Add a new line at the end of the *ButtonSubmitOrder_Click* event handler.

2. Put the following code on the new line:

   Response.Write("(" + Address1.Length + ")");

   ```
   protected void ButtonSubmitOrder_Click(object ser
   {
       if (Page.IsValid) Response.Write("OK!");
       string Address1 = TextBoxAddress1.Text;
       Address1 = "<br />" + Address1;
       Response.Write(Address1);
       Response.Write("(" + Address1.Length + ")");
   }
   ```

   You're actually joining 3 strings together here: an *opening bracket*, the *Length* property of the string and a *closing bracket*. This will show the length (number of characters) of the string in brackets.

3. View *buy.aspx* in your browser.

4. Fill in the required fields as before and click *Submit Order*.

This time you can see the length of the text you entered plus 6 (the number of characters in the <br /> tag) in brackets after the text.

5. Close your browser and return to Visual Studio.

OK!
test address 1 (21)

note

String methods

ToUpper and *ToLower* are both methods of string variables. You'll learn more about methods in: *Lesson 6-5: Create and use methods.*

Some other useful methods of string variables are:

Contains
Checks whether a string contains a certain piece of text.

IndexOf
Searches for a piece of text inside the string and tells you its position in the string.

Split
Splits a string into several strings separated by the character you choose.

5 Use the *ToUpper* method of the string variable to make a string all UPPER CASE.

Sometimes you might want to convert a string to upper case. Fortunately, C# makes this very easy.

1. Replace:

Response.Write(Address1);

With:

Response.Write(Address1.ToUpper());

2. View *buy.aspx* in your browser and test it in the same way as you have previously.

This time the Address 1 text is displayed in UPPER CASE.

You can use *ToLower()* in the same way to make a string all lower case. *ToUpper* and *ToLower* are methods (see sidebar).

3. Close the web browser.

6 Use the *Replace* method to remove all of the spaces from a string.

You can use the *Replace* method to replace letters inside a string.

1. Add a new line after: *Address1 = "<br />" + Address1;*

2. Add the following code on the new line:

Address1 = Address1.Replace(" ","");

This code will remove all of the spaces from the *Address1* string. By changing the contents of the two sets of quote marks, you could replace any part of a string with any other string.

```
if (Page.IsValid) Response.Write("OK!");
string Address1 = TextBoxAddress1.Text;
Address1 = "<br />" + Address1;
Address1 = Address1.Replace(" ","");
Response.Write(Address1.ToUpper());
Response.Write("(" + Address1.Length + ")");
```

note

Empty strings

You could create a string variable without a value using something like:

string TestString;

You might expect this to be the same as:

string TestString = "";

...but it is actually completely different.

The first example would create a string with a *null* value, while the second would create an empty string.

You'll learn more about *null* in: *Lesson 5-12: Understand null.*

3. View *buy.aspx* in your browser and test it again.

Make sure that you enter some text with spaces into the *Address 1* text box.

This time the spaces are removed from the string when it is displayed on the page after submitting.

4. Close the web browser.

7 Remove all of the code from the *ButtonSubmitOrder_Click* event handler.

Lesson 5-4: Use integer variables

An integer variable contains a whole number (a number with no decimal places).

Strings and integers make up the majority of variables in most ASP.NET applications.

1   Open *ShiningStone* from your sample files folder.

2   Open the code-behind file of *buy.aspx*.

3   Create an integer variable.

1.   Add the following code to the *Page_Load* event handler:

int TestInt = 10;
Response.Write(TestInt);

```
protected void Page_Load(obj
{
    int TestInt = 10;
    Response.Write(TestInt);
}
```

This code creates a new *int* variable called *TestInt* with a value of 10 and displays it on the page.

2.   View *buy.aspx* in your browser.

The number is displayed at the top of the page.

3.   Close the web browser.

4   Add a value to the *TestInt* variable.

Because C# understands that the *int* variable is a number rather than a piece of text, you can perform mathematical operations with it such as adding, subtracting, multiplying and dividing.

1.   Add the following line of code before the *Response.Write(TestInt);* line:

TestInt = TestInt + 5;

This code will add 5 to the value of the *TestInt* variable.

```
protected void Page_Load(obj
{
    int TestInt = 10;
    TestInt = TestInt + 5;
    Response.Write(TestInt);
}
```

2.   View *buy.aspx* in your browser.

This time *15* is displayed on the page (the sum of 10 + 5).

note

short, int and long

Along with *int*, there are two other integer variable types: *short* and *long*.

Much like *string* and *String*, the *int* variable has another name in the .NET framework which means exactly the same thing: *Int32*.

An *Int32* is a 32-bit integer. This means that an *Int32* (or *int*) variable can hold a number from minus 2,147,483,647 to 2,147,483,647 and takes up 32 bits of memory.

short and *long* correspond to the "real" variable names of *Int16* and *Int64*. An *Int16* variable can hold a number from minus 32,767 to 32,767 and an *Int64* can hold a number from minus 9,223,372,036,854,775,807 to 9,223,372,036,854,775,807!

If you found that your integers were using too much memory, you would probably convert them to *short* if you knew that their values would never exceed 32,767.

long is useful on the rare occasions where you need to work with numbers greater than 2,147,483,647.

General practice is to use *int* for all integer variables and only to change them to *short* or *long* if it becomes necessary.

15

3. Close the web browser.

5 **Retrieve the SelectedIndex property from a drop-down list control to indicate which item was chosen.**

Some properties of controls are integers, such as the *SelectedIndex* property of a *DropDownList* control.

1. Add the following line of code before the *Response.Write(TestInt);* line:

   TestInt = DropDownListCountry.SelectedIndex;

```
protected void Page_Load(object sender, EventArg
{
    int TestInt = 10;
    TestInt = TestInt + 5;
    TestInt = DropDownListCountry.SelectedIndex;
    Response.Write(TestInt);
}
```

2. View *buy.aspx* in your browser.

3. Complete the form.

   Make sure to choose a country from the drop-down list.

4. Click *Submit Order*.

   The *index* value for the country you selected is displayed.

   182

5. Change the country in the drop-down list.

6. Click *Submit Order* again.

   The index number that is displayed changes to the index number of the country that you selected.

   183

In a real-world web application you'd usually use the *SelectedValue* property instead of the *SelectedIndex* property to identify a user's drop-down choice. To keep things simple, you didn't use the *SelectedValue* property because it is a string rather than an integer.

6 **Remove all code from the *Page_Load* event handler.**

```
protected void Page_Load(object sender, EventArgs e)
{

}
```

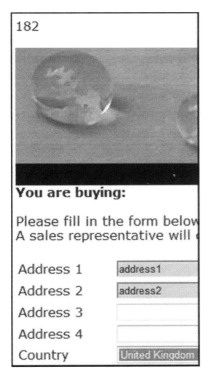

Lesson 5-5: Use floating point variables

Integers are great for working with whole numbers, but there will often be times when you will want to work with numbers that have decimal places, such as when working with currency values.

In C#, numbers with decimal places are stored as *floating point* numbers. The mathematics behind them is beyond the scope of this book, but you'll learn how to create and work with them in this lesson.

1   Open *ShiningStone* from your sample files folder.

2   Open the code-behind file of *buy.aspx*.

3   Add a *float* variable.

   1.   Add the following code to the *Page_Load* event handler:

   float TestFloat = 3.14159f;
   Response.Write(TestFloat);

   This code creates a new *float* variable called *TestFloat* with a value of *3.14159* and displays it on the page.

   You need to end a *float* value with an *f* in order for it to be recognised as a *float* value.

   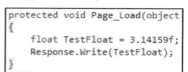

   2.   View *buy.aspx* in your browser.

   The number is displayed on the screen when the page loads.

   3.   Close your web browser.

4   Understand the accuracy problem with floating point numbers.

   Floating point values are only accurate within certain parameters (see sidebar).

   1.   Calculate **3.14159 * 3.14159** using a calculator or Microsoft Excel.

   You should find that the correct result is: *9.8695877281*

   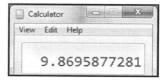

   2.   Change the second line of code that you added in the previous step to the following:

Response.Write(TestFloat * 3.14159f);

```
protected void Page_Load(object sender, EventArgs e)
{
    float TestFloat = 3.14159f;
    Response.Write(TestFloat * 3.14159f);
}
```

3. View *buy.aspx* in your browser.

9.869589

The result that is returned is *9.869589*. This happened because *float* variables are only accurate up to 7 digits!

4. Close your browser.

5   Fix the accuracy problem.

The *double* type is accurate up to at least 15 digits, so it should be capable of calculating the result correctly.

1. Change your code to:

    double TestDouble = 3.14159;
    Response.Write(TestDouble * 3.14159);

```
protected void Page_Load(object sender, E
{
    double TestDouble = 3.14159;
    Response.Write(TestDouble * 3.14159);
}
```

Remember how you had to put an f after the *float* value? You don't need to put any symbol after *double* values.

2. View *buy.aspx* in your browser.

This time the correct result of *9.8695877281* is displayed.

3. Close your browser.

6   Change the code to use a *decimal* variable instead of a *double* variable.

1. Change the code to:

    decimal TestDecimal = 3.14159m;
    Response.Write(TestDecimal * 3.14159m);

```
protected void Page_Load(object sender, Eve
{
    decimal TestDecimal = 3.14159m;
    Response.Write(TestDecimal * 3.14159m);
}
```

You'll notice that you add an *m* to the end of the *decimal* number in much the same way as you added an *f* for the *float*.

2. View *buy.aspx* in your browser.

Again, the result is correct: *9.8695877281*

7   Remove all of the code that you added to the *Page_Load* event handler.

Lesson 5-6: Use Boolean variables

You've already seen a lot of Boolean values when working with control properties. Wherever you saw a property that could be set to either *true* or *false*, you were looking at a Boolean value.

Booleans are always either *true* or *false* and are perfect for anything that can be expressed as a yes or no answer. In this lesson you'll work with C#'s Boolean variable type: *bool*.

1 Open *ShiningStone* from your sample files folder.

2 Open the code-behind file of *buy.aspx*.

3 Create a *bool* variable.

1. Add the following code to the *Page_Load* event handler:

    bool TestBool = true;
    Response.Write(TestBool);

    This code creates a new *bool* variable called *TestBool* and sets its value to *true*.

    ```
    protected void Page_Load(object sender, EventArgs e)
    {
        bool TestBool = true;
        Response.Write(TestBool);
    }
    ```

2. View *buy.aspx* in your browser.

    True is displayed at the top of the page.

3. Close the browser.

4 Change the value of the *bool* variable.

You can easily change the value of a *bool* variable in the same way as you would change the value of any other variable.

1. Add the following line of code after the *bool TestBool = true;* line:

    TestBool = false;

    Notice that there are no quote marks around *true* and *false*. They are not strings, but built-in values that C# understands.

    ```
    protected void Page_Load(object sender, EventArgs e)
    {
        bool TestBool = false;
        TestBool = false;
        Response.Write(TestBool);
    }
    ```

2. View *buy.aspx* in your browser.

    The value has been changed and *False* is displayed.

False

3. Close your web browser.

5 **Set the *bool* variable to the opposite of its current value.**

Booleans support logical operators, which you'll learn more about in: *Lesson 7-3: Use basic logical operators.* By using the exclamation mark (or NOT operator), you can change the bool variable to the opposite of its current value.

This is useful when you are using a *bool* variable to toggle a setting on or off.

1. Change the *TestBool = false;* line to:

TestBool = !TestBool;

```
protected void Page_Load(object sender, EventArgs e)
{
    bool TestBool = true;
    TestBool = !TestBool;
    Response.Write(TestBool);
}
```

2. View *buy.aspx* in your browser.

False is displayed again: the opposite of *True.*

False

3. Close your web browser.

4. Change the *bool Testbool = true;* line to:

bool TestBool = false;

```
protected void Page_Load(object sender, EventArgs e)
{
    bool TestBool = false;
    TestBool = !TestBool;
    Response.Write(TestBool);
}
```

5. View *buy.aspx* in your browser.

This time *True* is displayed: the second line of code has changed *TestBool* to its opposite. *True* is the opposite of *False.*

True

6. Close the web browser.

6 **Remove all code from the *Page_Load* event handler.**

note

Empty DateTime variables

If you create a *DateTime* variable without a value, its value will be *null*. You'll learn about *null* in: *Lesson 5-12: Understand null.*

Unlike the other variable types that you've worked with so far, there isn't a simple way to manually assign a value to a *DateTime* variable.

You will almost always create a date based on the value of a *Calendar* control or using *DateTime.Now.*

If you wanted to create a new *DateTime* variable containing an arbitrary date and time you'd do so by specifying arguments when creating a new instance of the *DateTime* class.

You'll learn how to do this in: *Lesson 6-2: Create an instance of a class.*

note

Regional calendars

Different calendars are used by different countries. The *DateTime* object supports all of these, but it will default to the calendar that is used by the computer that the web application is running on.

It's important to bear in mind that the web server you eventually place your site on may be using a different calendar to the computer you are developing the application on.

ASP.NET calls the regional rules for formatting dates, numbers, etc the *culture.*

You can use the *globalization* tag in the *Web.config* file to make sure that your site always runs using your chosen culture rather than using the culture of the server it is running on.

Lesson 5-7: Use DateTime variables

The *DateTime* variable is possibly the most specialized variable in C#. It is, as you would expect, used to store dates and times.

Date and time are often the most difficult things to work with in programming, since date and time systems are very complex. Fortunately, the *DateTime* variable does most of the work for you.

1 Open *ShiningStone* from your sample files folder.

2 Open the code-behind file of *buy.aspx.*

3 Add a *DateTime* variable.

1. Add the following code to the *Page_Load* event handler:

   DateTime TestDateTime = DateTime.Now;
   Response.Write(TestDateTime);

   ```
   protected void Page_Load(object sender, EventArgs e)
   {
       DateTime TestDateTime = DateTime.Now;
       Response.Write(TestDateTime);
   }
   ```

   The *Now* property of *DateTime* always contains the current date and time.

   This code will create a new *DateTime* variable containing the current date and time and display it on the page when it loads.

2. View *buy.aspx* in your browser.

   ```
   24/04/2013 15:23:26
   ```

   The date above represents 24th April 2013 in UK format. If your date and time are formatted differently from the example above see the *Regional calendars* sidebar for an explanation.

3. Close your browser.

4 Use the *AddDays* method to add three days to the *DateTime* variable.

The *DateTime* variable has several methods that allow you to easily manipulate the date and time stored inside it.

1. Add the following line of code after the line:
   DateTime TestDateTime = DateTime.Now;

   TestDateTime = TestDateTime.AddDays(3);

   ```
   protected void Page_Load(object sender, EventArgs e)
   {
       DateTime TestDateTime = DateTime.Now;
       TestDateTime = TestDateTime.AddDays(3);
       Response.Write(TestDateTime);
   }
   ```

   This code adds 3 days to value of the *TestDateTime* variable. This means that the result that is output to the page should be 3 days later than today.

```
27/04/2013 15:29:40
```

2. View *buy.aspx* in your browser and confirm that the date has changed.

3. Close your browser.

You can use the other *Add* methods of *DateTime* to add hours, months, years, etc. to a *DateTime* variable's value.

5 **Use the *Month* property to display the month from the value of the *DateTime* variable.**

Sometimes you'll just want to get a single component from a date, such as the month or year. The *DateTime* variable has properties that allow you to easily extract each component of a date.

1. Change the *Response.Write(TestDateTime);* line to:

    Response.Write(TestDateTime.Month);

    ```
    DateTime TestDateTime = DateTime.Now;
    TestDateTime = TestDateTime.AddDays(3);
    Response.Write(TestDateTime.Month);
    ```

    You might notice in the IntelliSense menu that the *Month* property is an *int* value.

2. View *buy.aspx* in your browser.

    The month is displayed as an integer.

3. Close your browser.

All of the components of the date have their own property. For example, you could get the year of the date using the *TestDateTime.Year* property.

6 **Use the *ToShortDateString* method to display the date in a shorter format.**

The *DateTime* variable offers a few methods that will format the date in different ways.

1. Change the *Response.Write(TestDateTime.Month);* line to:

    Response.Write(TestDateTime.ToShortDateString());

    ```
    DateTime TestDateTime = DateTime.Now;
    TestDateTime = TestDateTime.AddDays(3);
    Response.Write(TestDateTime.ToShortDateString());
    ```

    This will display a shorter date string. Notice that there are other similar methods such as *ToShortTimeString* and *ToLongDateString*.

2. View *buy.aspx* in your browser.

    ```
    27/04/2013
    ```

    The date is displayed in a shorter format.

You can customize the date string in a more sophisticated way using the *ToString* method. You'll learn how to do this in: *Lesson 5-9: Convert variables using cast and ToString.*

7 **Remove all code from the *Page_Load* event handler.**

Lesson 5-8: Convert variables using Convert and Parse

You now know how to create and work with the most common variable types in C#, but it's often necessary to convert variables from one type to another.

In this lesson you'll learn some of the ways that you can convert variables to different types.

1 Open *ShiningStone* from your sample files folder.

2 Open the code-behind file of *buy.aspx*.

3 Create a *string* variable.

Add the following code to the *ButtonSubmitOrder_Click* event handler:

string PhoneNumberText = TextBoxPhoneNumber.Text;

```
protected void ButtonSubmitOrder_Click(object sender, EventArgs e)
{
    string PhoneNumberText = TextBoxPhoneNumber.Text;
}
```

As you've seen before, this code will create a *string* variable called *PhoneNumberText* that contains the text that was entered into the *TextBoxPhoneNumber* control.

note

Converting other types

You don't have to use *Convert* exclusively on strings and integers; you could use it to convert an *int* to a *decimal*, a *float* to an *int*, or any other combination you can think of.

Obviously not all conversions are possible. Trying to convert a *bool* to a *DateTime*, for example, would cause an exception. Exceptions were covered in: *Lesson 3-5: Understand the Exception object.*

Although there is a *Convert.ToString* method, it's easier just to use *ToString*, as you'll see in: *Lesson 5-9: Convert variables using cast and ToString.*

4 Convert the contents of the *string* variable to *int* data using *Convert.ToInt32*.

In *Lesson 4-9: Use the RangeValidator and ValidationSummary controls,* you added a *RangeValidator* control with a *Type* property of *Integer*. This means that the user can only enter integer values into the *TextBoxPhoneNumber* control.

Because you know that the *TextBoxPhoneNumber* control's *Text* property will contain an integer, it will always be possible to convert the *string* variable from its *Text* property into an *int* variable.

Add the following code on the next line:

int PhoneNumber = Convert.ToInt32(PhoneNumberText);

```
protected void ButtonSubmitOrder_Click(object sender, EventArgs e)
{
    string PhoneNumberText = TextBoxPhoneNumber.Text;
    int PhoneNumber = Convert.ToInt32(PhoneNumberText);
}
```

This code converts the contents of the *PhoneNumberText* string variable into integer data which is stored in a new variable called *PhoneNumber*.

You could now perform mathematical operations on the *int* variable, something that you couldn't do with a *string* variable.

You'll notice that there are lots of other *Convert.To* options in the IntelliSense menu, including all of the types that you've worked with in this session.

5   Convert the contents of the *int* variable to *float* data using *Convert.ToSingle*.

Add the following code on the next line:

float PhoneNumberFloat = Convert.ToSingle(PhoneNumber);

```
protected void ButtonSubmitOrder_Click(object sender, EventArgs e)
{
    string PhoneNumberText = TextBoxPhoneNumber.Text;
    int PhoneNumber = Convert.ToInt32(PhoneNumberText);
    float PhoneNumberFloat = Convert.ToSingle(PhoneNumber);
}
```

Note that the method for converting to *float* is *ToSingle* rather than *ToFloat*. This is because the 'real' name of the *float* type is *Single* (see: *Lesson 5-5: Use floating point variables - sidebar*).

You could use the new *float* variable to carry out mathematical operations with decimal places, something that you couldn't do with *string* or *int* variables.

6   Convert the contents of the *string* variable to *int* data using the alternative *int.Parse* method.

Replace the *int PhoneNumber...* line with:

int PhoneNumber = int.Parse(PhoneNumberText);

```
protected void ButtonSubmitOrder_Click(object sender, EventArgs e)
{
    string PhoneNumberText = TextBoxPhoneNumber.Text;
    int PhoneNumber = int.Parse(PhoneNumberText);
    float PhoneNumberFloat = Convert.ToSingle(PhoneNumber);
}
```

The *Parse* method is an alternative to the *Convert* method, although it only converts from *string* to other types. There is a *Parse* method available for all of the types that you have worked with in this session.

7   Convert the contents of the *string* variable to *float* data using *float.Parse*.

Replace the *float PhoneNumberFloat...* line with:

float PhoneNumberFloat = float.Parse(PhoneNumberText);

```
protected void ButtonSubmitOrder_Click(object sender, EventArgs e)
{
    string PhoneNumberText = TextBoxPhoneNumber.Text;
    int PhoneNumber = int.Parse(PhoneNumberText);
    float PhoneNumberFloat = float.Parse(PhoneNumberText);
}
```

Here you're using the *Parse* method to convert the *PhoneNumberText* string data into *float* data.

Converting *string* values into numbers is very useful, since you cannot perform mathematical operations on *string* values.

8   Close Visual Studio.

note

The TryParse method

If the *Parse* or *Convert* methods are not able to convert a variable it will cause an exception. Exceptions were covered in: *Lesson 3-5: Understand the Exception object.*

The *TryParse* method doesn't cause an exception if conversion is impossible, but it requires the use of the *out* keyword.

TryParse and the *out* keyword are covered in the Expert Skills book in this series.

Lesson 5-9: Convert variables using cast and ToString

In this lesson, you'll use the *ToString* conversion method to convert any variable into a *string* and use the *cast* method to force C# to recognize a variable as a certain type.

1   Open *ShiningStone* from your sample files folder.

2   Open the code-behind file of *buy.aspx*.

3   Convert the contents of an *int* variable into *string* data using the *ToString* method.

You've seen the *ToString* method used a few times already in this course. Almost every type of variable has a *ToString* method that allows you to change its data into *string* data.

Add the following line to the end of the *ButtonSubmitOrder_Click* event handler:

string PhoneNumberText2 = PhoneNumber.ToString();

```
protected void ButtonSubmitOrder_Click(object sender, Even
{
    string PhoneNumberText = TextBoxPhoneNumber.Text;
    int PhoneNumber = int.Parse(PhoneNumberText);
    float PhoneNumberFloat = float.Parse(PhoneNumberText);
    string PhoneNumberText2 = PhoneNumber.ToString();
}
```

This converts the integer data in the *PhoneNumber* variable to string data and stores it in the new *PhoneNumberText2* string variable.

4   Format a date using *ToString*.

The *ToString* method behaves differently for different variable types. For some variable types, you can change how the resulting string is formatted by providing a *format string* as an argument.

Arguments are the values that you enter in the brackets when you call a method. You'll learn more about arguments in: *Lesson 6-6: Create methods with arguments.*

1.   Add the following code to the *Page_Load* event handler:

DateTime TodaysDate = DateTime.Now;
string FormattedDate = TodaysDate
.ToString("dd MMM yyyy");
Response.Write(FormattedDate);

```
protected void Page_Load(object sender, EventArgs e)
{
    DateTime TodaysDate = DateTime.Now;
    string FormattedDate = TodaysDate.ToString("dd MMM yyyy");
    Response.Write(FormattedDate);
}
```

This code creates a *DateTime* variable called *TodaysDate* containing today's date. The date is then converted into a *string* using the *ToString* method with an argument of *dd MMM yyyy* (this is a *format string* - see sidebar).

---

note

Format strings

In this lesson, you can see a basic format string to show a common representation of a date.

There are many different symbols that you can use in date format strings, but these are some of the most common:

d : Day
M : Month
y : Year
h : Hour
m : Minute
s : Second

You can learn more about date format strings from Microsoft's help files.

This *format string* tells the *ToString* method to display a 2-digit day, a 3-letter month and a 4-digit year.

2. View *buy.aspx* in your browser.

24 Apr 2013

The date appears in the format that you specified.

3. Close your browser.

5 Use *cast* to eliminate ambiguity.

The last way of converting variables is called *casting*. Casting is usually used when the type of the variable is ambiguous. For example, when faced with a value such as 123.45 C# cannot determine whether the number represents a *float, double* or *decimal* value.

1. Remove all code from the *Page_Load* event handler.

2. Add the following code to the *Page_Load* event handler:

decimal DecimalNumber = 100.75;

```
protected void Page_Load(object sender, EventArgs e)
{
    decimal DecimalNumber = 100.75;
}
```

The number *100.75* is underlined in red, and if you move your cursor over it you'll see that it is not being recognized as a decimal value (C# sees it as a *double* value). In *Lesson 5-5: Use floating point variables*, you discovered one solution for this problem when you suffixed the number with the letter *m*.

Using a *cast*, however, you can make sure that the value is recognized as a *decimal* value even without the *m* suffix.

3. Change the code to the following:

decimal DecimalNumber = (decimal)100.75;

```
protected void Page_Load(object sender, EventArgs e)
{
    decimal DecimalNumber = (decimal)100.75;
}
```

Putting the type in brackets before a value *casts* it to that type. Note that you could have done the same thing with the *Convert.ToDecimal* method.

4. Add the following code on the next line:

float FloatNumber = (float)DecimalNumber;

```
protected void Page_Load(object sender, EventArgs e)
{
    decimal DecimalNumber = (decimal)100.75;
    float FloatNumber = (float)DecimalNumber;
}
```

Here you have used *cast* to convert the *decimal* value into a *float* value.

There aren't *Convert* and *Parse* methods for all variable types, but *cast* works for every type.

6 Remove all code from both event handlers.

Lesson 5-10: Perform basic mathematical operations

You did some basic mathematics when working with integers and floating point numbers, but in this lesson you'll learn about all of the basic mathematical operations that are available to you.

1 Open *My Project* from your sample files folder.

2 Add a new Web Form to the project called: **calculator.aspx**

You learned how to do this in: *Lesson 1-7: Manage a project with the Solution Explorer.*

3 Add two new *TextBox* controls to the page.

Name the text boxes **TextBoxFirstNumber** and **TextBoxSecondNumber**.

4 Add a *Label* control to the page.

1. Add a *Label* control to the page, below the two text boxes.

2. Name the *Label* control: **LabelResult**

3. Clear the *Text* property of the *LabelResult* control.

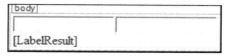

5 Add a Button control that will add together the contents of the two *TextBox* controls and display the result.

1. Add a *Button* control to the page, just after the two text boxes.

2. Set the *ID* property of the *Button* control to: **ButtonCalculate**

3. Set the *Text* property of the *ButtonCalculate* control to: **Calculate**

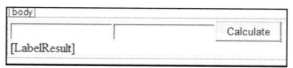

4. Add a *Click* event handler to the *ButtonCalculate* control.

Add the following code to the *ButtonCalculate_Click* event handler:

```
double FirstNumber =
Convert.ToDouble(TextBoxFirstNumber.Text);
double SecondNumber =
Convert.ToDouble(TextBoxSecondNumber.Text);
double Result = FirstNumber + SecondNumber;
LabelResult.Text = Result.ToString();
```

---

note

This example is easy to crash

You may have noticed that you can easily crash this web application in two ways:

1. By leaving both *TextBox* controls empty.

2. By entering text into the *TextBox* controls instead of numbers.

Later in the course, in: *Lesson 7-6: Use try and catch to handle errors*, you'll learn how to elegantly handle any errors that occur so that it is impossible for the user to crash your web pages.

note

Why use doubles?

You might be wondering why you're using the *double* type for the numbers in this lesson.

You could use the *int* type, but that would prevent you from using decimal places in your calculations. If you only wanted to work with whole numbers, you would use the *int* type.

You could also use the *float* and *decimal* types for speed or accuracy. If this were a currency calculator the best choice would be the *decimal* type for enhanced accuracy.

This lesson uses *double* as a compromise between the speed of *float* and the accuracy of *decimal*.

You learned more about the issues surrounding different numeric types in: *Lesson 5-5: Use floating point variables.*

---

note

Brackets (or Parentheses)

You can use brackets to eliminate ambiguity in mathematical operations, for example:

*int X = (1 + 2) * 2;*

...would make X equal 6.

*int X = 1 + (2 * 2);*

...would make X equal 5.

note

Modulo

Modulo is rarely seen outside of programming.

You can perform a modulo operation using the **%** symbol in the same way as you'd use the other mathematical operators (such as + and -).

Modulo divides two numbers and returns the remainder after dividing. For example 112 % 100 would return 12.

note

Shortcuts

There are a few shortcuts to perform the most basic mathematical operations.

Assume you have created an *int* variable called *Number*.

Number++;
Adds 1 to *Number*.

Number--;
Subtracts 1 from *Number*.

Number += 123;
Adds 123 to *Number*.

Number -= 123;
Subtracts 123 from *Number*.

Number *= 123;
Multiplies *Number* by 123.

Number /= 123;
Divides *Number* by 123.

```
protected void ButtonCalculate_Click(object sender, EventArgs e)
{
    double FirstNumber = Convert.ToDouble(TextBoxFirstNumber.Text);
    double SecondNumber = Convert.ToDouble(TextBoxSecondNumber.Text);
    double Result = FirstNumber + SecondNumber;
    LabelResult.Text = Result.ToString();
}
```

This code hopefully makes sense to you by now.

The text from each *TextBox* control is placed into a *double* variable, then the two doubles are added together and placed into another *double* variable called *Result*. Finally, *Result* is converted into a *string* and displayed in the *LabelResult* control.

5.   View *calculator.aspx* in your browser.

6.   Enter some numbers into the text boxes and click *Calculate*.

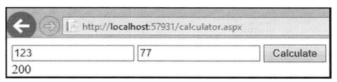

The result of adding the two numbers together appears in the *Label* control.

7.   Close your browser.

6   Change the calculation to multiply the two numbers.

This should be very straightforward to you by now.

1.   Change the line:

double Result = FirstNumber + SecondNumber;

to:

double Result = FirstNumber * SecondNumber;

```
protected void ButtonCalculate_Click(object sender, EventArgs e)
{
    double FirstNumber = Convert.ToDouble(TextBoxFirstNumber.Text);
    double SecondNumber = Convert.ToDouble(TextBoxSecondNumber.Text);
    double Result = FirstNumber * SecondNumber;
    LabelResult.Text = Result.ToString();
}
```

2.   View *calculator.aspx* in your browser.

3.   Enter some numbers into the text boxes and click the button.

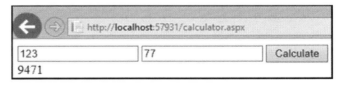

This time the numbers are multiplied.

In the same way, you can subtract using the minus operator - and divide using the forward slash operator: /.

7   Close Visual Studio.

Lesson 5-11: Use the Math library for advanced mathematics

note

Other Math methods

Sqrt
Returns the square root of a number.

Cos
Returns the cosine of an angle.

Tan
Returns the tangent of an angle.

Sin
Returns the sine of an angle.

Log
Returns the logarithm of a number in the specified base.

Floor
Returns the number if it is greater than or equal to the specified value.

Ceiling
Returns the number if it is less than or equal to the specified value.

This still isn't a complete list of the methods in the *Math* library. Feel free to explore the list of methods in *IntelliSense* to see what else *Math* can do.

note

The caret (^) in C#

In ordinary mathematical notation, the ^ operator indicates raising one number to the power of another.

For example, 12^5 would result in 248,832.

In Visual Basic, in fact, this will work.

In C#, however, the caret is used as a logical operator and will not work in mathematics.

You'll learn more about logical operators in: *Lesson 7-3: Use basic logical operators*.

As well as basic addition, subtraction, multiplication and division, C# offers a host of advanced mathematical functions inside the *Math* library.

In this lesson, you'll discover some of the most useful methods in the *Math* library.

1 Open *My Project* from your sample files folder.

2 Open the code-behind file of *calculator.aspx*.

3 Use the *Math* functions to raise one number to the power of another.

1. Change the line:

    *double Result = FirstNumber * SecondNumber;*

    to:

    double Result = Math.Pow(FirstNumber, SecondNumber);

    ```
    double FirstNumber = Convert.ToDouble(TextBoxFirstNumber.Text);
    double SecondNumber = Convert.ToDouble(TextBoxSecondNumber.Text);
    double Result = Math.Pow(FirstNumber, SecondNumber);
    LabelResult.Text = Result.ToString();
    ```

    This is the first method you've used that needs more than one argument. The first argument is the number to be raised (*FirstNumber*) and the second is the number to raise to (*SecondNumber*). You'll learn about arguments in greater depth in: *Lesson 6-6: Create methods with arguments*.

    After you type *Math.*, the IntelliSense menu lists all of the functions that you can use with *Math* (see sidebar for details of some of these).

2. View *calculator.aspx* in your browser.

3. Enter some numbers into the text boxes and press the button.

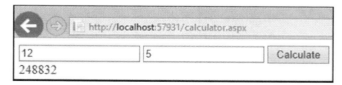

In this example the first number is raised to the power of the second (12^5).

Note that you could <u>not</u> have done this using the ^ operator. The ^ operator has a completely different purpose in C# (see sidebar).

4 Use the *Round* method of the the *Math* library to round a result to 2 decimal places.

1. Close your browser and return to the code-behind file of *calculator.aspx*.

2. Replace the *double Result...* line with:

double Result =
Math.Round(FirstNumber + SecondNumber, 2);

```
double FirstNumber = Convert.ToDouble(TextBoxFirstNumber.Text);
double SecondNumber = Convert.ToDouble(TextBoxSecondNumber.Text);
double Result = Math.Round(FirstNumber + SecondNumber, 2);
LabelResult.Text = Result.ToString();
```

This code adds *FirstNumber* and *SecondNumber* together, but the *Math.Round* method will round the result to 2 decimal places.

The *Round* method has two arguments: the number to round and the required number of decimal places. By changing the second argument (which is currently 2), you can change the number of decimal places returned.

3. View *calculator.aspx* in your browser.

4. Enter some numbers with decimal places and click the button.

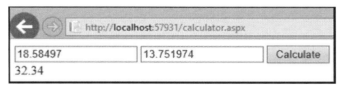

The numbers are added together and the result is rounded to 2 decimal places.

5 **Use the *Math.Max* method to get the larger of two numbers.**

1. Close your browser and return to the code-behind file of *calculator.aspx*.

2. Replace the *double Result...* line with:

double Result = Math.Max(FirstNumber, SecondNumber);

```
double FirstNumber = Convert.ToDouble(TextBoxFirstNumber.Text);
double SecondNumber = Convert.ToDouble(TextBoxSecondNumber.Text);
double Result = Math.Max(FirstNumber, SecondNumber);
LabelResult.Text = Result.ToString();
```

This code will return the larger of the two numbers entered into the text boxes.

3. View *calculator.aspx* in your browser.

4. Enter some numbers and click the button.

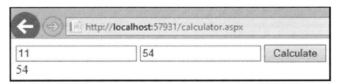

The largest number is displayed.

You can also use *Math.Min* to get the smaller of two numbers.

6 **Close Visual Studio.**

Lesson 5-12: Understand null

null is C#'s concept of 'nothing'. If you create a variable without assigning a value to it, it will often have a value of *null*.

1 Open *My Project* from your sample files folder.

2 Open the code-behind file of *calculator.aspx*.

3 Add a null string.

    1. Add the following code to the *Page_Load* event handler:

        string NullString;
        string EmptyString = "";

    2. Set a breakpoint at the end of the *Page_Load* event handler.

        You learned how to do this in: *Lesson 3-3: Use Breakpoints.*

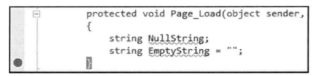

```
protected void Page_Load(object sender,
{
    string NullString;
    string EmptyString = "";
}
```

    3. Right-click *calculator.aspx* in the *Solution Explorer* and select *Set As Start Page* from the shortcut menu.

    4. Run *calculator.aspx* in *Debug* mode.

        You learned how to do this in: *Lesson 1-9: Run a project in debug mode.*

```
protected void Page_Load(object sender,
{
    string NullString;
    string EmptyString = "";
}
```

When the page loads, it pauses at the breakpoint and you are returned to the code editor.

    5. Check the values of the *NullString* and *EmptyString* variables.

        Hover your mouse cursor over the names *NullString* and *EmptyString* in the code editor to see their values.

        You can see that *NullString* has a value of *null*, while *EmptyString* has an empty *string* instead of *null*.

The distinction between *null* and an empty string is an important one. You can perform all string methods on an empty string, but many methods would cause an exception if you tried to use them with a *null* string.

If you tried to set the *Text* property of a *Label* control to *null*, for example, it would cause an exception.

4 Add an empty *int* variable.

    1. Stop debugging by clicking the stop button. ■

    2. Add the following line of code to the end of the *Page_Load* event handler:

---

note

string.IsNullOrEmpty

If you look at the IntelliSense menu for *string* by typing:

string.

...you'll see a method called *IsNullOrEmpty* which returns a *bool*.

IsNullOrEmpty is useful when you want to find out if a string is null or empty without having to check for both conditions.

You'll learn about checking conditions in: *Lesson 7-1: Use the if statement.*

---

int NullInt;

```
protected void Page_Load(obje
{
    string NullString;
    string EmptyString = "";
    int NullInt;
}
```

3. Run the page in Debug mode.

4. When the code pauses, check the value of *NullInt*.

```
int NullInt;
        NullInt  0
```

Rather than being null, the value is 0. This is because int variables aren't nullable by default (ie. they cannot be null). A normal int can never have a null value (and most of the time that's exactly what you want).

If you were to try to set *NullInt* to *null* using *NullInt = null;* you would see an error.

5. Stop debugging by clicking the stop button.

5 Make the *int* variable nullable.

There are times when you want an *int*, or other non-nullable variable to contain a null value, especially when working with databases as you'll discover in: *Lesson 12-8: Create a Search page.*

Fortunately, it's very easy to make a variable nullable.

1. Change the *int NullInt;* line to the following:

int? NullInt;

```
protected void Page_Load(obje
{
    string NullString;
    string EmptyString = "";
    int? NullInt;
}
```

Putting a question mark after *int* makes it nullable! You can do this with other non-nullable types, for example *double?* and *float?* would create nullable versions of those types.

You can't create a *string?* because *string* is already nullable.

2. Run the page in *Debug* mode.

3. Check the value of *NullInt*.

```
int? NullInt;
        NullInt  null
```

This time you can see that *NullInt* has a *null* value.

4. Stop debugging by clicking the stop button.

6 Remove all code from the *Page_Load* event handler.

7 Remove the breakpoint.

Lesson 5-13: Use object and var variables

An object is a self-contained piece of code that has its own set of properties, methods and events.

The .NET library that C# uses is actually a library of objects. Just about everything in C# is an object. Controls, web pages and even variables are all objects. In this lesson you'll learn about the *object* and *var* variable types.

1 Open *My Project* from your sample files folder.

2 Open the code-behind file of *calculator.aspx*.

3 Modify your code to use the *object* variable type.

> You used the *double* variable type for your calculations on this page, which is the correct approach, but since a *double* variable is an object you can also use the *object* variable type.
>
> An object variable can store any type of data. You typically use them when you need to store data but do not know its type in advance.
>
> Change the first line of code in *ButtonCalculate_Click* to the following:

object *FirstNumber = Convert.ToDouble(TextBoxFirstNumber.Text);*

```
protected void ButtonCalculate_Click(object sender, EventArgs e)
{
    object FirstNumber = Convert.ToDouble(TextBoxFirstNumber.Text);
    double SecondNumber = Convert.ToDouble(TextBoxSecondNumber.Text);
    double Result = Math.Max(FirstNumber, SecondNumber);
    LabelResult.Text = Result.ToString();
}
```

> You'll notice that the line that performs the calculation is now indicating an error using a red underline. This is because the *Math.Max* method expects numeric arguments and doesn't know what to do with an *object* variable.

note

GetType

You can use the *GetType* method of an *object* variable to return its current type.

4 Cast the *object* variable's value to a *double*.

> You can still make this code work by casting the *object* variable to the *double* variable type for the purposes of this calculation.
>
> Change the *double Result...* line to:

*double Result = Math.Max(**(double)**FirstNumber, SecondNumber);*

```
object FirstNumber = Convert.ToDouble(TextBoxFirstNumber.Text);
double SecondNumber = Convert.ToDouble(TextBoxSecondNumber.Text);
double Result = Math.Max((double)FirstNumber, SecondNumber);
LabelResult.Text = Result.ToString();
```

> The error disappears. You could also have solved the problem by converting the value of the *object* variable into a *double* with the *Convert.ToDouble* method.

5 Put today's date into the *object* variable.

Because an *object* variable doesn't have a fixed type, it is capable of storing any type of data.

1. Add the following line of code after the *object FirstNumber…* line:

   FirstNumber = DateTime.Now;

   ```
   object FirstNumber = Convert.ToDouble(TextBoxFirstNumber.Text);
   FirstNumber = DateTime.Now;
   ```

   This code changes the value of the *FirstNumber* variable to today's date.

   You can now see why C# needs to be explicity told the type of data that is stored in an *object*. It could literally be anything!

   Obviously trying to convert a *DateTime* value into a *double* value would cause an exception if you tried to run this code.

2. Remove the line that sets the *FirstNumber* variable's value to today's date.

6 **Use a *var* variable type.**

Just like the *object* variable type, the *var* variable type can be used to store data of any type. But there's an important twist.

The *var* data type establishes its type when it is created. From that point forward the type cannot be changed and the variable can be used in exactly the same way as the type that it has assumed.

1. Change the first line of code in *ButtonCalculate_Click* to the following:

   var FirstNumber = Convert.ToDouble(TextBoxFirstNumber.Text);

2. Remove the cast from the *double Result…* line:

   double Result = Math.Max(FirstNumber, SecondNumber);

   ```
   var FirstNumber = Convert.ToDouble(TextBoxFirstNumber.Text);
   double SecondNumber = Convert.ToDouble(TextBoxSecondNumber.Text);
   double Result = Math.Max(FirstNumber, SecondNumber);
   LabelResult.Text = Result.ToString();
   ```

3. View *calculator.aspx* in your browser and test the form.

   The calculation works without any problems. Even without casting the *var* into a *double,* C# knows that the *FirstNumber* variable's type is *double.* This is simply because you put a *double* value into the *var* variable when you created it, causing it to assume the *double* variable type.

4. Close your web browser.

7 **Change the code back to use *double*.**

Although the calculation will still work perfectly using *object* and *var* variables, it is best to use exactly the types you need whenever possible. Change the first line from a *var* back to a *double*.

   ```
   double FirstNumber = Convert.ToDouble(TextBoxFirstNumber.Text);
   ```

Session 5: Exercise

1   Open the *My Project* sample project and open *calculator.aspx* in Design view.

2   Add a new *Button* control to the page called: **ButtonCalculate2**

3   Add a *Click* event handler to the *ButtonCalculate2* control.

4   Create a *string* variable called **PIString** in the *ButtonCalculate2_Click* event handler with a value of: **"3.14159265"**

5   Create a *double* variable called **PIDouble** in the same event handler and set its value to the value of the *PIString* variable by using the *Convert* method.

6   Create an *int* variable in the same event handler called **CircleRadius** with a value of: **19**

7   Create a *double* variable in the same event handler called **CircleCircumference** with a value of: **PIDouble * CircleRadius**

8   Use the *Pow* function from the *Math* library to raise the *CircleCircumference* variable to the power of 2.

9   Convert the *CircleCircumference* variable to a *string* using the *ToString* method. Call the *string*: **OutputCircumference**

10   Create a *DateTime* variable called **TodaysDate** containing today's date.

My Project - start

My Project - end

If you need help slide the page to the left

Session 5: Exercise Answers

These are the four questions that students find the most difficult to answer:

Q 9	Q 8	Q 5	Q 4
Use the following line of code: **string OutputCircumference = CircleCircumference .ToString();** This was covered in: *Lesson 5-8: Convert variables using Convert and Parse.*	Use the following line of code: **CircleCircumference = Math.Pow (CircleCircumference, 2);** This was covered in: *Lesson 5-11: Use the Math library for advanced mathematics.*	Use the following line of code: **double PIDouble = Convert.ToDouble(PIString);** This was covered in: *Lesson 5-8: Convert variables using Convert and Parse.*	Use the following line of code: **string PIString = "3.14159265";** This was covered in: *Lesson 5-3: Use string variable properties and methods.*

If you have difficulty with the other questions, here are the lessons that cover the relevant skills:

1   Refer to: Lesson 1-7: Manage a project with the Solution Explorer.

2   Refer to: Lesson 1-15: Add controls to a page with the Toolbox.

3   Refer to: Lesson 3-2: Add event handlers to controls.

6   Refer to: Lesson 5-4: Use integer variables.

7   Refer to: Lesson 5-10: Perform basic mathematical operations.

10   Refer to: Lesson 5-7: Use DateTime variables.

Session Six: C# Classes, Namespaces and Methods

Though this be madness, yet there is method in it.

William Shakespeare, English poet and playwright (1564 – 1616)

Classes can be thought of as containers that C# code is separated into.

All C# code must be contained within a class. For example, the code-behind files that are automatically created with your pages are classes.

.NET programming may seem complicated with its hierarchical system of classes and extensive library of functions, but it's really not all that difficult when you have an understanding of classes.

In this session you'll learn the essentials of how to use C# classes, and even how to create some new classes of your own.

Session Objectives

By the end of this session you will be able to:

- Create a class
- Create an instance of a class
- Use the .NET framework
- Work with namespaces
- Create and use methods
- Create methods with arguments
- Create methods that return a value
- Create a private method
- Create a static method
- Create and dispose of instances
- Create a class constructor method

note

Everything in an ASP.NET application is part of a class

You might remember that C#'s code-behind files end in *.cs*, the same file extension as *MyClass.cs*. That's because your pages are classes too!

An ASP.NET application consists of many classes co-operating with each other to produce the web site that you see in your browser.

note

Protection levels

In this lesson you created both your property and your method using the prefix *public*.

public means that the property or method is available within any instance created from the class. For example the *Text* property of a *Label* control is a public property of the *Label* class.

If you'd created a property with the prefix *private*, it would only be available to code inside the class. In other words it would be hidden in any instance created from the class.

public and *private* are called *protection levels*.

You'll learn more about protection levels in: *Lesson 6-8: Create a private method*.

If you are not completing the course incrementally use the sample file: **Lesson 6-1** to begin this lesson.

Sample files with the starting point for each lesson are also provided for all of the other lessons in this session.

Lesson 6-1: Create a class

C# code is organized into classes, which can have properties, methods and events.

Classes can be thought of as templates from which any number of instances of the class (also called objects) may be created.

In previous lessons you created many variables. You were actually creating many instances of the relevant variable's class.

For example, the *DateTime* class defines all of the properties, methods and events of a *DateTime* variable.

In this lesson you'll create a brand new custom class of your own.

1   Open *My Project* from your sample files folder.

2   Create a new class.

1.   Right-click *My Project* in the *Solution Explorer* and then click Add→New Item... from the shortcut menu.

2.   Click *Code* under the *Visual C#* list on the left-hand side.

3.   Click *Class* from the central list of item types.

4.   Name the class: **MyClass.cs**

5.   Click *Add*.

Add

```
using System;
using System.Collections.Generic;
using System.Linq;
using System.Web;

namespace My_Project
{
    public class MyClass
    {
    }
}
```

Your new class appears in the *Solution Explorer* and its code is automatically displayed.

3   Add a property to your class.

Add the following line of code to your class:

public int IntProperty;

```
public class MyClass
{
    public int IntProperty;
}
```

This code will create a new property called *IntProperty* in your class, using the *int* data type.

tip

Adding classes quickly

You can skip straight to *Class* in the *Add New Item* dialog by right-clicking in the *Solution Explorer* window and clicking Add→Class instead of Add→New Item…

This saves some time when creating classes.

After you have created an instance of the class, you will be able to access this new property using: *MyClassInstance.IntProperty*

4 Add a method to your class.

1. Add the following code to your class:

   public void AddToProperty()
   {
   }

   ```
   public class MyClass
   {
       public int IntProperty;
       public void AddToProperty()
       {
       }
   }
   ```

   This code creates a new method called *AddToProperty*.

   After you have created an instance of the class, you will be able to call the new method using: *MyClassInstance.AddToProperty()*

2. Add the following code inside the *AddToProperty* method:

   IntProperty = IntProperty + 1;

   ```
   public void AddToProperty()
   {
       IntProperty = IntProperty + 1;
   }
   ```

   Now the *AddToProperty* method will add 1 to the value of the *IntProperty* property whenever it is called.

   You can use classes to create your own objects when none of the built-in classes provide the functionality you need.

   Before you can use your new class, you will need to create an *instance* of it. You'll learn how to do this in the next lesson: *Lesson 6-2: Create an instance of a class.*

5 Close Visual Studio.

Lesson 6-2: Create an instance of a class

Before you can use your class you must create an instance of it. You can do this in almost exactly the same way as you would with a variable.

In this lesson, you'll create and use an instance of the class that you created in: *Lesson 6-1: Create a class*.

1   Open *My Project* from your sample files folder.

2   Open the code-behind file of *calculator.aspx*.

3   Create an instance of your class.

Add the following code to the *Page_Load* event handler:

MyClass MyClassInstance = new MyClass();

```
protected void Page_Load(object sender, EventArgs e)
{
    MyClass MyClassInstance = new MyClass();
}
```

This code creates a new instance of the *MyClass* class called *MyClassInstance*.

As you can see, creating instances of classes is very similar to creating variables.

4   Use the new instance.

You can use an instance of your class in exactly the same way as you'd use a variable.

1.   Add the following line of code to the end of the *Page_Load* event handler:

MyClassInstance.IntProperty = 10;

```
protected void Page_Load(object sender, EventArgs e)
{
    MyClass MyClassInstance = new MyClass();
    MyClassInstance.IntProperty = 10;
}
```

This code will set the *IntProperty* property of the *MyClassInstance* object to *10*.

2.   Add the following line of code on the next line:

MyClassInstance.AddToProperty();

```
protected void Page_Load(object sender, EventArgs e)
{
    MyClass MyClassInstance = new MyClass();
    MyClassInstance.IntProperty = 10;
    MyClassInstance.AddToProperty();
}
```

In *Lesson 6-1: Create a class*, you created the *AddToProperty* method which adds 1 to the *IntProperty* property whenever it is called.

3.   Add the following line of code on the next line:

Response.Write(MyClassInstance.IntProperty);

```
protected void Page_Load(object sender, EventArgs e)
{
    MyClass MyClassInstance = new MyClass();
    MyClassInstance.IntProperty = 10;
    MyClassInstance.AddToProperty();
    Response.Write(MyClassInstance.IntProperty);
}
```

This code will display the value of the *IntProperty* property of the *MyClassInstance* object on the page so that you can check whether the method worked.

Since you set the *IntProperty* property to *10* and then called the *AddToProperty* method once, you are expecting a result of *11*.

4. View *calculator.aspx* in your browser.

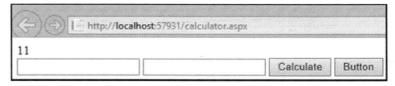

The number *11* appears at the top of the screen as expected.

5. Close your browser.

5   Remove all code from the *Page_Load* event handler.

```
protected void Page_Load(object sender, EventArgs e)
{

}
```

6   Close Visual Studio.

Lesson 6-3: Use the .NET framework

You have already used several components of the .NET framework, but you have only seen a tiny fraction of what is available.

In this lesson you'll use the *using* keyword in your class to enable quick access to an even larger selection of objects from the .NET framework.

1 Open *My Project* from your sample files folder.

2 Open *MyClass.cs*.

3 Examine the *using* lines.

At the top of the class, you can see the *using* lines that were added automatically when the class was created:

```
using System;
using System.Collections.Generic;
using System.Linq;
using System.Web;
```

These lines are all references to different parts (or *namespaces*) of the .NET framework (see sidebar).

You'll learn more about namespaces in: *Lesson 6-4: Work with namespaces*.

note

The default .NET namespaces

When you create a new page, references to several default namespaces are automatically added. These are:

System
The root namespace that contains all of the others. *System* contains all of the core functionality (such as all of the variable types), so you'll want this line of code in every class.

System.Collections.Generic
Contains the generic collection types. You'll learn more about collections in: *Lesson 8-2: Create a collection*.

System.Linq
Contains objects for LINQ, which you'll learn about in: *Lesson 10-3: Retrieve a single row of data using LINQ*.

System.Web
Contains all of the web controls such as *Button* and *DropDownList*. You'll always want this when working with web pages.

4 Add a new method to the *MyClass* class called: **TestMethod**

As you did with the *AddToProperty* method, add the following code to add a second method to the class:

public void TestMethod()
{
}

```
public void AddToProperty()
{
    IntProperty = IntProperty + 1;
}
public void TestMethod()
{
}
```

5 Create a *StringBuilder* object from the .NET framework.

The *StringBuilder* object is a more advanced version of the *string* variable that is designed to work better with very large strings. It's in the *System.Text* namespace, so it isn't easily accessible by default.

Add the following code to the *TestMethod* method:

System.Text.StringBuilder TestStringBuilder =
new System.Text.StringBuilder();

```
public void TestMethod()
{
    System.Text.StringBuilder TestStringBuilder =
        new System.Text.StringBuilder();
}
```

This code creates a new instance of the *StringBuilder* class called *TestStringBuilder*.

Notice that you have to type *System.Text* in order to access the *System.Text* namespace.

6 Add a *using* line for *System.Text*.

Although it's easy enough to type *System.Text* when you need to access the *System.Text* namespace, this may make your code harder to read and more cumbersome to edit.

Fortunately a short-cut to any namespace may be created by adding a new *using* line.

1. Add the following line of code to the *using* lines at the top of the page:

using System.Text;

```
using System.Linq;
using System.Web;
using System.Text;
```

This code creates a short-cut so that objects in the *System.Text* namespace can be accessed directly.

2. Change the *System.Text.StringBuilder...* line to:

StringBuilder TestStringBuilder = new StringBuilder();

```
public void TestMethod()
{
    StringBuilder TestStringBuilder = new StringBuilder();
}
```

This is much easier to read.

Note that if the *using* line had not been added, this code would have caused a build error.

7 Close Visual Studio.

---

note

Namespace confusion

Using a reference to a namespace makes your code a little less readable.

System.Text.StringBuilder

... makes it clear that the *StringBuilder* class is defined in the *System.Text* namespace.

StringBuilder

... does not make it clear which namespace *StringBuilder* originated from.

Fortunately, you can easily see which namespace an object originates from by hovering your mouse cursor over it.

If you try this with *StringBuilder* you'll see which namespace it originated from and a short description of what the class does.

```
StringBuilder TestStringB

    class System.Text.StringBuilder
    Represents a mutable string of
```

Lesson 6-4: Work with namespaces

You worked with some of the namespaces of the .NET framework in *Lesson 6-3: Use the .NET framework*, but your project has namespaces of its own too.

For most projects you won't need to change the namespaces that are automatically generated, but it's useful to understand what they do and how to modify them if you need to.

1   Open *My Project* from your sample files folder.

2   Open *MyClass.cs*.

3   Change the namespace of the *MyClass* class.

1.   Look for the following line of code:

```
namespace My_Project
```

This line tells C# that everything inside its curly brackets { } is part of the *My_Project* namespace.

Whenever you create a project, a default namespace is created with the same name as the project. Because this project is called *My Project*, everything is placed in the automatically-generated *My_Project* namespace by default.

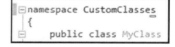

2.   Change the *namespace* line to:

namespace CustomClasses

3.   Open the code-behind file of *calculator.aspx*.

4.   Try adding the following code to the *Page_Load* event handler:

MyClass MyClassInstance = new MyClass();

```
protected void Page_Load(object sender, Event
{
    MyClass MyClassInstance = new MyClass();
}
```

Errors appear immediately, and you will notice that *MyClass* is not displayed in the IntelliSense menu as you type.

This same line of code worked fine in *Lesson 6-2: Create an instance of a class*. That was because *calculator.aspx.cs* shared the same namespace as the *MyClass* class (*My_Project*).

5.   Change the *MyClass...* line of code to:

CustomClasses.MyClass MyClassInstance = new CustomClasses.MyClass();

```
protected void Page_Load(object sender, EventArgs e)
{
    CustomClasses.MyClass MyClassInstance =
        new CustomClasses.MyClass();
}
```

Now that you've told your code to look in the *CustomClasses* namespace, it can find *MyClass* without any problems.

By using namespaces, you can separate your classes into their own groups. This keeps the number of items in the IntelliSense menu manageable.

4 Add a *using* line for the *CustomClasses* namespace.

Just as you did with the *System.Text* namespace in *Lesson 6-3: Use the .NET framework*, you can also add *using* lines that reference your own namespaces.

1. Add the following line to the *using* lines at the top of *calculator.aspx*'s code-behind file:

    using CustomClasses;

    ```
    using System.Web.UI;
    using System.Web.UI.WebControls;
    using CustomClasses;
    ```

2. Change the *CustomClasses.MyClass…* line back to:

    MyClass MyClassInstance = new MyClass();

    ```
    protected void Page_Load(object sender, Event
    {
        MyClass MyClassInstance = new MyClass();
    }
    ```

Now that you've added a *using* line for the *CustomClasses* namespace, you can directly access every class in that namespace.

5 Add a sub-namespace.

The namespaces of the .NET framework don't just have a single level, but are arranged in a hierarchy. It's very easy to create the same kind of hierarchy yourself.

1. Return to *MyClass.cs*.

2. Change the *namespace* line to:

    namespace CustomClasses.TestClasses

    ```
    namespace CustomClasses.TestClasses
    ```

    This code tells C# that the *MyClass* class is in the *TestClasses* namespace, which is inside the *CustomClasses* namespace.

3. Return to the code-behind file of *calculator.aspx*.

    ```
    MyClass MyClassInstance = new MyClass();
    ```

    The reference to *MyClass* is displaying an error again. That's because *MyClass* isn't in the root *CustomClasses* namespace any more, so it can't be found.

4. Add the following *using* line:

    using CustomClasses.TestClasses;

    ```
    using System.Web.UI.WebControls;
    using CustomClasses;
    using CustomClasses.TestClasses;
    ```

    This fixes the error by making all of the classes in the *TestClasses* sub-namespace available to your code.

    You could also have accessed the *MyClass* class by typing *CustomClasses.TestClasses.MyClass*.

Lesson 6-5: Create and use methods

You have already created a method in: *Lesson 6-1: Create a class*. In this lesson you'll create a new class with some more useful methods.

1   Open *My Project* from your sample files folder.

2   Create a new class named: **CalculatorFunctions.cs**

You learned how to do this in: *Lesson 6-1: Create a class*.

This class will be used to perform useful mathematical functions.

3   Add properties to the class.

1.   Add a public *double* property called: **FirstNumber**

2.   Add another public *double* property called: **SecondNumber**

3.   Add a third public *double* property called: **Result**

Your class should now look like this:

```
public class CalculatorFunctions
{
    public double FirstNumber;
    public double SecondNumber;
    public double Result;
}
```

4   Create a method that adds together the values of the *FirstNumber* and *SecondNumber* properties.

1.   Create a new method using the following code:

public void Add()
{
}

This code creates a new method called *Add*. The word v*oid* means that the method doesn't return a value, but you'll learn more about that in: *Lesson 6-7: Create methods that return a value*.

2.   Add the following code to the *Add* method:

Result = FirstNumber + SecondNumber;

```
public void Add()
{
    Result = FirstNumber + SecondNumber;
}
```

This code will add together the values of the *FirstNumber* and *SecondNumber* properties and place the resulting value in the *Result* property.

5   Create methods for other common mathematical functions.

1.   Add a **Subtract** method that works in exactly the same way as the *Add* method.

The code should be:

```
public void Subtract()
{
    Result = FirstNumber - SecondNumber;
}
```

public void Subtract()
{
    Result = FirstNumber - SecondNumber;
}

2. Add a **Multiply** method in the same way.

3. Add a **Divide** method in the same way.

6   Use your methods to perform calculations.

1. Open the code-behind file of *calculator.aspx*.

2. Remove all code from the *ButtonCalculate_Click* event handler.

3. Add the following code to the *ButtonCalculate_Click* event handler:

CalculatorFunctions Functions = new CalculatorFunctions();

```
protected void ButtonCalculate_Click(object sender, EventArgs e)
{
    CalculatorFunctions Functions = new CalculatorFunctions();
}
```

This code creates a new instance of the *CalculatorFunctions* class called *Functions*.

4. Add the following code on the next line:

Functions.FirstNumber = Convert.ToDouble(TextBoxFirstNumber.Text);
Functions.SecondNumber = Convert.ToDouble(TextBoxSecondNumber.Text);

```
CalculatorFunctions Functions = new CalculatorFunctions();
Functions.FirstNumber = Convert.ToDouble(TextBoxFirstNumber.Text);
Functions.SecondNumber = Convert.ToDouble(TextBoxSecondNumber.Text);
```

This code sets the *FirstNumber* and *SecondNumber* properties of the *Functions* object to the values entered in the textboxes.

5. Add the following code on the next line of the event handler:

Functions.Add();

This code calls the *Add* method that you defined in the *CalculatorFunctions* class. It will add together the *FirstNumber* and *SecondNumber* properties and place the resulting value in the *Result* property.

6. Add the following code on the next line:

LabelResult.Text = Functions.Result.ToString();

This code displays the value of the *Result* property in the *LabelResult* control.

```
CalculatorFunctions Functions = new CalculatorFunctions();
Functions.FirstNumber = Convert.ToDouble(TextBoxFirstNumber.Text);
Functions.SecondNumber = Convert.ToDouble(TextBoxSecondNumber.Text);
Functions.Add();
LabelResult.Text = Functions.Result.ToString();
```

All of the calculations on the *calculator.aspx* page are now done by your *CalculatorFunctions* class. If you like, try it out by viewing *calculator.aspx* in your browser.

Lesson 6-6: Create methods with arguments

Although the *CalculatorFunctions* class works, it could be much easier to use. Rather than setting two properties in order to perform calculations, you could make the numbers into arguments of each of the methods.

By using arguments, you can make methods accept values when they are called. You'll change your mathematical methods to use arguments in this lesson.

1   Open *My Project* from your sample files folder.

2   Open *CalculatorFunctions.cs*.

3   Remove the *FirstNumber* and *SecondNumber* properties.

    Since you will be providing these numbers through arguments, the *FirstNumber* and *SecondNumber* properties are no longer needed.

```
public class CalculatorFunctions
{
    public double Result;
    public void Add()
    {
        Result = FirstNumber + SecondNumber;
```

    Some errors appear when you remove the properties.

4   Change all of the methods to require arguments.

    1. Change the line that starts the *Add* method to:

        *public void Add(***double FirstNumber, double SecondNumber***)*

```
public void Add(double FirstNumber, double SecondNumber)
{
    Result = FirstNumber + SecondNumber;
}
```

        This code makes the *Add* method ask for two *double* variables called *FirstNumber* and *SecondNumber* when you call it.

        Since these arguments have the same names as the properties that you removed in the previous step, you don't need to make any further changes to the code.

    2. Add arguments to the *Subtract*, *Multiply* and *Divide* methods in the same way so there are no more errors.

5   Call the *Add* method from the *calculator.aspx* page.

    Since you've changed the *Add* method to require arguments instead of using properties, you'll need to change how you call it.

```
Functions.FirstNumber =
Functions.SecondNumber
Functions.Add();
```

    1. Open the code-behind file of *calculator.aspx*.

        Some of your code is marked in red because it is no longer valid.

    2. Remove all code from the *ButtonCalculate_Click* event handler.

important

Overloading

Some methods are *overloaded*, which means that they can process multiple groups of arguments.

The *ToString* method is a good example:

You can use *ToString()* on its own to turn a value into a string without any arguments.

You could use:

ToString("yyyy")

…to convert a *DateTime* variable into a string containing just the year.

Finally, you could use:

.ToString("yyyy", System.Globalization.CultureInfo. GetCultureInfo("fr-FR"));

…to get the year from a date using the French culture (which would be the same as other European formats).

When multiple sets of arguments are available, you will see these arrows in the IntelliSense menu:

You can click on the arrows to cycle through the different groups of arguments, or you can cycle through the groups using the up and down arrow keys.

Creating your own overloaded methods is covered in the Expert Skills course in this series.

3. Add the following code to the *ButtonCalculate_Click* event handler:

double FirstNumber = Convert.ToDouble(TextBoxFirstNumber.Text); double SecondNumber = Convert.ToDouble(TextBoxSecondNumber.Text);

```
protected void ButtonCalculate_Click(object sender, EventArgs e)
{
    double FirstNumber = Convert.ToDouble(TextBoxFirstNumber.Text
    double SecondNumber = Convert.ToDouble(TextBoxSecondNumber.Te
}
```

This code creates *FirstNumber* and *SecondNumber* variables containing the numbers that were entered by the user.

4. Add the following code on the next line of the event handler:

CalculatorFunctions Functions = new CalculatorFunctions();

```
double FirstNumber = Convert.ToDouble(TextBoxFirstNumber.Text);
double SecondNumber = Convert.ToDouble(TextBoxSecondNumber.Text);
CalculatorFunctions Functions = new CalculatorFunctions();
```

This code creates a new instance of the *CalculatorFunctions* class called *Functions*.

5. Add the following code on the next line of the event handler:

Functions.Add(FirstNumber, SecondNumber);

```
double FirstNumber = Convert.ToDouble(TextBoxFirstNumber.Text);
double SecondNumber = Convert.ToDouble(TextBoxSecondNumber.Text);
CalculatorFunctions Functions = new CalculatorFunctions();
Functions.Add(FirstNumber, SecondNumber);
```

This code calls the *Add* method with the *FirstNumber* and *SecondNumber* variables as arguments.

6. Add the following code on the next line of the event handler:

LabelResult.Text = Functions.Result.ToString();

```
double FirstNumber = Convert.ToDouble(TextBoxFirstNumber.Text);
double SecondNumber = Convert.ToDouble(TextBoxSecondNumber.Text);
CalculatorFunctions Functions = new CalculatorFunctions();
Functions.Add(FirstNumber, SecondNumber);
LabelResult.Text = Functions.Result.ToString();
```

The majority of the methods in the .NET library require arguments. Some methods can even accept multiple sets of arguments. This is called *overloading* (see sidebar).

6 Test the new functionality.

1. View *calculator.aspx* in your browser.

2. Fill in the two text boxes with numbers and click the *Calculate* button.

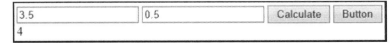

The calculation works correctly.

7 Close your browser and close Visual Studio.

Lesson 6-7: Create methods that return a value

note

What are functions?

In C#, the code for creating methods that return values is almost exactly the same as the code for methods that don't return a value.

Visual Basic, however, has a clear distinction between the two. Methods that return a value are called *functions* in Visual Basic.

In C#, methods are usually referred to as methods regardless of whether they return a value or not.

This information is provided because you might hear some developers use the word 'function' when they refer to a method that returns a value.

Your *CalculatorFunctions* class is more useful now, but it would be even easier to use if it didn't store the results of calculations in the *Result* property.

In this lesson you'll convert your mathematical methods so that they return results by themselves, without needing to use properties.

1   Open *My Project* from your sample files folder.

2   Open *CalculatorFunctions.cs*.

3   Remove the *Result* property.

Since the methods are going to return values by themselves, you won't need the *Result* property to store results any more.

Errors appear when you do this, but you'll fix the errors in the course of this lesson.

4   Change your methods to return values.

1. Change the line that starts the *Add* method to:

public **double** *Add(double FirstNumber, double SecondNumber)*

```
public double Add(double FirstNumber, double SecondNumber)
{
    Result = FirstNumber + SecondNumber;
}
```

You've changed the method from *public void* to **public double**. This tells C# that the method will return a *double* value.

void is used for methods that don't return any values.

2. Change the line inside the *Add* method to:

return FirstNumber + SecondNumber;

```
public double Add(double FirstNumber, double SecondNumber)
{
    return FirstNumber + SecondNumber;
}
```

return tells the method to return its value. Note that the *return* line will always end the method, so any code placed after this line will never run.

3. Make the *Subtract, Multiply* and *Divide* methods return a *double* value in the same way as you did with the *Add* method.

Simply change *void* to **double** in each method and replace *Result =* with: **return**

5   Call the *Add* method on the *calculator.aspx* page.

You will need to change how you call the *Add* method to account for the fact that the method now returns a value.

1. Open the code-behind file of *calculator.aspx*.

Some of your code is marked with red underlines because it is no longer valid.

```
Functions.Add(FirstNumber, SecondNumber);
LabelResult.Text = Functions.Result.ToString();
```

2. Change the *Functions.Add…* line to:

    double Result = Functions.Add(FirstNumber, SecondNumber);

```
protected void ButtonCalculate_Click(object sender, EventArgs e)
{
    double FirstNumber = Convert.ToDouble(TextBoxFirstNumber.Text);
    double SecondNumber = Convert.ToDouble(TextBoxSecondNumber.Text);
    CalculatorFunctions Functions = new CalculatorFunctions();
    double Result = Functions.Add(FirstNumber, SecondNumber);
    LabelResult.Text = Functions.Result.ToString();
}
```

This code stores the value returned by the *Add* method in a new *double* variable called *Result*.

3. Change the line that sets the *LabelResult.Text* property to:

    LabelResult.Text = Result.ToString();

```
protected void ButtonCalculate_Click(object sender, EventArgs e)
{
    double FirstNumber = Convert.ToDouble(TextBoxFirstNumber.Text);
    double SecondNumber = Convert.ToDouble(TextBoxSecondNumber.Text);
    CalculatorFunctions Functions = new CalculatorFunctions();
    double Result = Functions.Add(FirstNumber, SecondNumber);
    LabelResult.Text = Result.ToString();
}
```

This code uses the *Result* variable that you created on the previous line instead of the property of the *Functions* class that you used in: *Lesson 6-6: Create methods with arguments.*

6   Test your code.

1. View *calculator.aspx* in your browser.

2. Fill in the two boxes with numbers and click the *Calculate* button.

    | 3141 | 59 | Calculate |
    | 3200 | | |

    The calculation works correctly using your class method.

3. Close your browser.

Your calculation methods now work in the best possible way. Using arguments and return values in this way prevents any confusion that might result from the values of properties being set by other processes (see sidebar).

It is best practice to use arguments and return values wherever possible.

7   Close Visual Studio.

note

Why return values?

You might be wondering why returning a value from your methods is better than setting a property as you did in earlier lessons.

In this case it's undoubtedly better because it eliminates potential errors.

Previously there was no way of knowing which calculation had produced the result found in the *Result* variable.

There's nothing stopping you from taking whichever approach you think is best for whatever you're trying to achieve, but it is generally best to return values from methods using the *return* keyword.

Lesson 6-8: Create a private method

So far all of the methods and properties that you've created have been *public*, meaning that they can be accessed freely when an instance of the class is created (or *instantiated*).

public is a protection level. You can use different protection levels to change the accessibility of methods and properties. You'll learn how to use the *private* protection level in this lesson.

1   Open *My Project* from your sample files folder.

2   Open *CalculatorFunctions.cs*.

3   Add a private method to the class.

Add the following method to the *CalculatorFunctions* class:

private double RoundNumber(double Number)
{
    return Math.Round(Number, 2);
}

```
public class CalculatorFunctions
{
    private double RoundNumber(double Number)
    {
        return Math.Round(Number, 2);
    }
}
```

This method accepts a *double* value as an argument and returns it as a *double* value rounded to 2 decimal places.

What makes this method different to the methods that you've added so far is that it is *private*. This means that it can only be accessed by code that is within the *CalculatorFunctions* class itself.

4   Try to access the *RoundNumber* method from *calculator.aspx*.

1.   Open the code-behind file of *calculator.aspx*.

2.   Add a new line at the end of the *ButtonCalculate_Click* event handler.

3.   Type the following on the new line:

Functions.

```
Functions.
          ⊗  Add
          ⊗  Divide
          ⊗  Equals
          ⊗  GetHashCode
          ⊗  GetType
          ⊗  Multiply
          ⊗  Subtract
          ⊗  ToString
```

The IntelliSense menu should appear. This lists all of the methods in the *Functions* object, which is an instance of the *CalculatorFunctions* class.

4. Look for the *RoundNumber* method in the IntelliSense menu.

    You won't see *RoundNumber* in the list, as it's been declared *private*. If you tried to use the *Functions.RoundNumber* method here, you would get an error message.

5. Remove the *Functions.* code that you added.

```
protected void ButtonCalculate_Click(object sender, EventArgs e)
{
    double FirstNumber = Convert.ToDouble(TextBoxFirstNumber.Text);
    double SecondNumber = Convert.ToDouble(TextBoxSecondNumber.Text);
    CalculatorFunctions Functions = new CalculatorFunctions();
    double Result = Functions.Add(FirstNumber, SecondNumber);
    LabelResult.Text = Result.ToString();
}
```

5 Use the *RoundNumber* method inside *CalculatorFunctions.cs*.

1. Return to *CalculatorFunctions.cs*.

2. Change the *return* line in the *Add* method to:

    return RoundNumber(FirstNumber + SecondNumber);

```
public double Add(double FirstNumber, double SecondNumber)
{
    return RoundNumber(FirstNumber + SecondNumber);
}
```

This time there are no errors. The private *RoundNumber* function is available because your code is inside the *CalculatorFunctions* class.

Anything that is created with the *private* protection level can only be accessed inside its own class.

3. View *calculator.aspx* in your browser and test the calculation to confirm that it is rounding correctly.

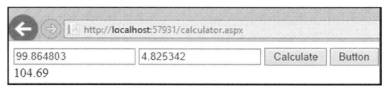

4. Close your browser.

6 Close Visual Studio.

Lesson 6-9: Create a static method

In order to use all of the properties and methods that you've created in the *CalculatorFunctions* class so far, you have had to first create an instance of the class.

Some properties, such as the *DateTime.Now* property that you saw in *Lesson 5-7: Use DateTime variables* can be accessed without creating an instance of the class.

These are called *static* properties and methods. You'll create some of these in this lesson.

1   Open *My Project* from your sample files folder.

2   Open *CalculatorFunctions.cs*.

3   Make the *Add* method static.

A static method can be called without creating an instance of its class. The methods in the *Math* class that you saw in *Lesson 5-11: Use the Math library for advanced mathematics* were all static methods.

Change the line that begins the *Add* function to:

public static double Add(double FirstNumber, double SecondNumber)

```
public static double Add(double FirstNumber, double SecondNumber)
{
    return RoundNumber(FirstNumber + SecondNumber);
}
```

All you need to do to make a method static is to add the word *static* after its protection level. You can do exactly the same thing to make classes and properties static.

Note that you should avoid using static properties wherever possible (see sidebar).

4   Make the *RoundNumber* method static.

You can see that there is an error inside your *Add* method. If you move your mouse cursor over the error, you'll see a message complaining that the *RoundNumber* method is not static.

Static methods are isolated from ordinary methods, since ordinary methods can only be used via an instance of the class. The only way to allow the *Add* method to call the *RoundNumber* method is to make the *RoundNumber* method static as well.

In the same way as you did with the *Add* method, make the *RoundNumber* method static:

private static double RoundNumber(double Number)

```
private static double RoundNumber(double Number)
{
    return Math.Round(Number, 2);
}
```

important

Static properties are bad programming practice

Static methods can be very useful but static properties are a very bad idea.

When you create a static property it is available to your entire application. This means that every class in the application is able to change its value. For this reason you can never be sure what value the static property has, rendering it worthless.

The use of static properties can introduce many errors that are almost impossible to debug.

My advice is to never use them in your code.

The errors disappear.

```
public static double Add(double FirstNumber, double SecondNumber)
{
    return RoundNumber(FirstNumber + SecondNumber);
}
```

5   **Call the static method from the** *calculator.aspx* **page.**

Because the *Add* method is now static, you no longer need to create an instance of the class to call it.

1. Open the code-behind file of *calculator.aspx*.

2. Remove the line:

   CalculatorFunctions Functions = new CalculatorFunctions();

```
protected void ButtonCalculate_Click(object sender, EventArgs e)
{
    double FirstNumber = Convert.ToDouble(TextBoxFirstNumber.Text);
    double SecondNumber = Convert.ToDouble(TextBoxSecondNumber.Text);
    double Result = Functions.Add(FirstNumber, SecondNumber);
    LabelResult.Text = Result.ToString();
}
```

Since you're going to use a static method for the calculation, you don't need an instance of the class any more.

The line that calls the *Add* method is now marked as an error. This is because the *Functions* instance of the *CalculatorFunctions* class no longer exists.

3. Change the line beginning with *double Result* to:

   double Result = CalculatorFunctions.Add(FirstNumber, SecondNumber);

```
protected void ButtonCalculate_Click(object sender, EventArgs e)
{
    double FirstNumber = Convert.ToDouble(TextBoxFirstNumber.Text);
    double SecondNumber = Convert.ToDouble(TextBoxSecondNumber.Text);
    double Result = CalculatorFunctions.Add(FirstNumber, SecondNumber);
    LabelResult.Text = Result.ToString();
}
```

4. View *calculator.aspx* in your browser.

5. Test the calculation.

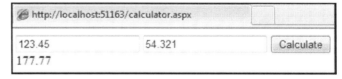

The calculation still works without any problems, but you've reduced the amount of code needed to call the method by making it static.

Static methods are ideal for methods that stand alone and don't need access to any properties. The calculations in the *CalculatorFunctions* class are a perfect example of this.

6   **Close Visual Studio.**

Lesson 6-10: Create and dispose of instances

You've already created an instance of your own class and have seen how static methods work.

In this lesson you'll learn about best practice when working with classes.

1   Open *ShiningStone* from your sample files folder.

2   Open the code-behind file of *buy.aspx*.

3   Create a new instance of a data class.

The *ShiningStone* project has a LINQ data class that allows it to communicate with its database. You'll learn how to use the LINQ data class in *Lesson 10-3: Retrieve a single row of data using LINQ.* For now it's a good class to practice creating and disposing of instances.

1.   Add the following code to the *ButtonSubmitOrder_Click* event handler:

ShiningStoneDataContext Data = new ShiningStoneDataContext();

```
protected void ButtonSubmitOrder_Click(object sender, EventArgs e)
{
    ShiningStoneDataContext Data = new ShiningStoneDataContext();
}
```

This code creates a new instance of the *ShiningStoneDataContext* class called *Data.*

2.   Add the following code on the next line:

Data.SubmitChanges();

This method won't actually do anything at this stage. It's just an example of a method that you might call from the *Data* object.

```
protected void ButtonSubmitOrder_Click(object sender, EventArgs e)
{
    ShiningStoneDataContext Data = new ShiningStoneDataContext();
    Data.SubmitChanges();
}
```

4   Dispose of the *Data* instance.

Many classes have a method called *Dispose.* The *Dispose* method is used to clear the class from memory.

Some classes don't have *Dispose* methods. This is usually because they don't have any properties that stay in memory.

A LINQ data class like the *ShiningStoneDataContext* class can load a lot of data into memory when it is used, so it is good practice to dispose of it as soon as you no longer need it.

Add the following line of code on the next line:

Data.Dispose();

note

Garbage collection

C# has a garbage collector that automatically disposes of objects that are no longer in scope.

In this case, for example, the C# garbage collector would dispose of the *Data* instance after *ButtonSubmitOrder_Click* was finished, since it wouldn't be usable any more.

Despite this, it's always best to dispose of instances manually when you can, since the garbage collector doesn't always clean up memory immediately.

```
protected void ButtonSubmitOrder_Click(object sender, EventArgs e)
{
    ShiningStoneDataContext Data = new ShiningStoneDataContext();
    Data.SubmitChanges();
    Data.Dispose();
}
```

This code will remove the *Data* instance from memory. If you were to try to work with the *Data* instance after this line, you would cause an exception.

5   Use the *using* statement to automatically dispose of an instance.

As well as disposing of instances using the *Dispose* method, you can use a *using* statement to automatically dispose of an instance.

Note that working with *using* statements inside your code is completely different to the *using* lines at the top of the page.

1. Remove all code from the *ButtonSubmitOrder_Click* event handler.

2. Add the following code to the *ButtonSubmitOrder_Click* event handler:

   using (ShiningStoneDataContext Data =
   new ShiningStoneDataContext())
   {
   **   Data.SubmitChanges();**
   }

```
protected void ButtonSubmitOrder_Click(object sender, EventArgs e)
{
    using (ShiningStoneDataContext Data = new ShiningStoneDataContext())
    {
        Data.SubmitChanges();
    }
}
```

This code does exactly the same thing as calling the *Dispose* method, but is much easier to understand and work with.

The *using* statement creates the *Data* instance and then automatically disposes of it after the last curly bracket *}*.

It is generally best to use *using* statements wherever possible as it eliminates the possibility of forgetting to dispose of an object.

6   Close Visual Studio.

Lesson 6-11: Create a class constructor method

A constructor is a method that runs whenever an instance of a class is created. In this lesson you'll learn how to use constructors and add them to your own classes.

1   Open *My Project* from your sample files folder.

2   Open *MyClass.cs*.

3   Add a constructor method to the class.

1.   Add the following method to the class:

public MyClass()
{
}

This is a simple constructor method. Any code that you place inside this method will run when a new instance of the class is created.

In order to be recognized as a constructor, the method must have the same name as the class it belongs to.

Notice how the syntax differs from a normal method. There is no *void* (or other return value type) specified before the method name. This syntax is peculiar to constructors.

```
public MyClass()
{
    IntProperty = 15;
}
```

2.   Add the following code to the constructor method:

IntProperty = 15;

This code will set the value of the *IntProperty* property to *15* whenever a new instance of the class is created.

4   See the constructor in action on the *calculator.aspx* page.

1.   Open the code-behind file of *calculator.aspx*.

In *Lesson 6-4: Work with namespaces,* you created an instance of the *MyClass* class in the *Page_Load* event handler.

2.   Set a breakpoint at the end of the *Page_Load* event handler.

You learned how to do this in: *Lesson 3-3: Use Breakpoints.*

```
        protected void Page_Load(object sender, EventArgs e)
        {
            MyClass MyClassInstance = new MyClass();
```

3.   Run *calculator.aspx* in debug mode.

4.   When the code is paused, check the value of the *MyClassInstance.IntProperty* property.

You can see that the constructor has set the value of the property to 15.

```
MyClass MyClassInstance = new MyClass();
        MyClassInstance {CustomClasses.TestClasses.MyClass}
            IntProperty  15
```

5. Stop debugging but leave the breakpoint in place.

5 **Add arguments to your constructor.**

Just like any other method, constructors can have arguments.

1. Return to *MyClass.cs*.

2. Change the code of the constructor to:

public MyClass(int StartingNumber)
{
IntProperty = StartingNumber;
}

```
public MyClass(int StartingNumber)
{
    IntProperty = StartingNumber;
}
```

This code adds an argument to the constructor called *StartingNumber* and sets the *IntProperty* property to the number provided in the argument.

This should look very familiar to you. It's exactly the same as adding arguments to any other method. This was covered in: *Lesson 6-6: Create methods with arguments.*

6 **Instantiate the *MyClass* class with arguments.**

1. Return to the code-behind file of *calculator.aspx*.

```
MyClass MyClassInstance = new MyClass();
```

The line that creates the instance of the *MyClass* class is now marked as an error.

This is because it's trying to create an instance of the *MyClass* class without providing the required argument.

2. Change the code in the *Page_Load* event handler to:

MyClass MyClassInstance = new MyClass(17);

```
MyClass MyClassInstance = new MyClass(17);
```

This provides the number 17 as the constructor argument.

This means that when the constructor runs, it will set the value of *IntProperty* to 17.

You could provide any *int* value for this argument.

3. Run *calculator.aspx* in debug mode.

The breakpoint should still be in place, so execution will be paused at the end of *Page_Load* event handler.

4. Check the value of the *MyClassInstance.IntProperty* property.

Tthe constructor has set the value of the property to 17.

5. Stop debugging and remove the breakpoint.

Session 6: Exercise

1   Open the *My Project* sample project and add a new class called: **Circle.cs**

2   Add a public *double* property to the *Circle* class called: **CircleCircumference**

3   Add a public method to the *Circle* class called: **CalculateDiameter**

4   Make the *CalculateDiameter* method return a *double* value.

    (Don't worry about the indicated error, this will be overcome in question 6).

5   Make the *CalculateDiameter* method ask for a *double* argument called: **Radius**

6   Add code to the *CalculateDiameter* method to multiply the *Radius* argument by 2 and return the result.

7   Add a constructor method to the *Circle* class.

8   Make the constructor method require a *double* value as an argument called: **Circumference**

9   Make the constructor method set the *CircleCircumference* property to the value of the *Circumference* argument.

10   Make the *CalculateDiameter* method into a static method.

11   Add a new Web Form to the project called: **circlecalculator.aspx**

12   Open the code-behind file of *circlecalculator.aspx*.

13   Add code to the *Page_Load* event handler to create an instance of the *Circle* class named **MyCircle** using a *Circumference* argument of: **50**

14   Add code on the next line to create a new *double* variable called: **MyCircleDiameter**

15   Add code on the next line to call the static *CalculateDiameter* method of the *Circle* class with a *Radius* argument of **7.95**, storing the resulting value in the *MyCircleDiameter* variable.

    (Remember that *CalculateDiameter* is a static method and is called in a different way to normal methods).

16   Add code to output the value of *MyCircleDiameter* using *Response.Write*.

17   View *circlecalculator.aspx* in your browser.

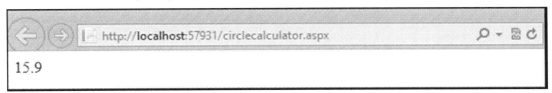

My Project - start   My Project - end   If you need help slide the page to the left

Session 6: Exercise Answers

These are the four questions that students find the most difficult to answer:

Q 10	Q 7	Q 6	Q 3
Change the line that starts the *CalculateDiameter* method to: **public static double CalculateDiameter (double Radius)** This was covered in: *Lesson 6-9: Create a static method.*	Use the following code: **public Circle()** **{** **}** This was covered in: *Lesson 6-11: Create a class constructor method.*	Use the following line of code: **return Radius * 2;** This was covered in: *Lesson 6-7: Create methods that return a value.*	Use the following code to add the public method: **public void CalculateDiameter()** **{** **}** This was covered in: *Lesson 6-5: Create and use methods.*

If you have difficulty with the other questions, here are the lessons that cover the relevant skills:

1   Refer to: Lesson 6-1: Create a class.

2   Refer to: Lesson 6-1: Create a class.

4   Refer to: Lesson 6-7: Create methods that return a value.

5   Refer to: Lesson 6-6: Create methods with arguments.

8   Refer to: Lesson 6-11: Create a class constructor method.

9   Refer to: Lesson 6-11: Create a class constructor method.

11   Refer to: Lesson 1-7: Manage a project with the Solution Explorer.

12   Refer to: Lesson 1-7: Manage a project with the Solution Explorer.

13   Refer to: Lesson 6-11: Create a class constructor method.

14   Refer to: Lesson 5-5: Use floating point variables.

15   Refer to: Lesson 6-9: Create a static method.

16   Refer to: Lesson 3-7: Understand Request and Response.

17   Refer to: Lesson 1-9: Run a project in debug mode.

Session Seven: C# Logical constructs and error handling

> Logic and mathematics are nothing but specialised linguistic structures.
>
> *Jean Piaget, Swiss psychologist and philosopher (1896 – 1980)*

Now that you know how C# code is structured and organized, it's time to add some programming logic to enable your code to respond intelligently to different conditions.

In this session you'll learn the basics of programming logic and a little more about best coding practice.

Session Objectives

By the end of this session you will be able to:

- Use the if statement
- Use else and else if
- Use basic logical operators
- Use advanced logic
- Use get and set
- Use try and catch to handle errors
- Use comments
- Use summaries

note

Single line if statements

As well as using curly brackets {}, you can put an *if* statement on a single line. For example:

if (Page.IsValid)
Response.Write("Validation OK");

Of course, this is useful only if you have just one line of code that you intend your *if* statement to run.

Some programmers prefer to use the curly brackets even when they want to run only a single line of code, as this is more consistent and makes the code easier to understand.

important

The = assignment operator and the == equality operator

Some programming languages use the equals sign (=) for both assignment and equality.

C# uses the double equals sign (==) for equality and the single equals sign (=) for assignment.

Examples

AcceptedTerms = true

Assigns the value of *true* to the *AcceptedTerms* Boolean variable.

AcceptedTerms == true

Checks whether the value of the *AcceptedTerms* variable is equal to *true*. Returns *true* if it is, and *false* if it isn't.

If you are not completing the course incrementally use the sample file: **Lesson 7-1** to begin this lesson.

Sample files with the starting point for each lesson are also provided for all of the other lessons in this session.

Lesson 7-1: Use the if statement

1   Open *ShiningStone* from your sample files folder.

2   Open the code-behind file of *buy.aspx*.

3   Create an *if* statement.

1. Remove all existing code from the *ButtonSubmitOrder_Click* event handler.

2. Add the following code to the event handler:

   bool AcceptedTerms = CheckBoxAcceptTerms.Checked;

   ```
   protected void ButtonSubmitOrder_Click(object sender, EventArgs e)
   {
       bool AcceptedTerms = CheckBoxAcceptTerms.Checked;
   }
   ```

   This code should make sense to you by now. It creates a Boolean variable called *AcceptedTerms* which will be *true* if the *CheckBoxAcceptTerms* control is checked and *false* if it is not.

   You created the *CheckBoxAcceptTerms* control in the session 4 exercise.

3. Add the following code on the next line:

   if (AcceptedTerms == true)
   {
   }

   This is the first time you've seen the == equality operator. See sidebar for more on this.

   This is a very simple *if* statement. As you can see, the code is very similar to the code that you've used to create methods. Everything inside the curly brackets { } will only run if the *AcceptedTerms* variable has a value of *true*.

   In other words, the code inside the curly brackets { } will only run if the user has checked the *CheckBoxAcceptTerms* control.

4. Add the following code inside the *if* statement (between { }):

   Response.Write("Terms OK");

   ```
   protected void ButtonSubmitOrder_Click(object sender, EventArgs e)
   {
       bool AcceptedTerms = CheckBoxAcceptTerms.Checked;
       if (AcceptedTerms == true)
       {
           Response.Write("Terms OK");
       }
   }
   ```

5. View *buy.aspx* in your browser.

6. Complete the form (without checking *I accept the terms and conditions*) and then click the *Submit Order* button.

   The page posts back, but nothing interesting happens.

Terms OK

7. Check the *I accept the terms and conditions* box.

8. Click *Submit Order* again.

   This time the logical test in the *if* statement returns *true* and *Terms OK* appears on the page.

4 Create a nested *if* statement.

As you can see, it's quite simple to test for a single condition. You can make your program's logic more complex by putting *if* statements inside other *if* statements.

Just like putting HTML tags inside each other, this is known as *nesting*.

1. Close your browser and return to the code-behind file of *buy.aspx*.

2. Add the following code inside the *if* statement that you created before (just after the *Response.Write* line):

   if (Page.IsValid)
   {
      Response.Write("Validation OK");
   }

```
protected void ButtonSubmitOrder_Click(object sender, EventArgs e)
{
    bool AcceptedTerms = CheckBoxAcceptTerms.Checked;
    if (AcceptedTerms == true)
    {
        Response.Write("Terms OK");
        if (Page.IsValid)
        {
            Response.Write("Validation OK");
        }
    }
}
```

As you may remember from *Lesson 4-8: Use the RequiredFieldValidator control, Page.IsValid* is the server-side confirmation that your form's validation controls are happy with the form's content.

The *if* statement will now check if the *AcceptedTerms* variable is *true* and will only check the *Page.IsValid* property if so.

You might want to do this if you intend to reject the user's order if they do not accept the terms and conditions (making any further validation checks pointless).

3. View *buy.aspx* in your browser.

4. Complete the form without checking the *CheckBoxAcceptTerms* control and click the *Submit Order* button.

   Nothing happens. The *CheckBoxAcceptTerms* control wasn't checked so neither of the *if* statements succeeded.

5. Check the *CheckBoxAcceptTerms* control and click *Submit Order* again.

   This time both *if* statements succeed and the results are shown on the page.

6. Close your web browser.

Terms OKValidation OK

Lesson 7-2: Use else and else if

The *if* statements that you've used so far are great for testing a single condition, but sometimes you will need to test for multiple conditions with different outcomes for each condition.

This could be done by creating separate *if* statements for every condition, but it's easier and tidier to use *else* and *else if* to do this.

In this lesson you'll use *else* and *else if* to extend the logic of your *if* statements.

1   Open *ShiningStone* from your sample files folder.

2   Open the code-behind file of *buy.aspx*.

3   Add an *else* statement.

Add the following code at the end of the *ButtonSubmitOrder_Click* event handler:

else
{
   Response.Write
   ("You must accept the terms and conditions to continue");
}

```
if (AcceptedTerms == true)
{
    Response.Write("Terms OK");
    if (Page.IsValid)
    {
        Response.Write("Validation OK");
    }
}
else
{
    Response.Write("You must accept the terms and conditions to continue");
}
```

This code follows on from the *if* statement that checks whether the *CheckBoxAcceptTerms* control is checked. As you might have guessed, it will run if the *CheckBoxAcceptTerms* control is not checked.

else means 'otherwise', ie if the *CheckBoxAcceptTerms* control is checked, write *Terms OK,* otherwise write *You must accept the terms and conditions to continue.*

4   Add an *else if* statement.

As well as using *else* to run some code if an *if* statement's logic fails, you can use *else if* to create chains of logical procedures.

1.   Add the following code to the end of the *ButtonSubmitOrder_Click* event handler:

string SelectedCountry =
DropDownListCountry.SelectedItem.Text;

```
      Response.Write("You must accept the terms and conditions to
}
string SelectedCountry = DropDownListCountry.SelectedItem.Text;
```

This code will put the name of the country chosen from the drop-down list into a *string* variable called *SelectedCountry*.

2. Add the following code on the next line:

if (SelectedCountry == "Canada")
{
    Response.Write("We cannot currently deliver to Canada");
}

As you know from *Lesson 7-1: Use the if statement*, this code checks whether the selected country is *Canada* and outputs the shown text if it is.

3. Add the following code on the next line:

else if (SelectedCountry == "United Kingdom")
{
    Response.Write("Eligible for free delivery");
}

Because you used *else if*, this *if* statement will follow on from the first one. It will only run if the value of the *SelectedCountry* variable is not *Canada*, but is *United Kingdom*.

4. Add the following code on the next line:

else
{
    Response.Write("Standard delivery charges apply");
}

```
string SelectedCountry = DropDownListCountry.SelectedItem.Text;
if (SelectedCountry == "Canada")
{
    Response.Write("We cannot currently deliver to Canada");
}
else if (SelectedCountry == "United Kingdom")
{
    Response.Write("Eligible for free delivery");
}
else
{
    Response.Write("Standard delivery charges apply");
}
```

This ends the chain of logic. It will only run if the value of the *SelectedCountry* variable is not *Canada* or *United Kingdom*.

5. View *buy.aspx* in your browser.

Try completing the form and setting the *Country* drop-down list to *Canada*, *United Kingdom* and any other country to see the difference.

Because *Response.Write* is being used, the text is all output together at the top of the page. In the final version of this page, you'd use a *Label* control to show the results instead.

Lesson 7-3: Use basic logical operators

note

&& and &

It's possible to use a single *&* instead of *&&*, but there are very few (if any) situations where this would be a good idea.

With *&&*, C# will stop checking your conditions as soon as it finds one that doesn't match.

For example consider the following code:

bool FirstBool = false;
bool SecondBool = true;
if (FirstBool && SecondBool)

When C# sees this, it will check *FirstBool*, see that it is *false* and stop checking. It won't bother checking *SecondBool*.

If you used:

if (FirstBool & SecondBool)

...C# would check both, even though it knows that the code won't run after seeing that *FirstBool* is false.

There's only one circumstance I can think of where a single ampersand would make any sense. This would be when the second logical test called a method and the programmer was relying upon the method being called.

This would, of course, be very poor programming practice.

You could create a great deal of programming logic with the techniques that you've already learned in this session, but you can use *logical operators* to make your *if* statements even more powerful.

1 Open *ShiningStone* from your sample files folder.

2 Open the code-behind file of *buy.aspx*.

3 Use && to check two conditions in a single *if* statement.

&& is the *AND* logical operator.

By using *&&*, you can check many different conditions in a single *if* statement.

1. Change the *if (AcceptedTerms...* line to:

   if (AcceptedTerms == true && Page.IsValid)

   This code makes the single *if* statement check both conditions. The code inside the *if* statement will only run if both the *AcceptedTerms* variable and the *Page.IsValid* property are *true*.

2. Remove the following code:

   if (Page.IsValid)
   {
   *   Response.Write("Validation OK");*
   }

   Since your first *if* statement now handles the *Page.IsValid* property as well, you don't need this code any more.

```
if (AcceptedTerms == true && Page.IsValid)
{
    Response.Write("Terms OK");
}
else
{
    Response.Write("You must accept the ter
}
```

4 Use || to check whether either one of two conditions is true.

|| is the *OR* logical operator.

By using ||, you can check whether any of several conditions are true. *&&* is different because it will only run if every condition is true.

1. Change the *else if (SelectedCountry...* line to:

   else if (SelectedCountry == "United Kingdom"
   || SelectedCountry == "Ireland")

```
else if (SelectedCountry == "United Kingdom"
    || SelectedCountry == "Ireland")
{
    Response.Write("Eligible for free delivery");
}
```

note

Greater than and less then

You can use > and < to check whether one numeric value is greater than or less than another.

You can also use >= and <= for greater-than-or-equal and less-than-or-equal comparisons.

© 2014 The Smart Method Ltd

note

The ^ operator

The ^ operator is the XOR (exclusive-or) operator. XOR returns *true* if only one of the two conditions are *true*.

For example:

Condition1 ^ Condition2

...would return *true* if only one of the two conditions was *true*. It would return *false* if both conditions were *true* or if both conditions were *false*.

XOR is very rarely used, as it is possible to achieve the same thing using the && and || operators.

note

Other ways to use !

The *!* operator is more versatile than the others, and can be used in a number of ways.

For example, if you had a *bool* variable called *MyBool*, all of the following would check if the value of *MyBool* is *false*:

if (MyBool != true)

if (!MyBool == true)

if (!MyBool)

In *Lesson 7-4: Use advanced logic* you'll learn about bracketing logical operators, which can be used to make logical operations even more versatile.

By using the || operator, you've made this *if* statement execute its code if the value of the *SelectedCountry* variable is either *United Kingdom* or *Ireland*.

2. View *buy.aspx* in your browser.

3. Complete the form and try selecting either *United Kingdom* or *Ireland* from the drop-down menu.

> Terms OKValidation OKEligible for free delivery

Both options cause the *if* statement to run and print *Eligible for free delivery* at the top of the page.

4. Close your browser.

5 **Use *!* to check if a condition is not true.**

! is the *NOT* operator. You have actually used it once already in: *Lesson 5-6: Use Boolean variables.*

So far all of your *if* statements have been used to check whether a condition was *true*. You can use *!* to check whether a condition is *false*. Of course, you could also use *== false* to accomplish the same result, but the *!* operator requires less code.

1. Return to the code-behind file of *buy.aspx*.

2. Change the *if (AcceptedTerms...* line to:

if (!AcceptedTerms == true || !Page.IsValid)
{
   Response.Write
   ("You must accept the terms and conditions to continue");
}

```
if (!AcceptedTerms == true || !Page.IsValid)
{
    Response.Write("You must accept the term
}
```

By using the *!* operator, you've made the *if* statement do the opposite of what it did previously.

You'll notice that you've also used the || (OR) operator instead of the && (AND) operator.

This is because you want the code to run if either the value of the *AcceptedTerms* variable is *false* (NOT true) <u>OR</u> the value of the *Page.IsValid* property is *false* (NOT true).

3. Remove the redundant code:

else
{
   Response
   .Write("You must accept the terms and conditions to continue");
}

```
bool AcceptedTerms = CheckBoxAcceptTerms.Checked;
if (!AcceptedTerms == true || !Page.IsValid)
{
    Response.Write("You must accept the terms and conditions to
}
string SelectedCountry = DropDownListCountry.SelectedItem.Text;
if (SelectedCountry == "Canada")
```

Lesson 7-4: Use advanced logic

You now know how to check for multiple conditions using logical operators. Even more can be done by using brackets to control precedence in the same way as you would with mathematical operations.

1   Open *ShiningStone* from your sample files folder.

2   Open the code-behind file of *buy.aspx*.

3   Remove all of the code from the *ButtonSubmitOrder_Click* event handler.

You're going to start from the beginning again and try to make the logic as streamlined as possible.

4   Create a complex *if* statement.

1.   Add the following code to the *ButtonSubmitOrder_Click* event handler:

string SelectedCountry = DropDownListCountry.SelectedItem.Text;

```
protected void ButtonSubmitOrder_Click(object sender, EventArgs e)
{
    string SelectedCountry = DropDownListCountry.SelectedItem.Text;
}
```

You need this code to extract the name of the selected country from the dropdown list control.

2.   Add the following code to the next line:

if (Page.IsValid
&& CheckBoxAcceptTerms.Checked
&& SelectedCountry == "United Kingdom"
|| SelectedCountry == "Ireland")
{
**   Response.Write("Logic succeeded!");**
}

```
if (Page.IsValid
    && CheckBoxAcceptTerms.Checked
    && SelectedCountry == "United Kingdom"
    || SelectedCountry == "Ireland")
{
    Response.Write("Logic succeeded!");
}
```

Here's the logic that you're trying to define:

The page must be valid AND The terms and conditions checkbox must be checked.

AND also…

The selected country must be either the United Kingdom OR Ireland.

Unfortunately the code above does not model this correctly.

note

Multi-line if statements

As you can see in the screenshot to the right, you can put C# code across multiple lines to make it easier to read.

Whether you do this or not is up to you. Personally I prefer to keep my *if* statements on a single line when possible and only break them up if they are very long.

3. View *buy.aspx* in your browser.

4. Complete the form, selecting *Ireland* from the *Country* drop-down and leaving the *terms and conditions* checkbox unchecked.

   Although the *terms and conditions* checkbox was left unchecked, the *if* statement still executes its code. This is because there were no brackets to clarify precedence.

   Here's what C# saw:

   The terms and conditions check box isn't checked

   AND

   The SelectedCountry is not United Kingdom

   …. So that's a fail on two counts… except you then indicated:

   OR Selected Country = Ireland

   … which is *true* so C# thought you wanted the code to run.

   To solve the problem you need to add brackets to tell C# what you really meant. In other words you need to define precedence rules. This is indicated by the use of brackets like this:

   (The page must be valid AND The terms and conditions checkbox must be checked)

   AND

   (The selected country must be either the United Kingdom OR Ireland.)

Logic succeeded!

5 Close your browser and add brackets to clarify precedence.

1. Change the *if* statement to the following:

   if ((Page.IsValid && CheckBoxAcceptTerms.Checked)
   && (SelectedCountry == "United Kingdom"
   || SelectedCountry == "Ireland"))

```
if (
    (Page.IsValid && CheckBoxAcceptTerms.Checked)
    &&
    (SelectedCountry == "United Kingdom" || SelectedCountry == "Ireland")
)
{
    Response.Write("Logic succeeded!");
}
```

5. View *buy.aspx* in your browser.

6. Complete the form, selecting *Ireland* from the *Country* drop-down and leaving the *terms and conditions* check box unchecked.

   This time nothing happens, since the *terms and conditions* checkbox isn't checked.

7. Check the *terms and conditions* check box and resubmit the form.

   This time all of the logic that you specified succeeds correctly and the code runs.

Logic succeeded!

Lesson 7-5: Use get and set

There are two special methods that you can add to properties: *get* and *set*. It's fairly rare to want to do this, but it's important that you understand the technique.

1   Open *ShiningStone* from your sample files folder.

2   Open the code-behind file of *buy.aspx*.

3   Create a *bool* property.

In *Lesson 6-1: Create a class (sidebar)*, you discovered that your code-behind file is actually a class.

You can add properties to your code-behind files, just as you would add a property to any other class.

Add the following code (outside any event handlers):

private bool AcceptedTerms;

```
public partial class buy : System.Web.UI.Page
{
    protected void Page_Load(object sender, EventArgs e)
    {

    }

    private bool AcceptedTerms;
}
```

This code creates an ordinary *bool* property that can be accessed only within the code-behind file, since it is private.

There's very rarely any reason to make properties in a code-behind file public.

4   Add a *get* method to the property.

By adding a *get* method, you can change what is returned when any code requests the value of the property.

1.   Change the property code to the following:

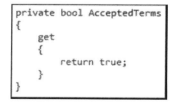

private bool AcceptedTerms
{
  get
  {
    return true;
  }
}

Note that there is no longer a semi-colon after *AcceptedTerms*.

This very simple *get* method will always return *true* whenever anything asks for the value of the *AcceptedTerms* property.

The *AcceptedTerms* property is now also read-only. If you tried to change the value of *AcceptedTerms* you would see an error.

2.   Change the *return true;* line to:

return CheckBoxAcceptTerms.Checked;

```
private bool AcceptedTerms
{
    get
    {
        return CheckBoxAcceptTerms.Checked;
    }
}
```

Now the *AcceptedTerms* property will always have the same value as the *Checked* property of the *CheckBoxAcceptTerms* control.

5   Add a *set* method to the property.

At the moment the *AcceptedTerms* property will retrieve the value of *CheckBoxAcceptTerms.Checked*, but the property is read-only so you can't set its value.

1.   Add the following code after the end of the *get* method:

set
{
   CheckBoxAcceptTerms.Checked = value;
}

```
private bool AcceptedTerms
{
    get
    {
        return CheckBoxAcceptTerms.Checked;
    }
    set
    {
        CheckBoxAcceptTerms.Checked = value;
    }
}
```

value acts as a placeholder for any value that is assigned to the property.

This code will set the *CheckBoxAcceptTerms.Checked* property to the value that is provided if you change the value of the *AcceptedTerms* property.

2.   Add the following code to the *Page_Load* event handler:

AcceptedTerms = true;

```
protected void Page_Load(object sender, EventArgs e)
{
    AcceptedTerms = true;
}
```

Since assigning a value to the *AcceptedTerms* property will call the *set* method that you created, the *CheckBoxAcceptTerms* control will be checked when the page loads.

3.   View *buy.aspx* in your browser.

☑ I accept the terms and conditions
Submit Order

The *CheckBox* is checked. Your *set* method successfully passed the assigned value to the control's *Checked* property.

4.   Close your browser.

Lesson 7-6: Use try and catch to handle errors

note

Handling errors for a whole site

try and *catch* are great for handling errors in specific methods. You should use *try* and *catch* whenever you have code that could cause an error, especially if it deals with data that was entered by the user.

By using *try* and *catch*, you can inform the user if something goes wrong instead of displaying a default error message.

It's possible, however, to handle errors for your entire site. You'll learn how to do this in: *Lesson 12-2: Handle errors with Global.asax.*

Unfortunately, no matter how hard you try to limit the possibility of errors they will still happen, usually because the user did something you didn't expect.

Fortunately, you can use the *try* and *catch* statements to handle errors without the page crashing and displaying an ugly error page.

1   Open *My Project* from your sample files folder.

2   Open the code-behind file of *Default.aspx*.

3   Add code that will cause an exception.

If you think back to *Lesson 3-5: Understand the Exception object*, you'll remember that one of the easiest ways to cause an exception (error) is to try to divide by zero.

Add the following code to the *Page_Load* event handler:

int Zero = 0;
int Error = 1 / Zero;

```
protected void Page_Load(object sender, EventArgs e)
{
    int Zero = 0;
    int Error = 1 / Zero;
}
```

4   View *Default.aspx* in your browser.

If your code pauses, minimize your browser and then press the continue button. ▶ Continue ▾

An error page appears.

Server Error in '/' Application.

Attempted to divide by zero.

5   Handle the error using *try* and *catch*.

1.   Close your browser.

2.   Change the code in the *Page_Load* event handler to the following:

```
try
{
   int Zero = 0;
   int Error = 1 / Zero;
}
catch
{
}
```

```
try
{
    int Zero = 0;
    int Error = 1 / Zero;
}
catch
{
}
```

This C# code will try to run the code between the first set of curly brackets { } (the *try* statement) and will only run the code between the second set (the *catch* statement) if an exception occurs.

Since there is no code in the *catch* statement, nothing will happen if there is an error. This is known as *swallowing* the error, and is considered to be bad practice.

3. View *Default.aspx* in your browser.

Home Page.

This time the page is displayed normally. The error still happened, but your *try* and *catch* code handled it.

4. Close your browser.

6   **Retrieve the details of the error in the *catch* statement.**

If you want to tell the user what went wrong or record any errors in a log, you can retrieve the *Exception* object in your *catch* statement.

You examined the *Exception* object in: *Lesson 3-5: Understand the Exception object.*

1. Change the *catch* line to the following:

   catch (Exception Ex)

   This code is very similar to adding an argument to a method, as you did in: *Lesson 6-6: Create methods with arguments.* It creates an object called *Ex* which contains the *Exception* object that was generated by the error.

2. Add the following code to the *catch* statement (between the curly brackets { }):

   Response.Write(Ex.Message);

   ```
   catch (Exception Ex)
   {
       Response.Write(Ex.Message);
   }
   ```

   This code will display the *Message* property of the *Exception* object at the top of the page.

3. View *Default.aspx* in your browser.

   This time the error message appears at the top of the page.

Attempted to divide by zero.

4. Close your browser.

Lesson 7-7: Use comments

You can tell when code has been written by a true professional because it is easy to understand and maintain. Using a consistent naming convention and following best practice is part of this, but adding comments to your code can also help immensely.

The best programmers always add comments to their code wherever it might be confusing. In this lesson you'll discover several different ways of adding comments.

1   Open *My Project* from your sample files folder.

2   Open *CalculatorFunctions.cs*.

3   Add a basic comment.

    1.   Add a new line before:

       return RoundNumber(FirstNumber + SecondNumber);

    2.   Add a comment to the new line with the code:

       //Add FirstNumber and SecondNumber

```
public static double Add(double FirstNumber, double SecondNumber)
{
    //Add FirstNumber and SecondNumber
    return RoundNumber(FirstNumber + SecondNumber);
}
```

The comment is shown in green.

By adding the two forward-slashes, you have defined the piece of text as a comment. Comments don't affect the code in any way; their only purpose is to explain the code to someone reading it.

4   Use /* */ to comment a large area.

    1.   On the line before the *Divide* method, type:

       /*

    This begins a commented area.

    2.   On the line after the end of the *Divide* method, type:

       */

    This ends the commented area.

```
/*
public double Divide(double FirstNumber, double SecondNumber)
{
    return FirstNumber / SecondNumber;
}
*/
```

Because it's now commented, the *Divide* method can no longer be called. It won't be recognized as a method any more, since it's now considered to be a comment.

This technique is used widely and is known as "commenting out" a method. It is more useful than deleting the method because if you later find that you need it again you only need to remove the comment markers.

tip

Comment shortcuts

You can quickly comment and uncomment code using the comment buttons on the toolbar:

Clicking these buttons will comment or uncomment any lines of code that are selected. You can use them to comment and uncomment large amounts of code very quickly.

These buttons work on HTML, JavaScript and CSS code as well as C#.

You can use /* */ comments to create large, multi-line comments.

3. Remove the comment marks from the *Divide* method so that it is recognized as a method again.

```
public double Divide(double FirstNumber, double SecondNumber)
{
    return FirstNumber / SecondNumber;
}
```

note

When to comment

You don't need to add comments to every line of code; most of the code that you've written so far is easy enough to understand without any comments.

Comments become necessary when you have written a complex piece of code that can't be understood at a glance.

5 Add a comment at the end of a line.

It's often tidier to add your comments at the end of the line they explain rather than before it. This is known as an "in-line comment".

1. Remove the line:

   //Add FirstNumber and SecondNumber

2. Change the line:

   return RoundNumber(FirstNumber + SecondNumber);

   to:

   **return RoundNumber(FirstNumber + SecondNumber);
   //Add FirstNumber and SecondNumber**

```
public static double Add(double FirstNumber, double SecondNumber)
{
    return RoundNumber(FirstNumber + SecondNumber); //Add FirstNumber and SecondNumber
}
```

This is usually the best way to comment short lines of code.

6 Add a comment in mid-line using /* */.

Using /* */, you can even add comments in the middle of a line of code. This can make the code confusing to read, so think carefully before doing so.

Change the line:

public double Divide(double FirstNumber, double SecondNumber)

to:

**public double Divide(double FirstNumber,
double SecondNumber /* Denominator */)**

```
public double Divide(double FirstNumber, double SecondNumber /* Denominator */)
{
    return FirstNumber / SecondNumber;
}
```

7 Close Visual Studio.

Lesson 7-8: Use summaries

In *Lesson 5-1: Use IntelliSense*, you saw that descriptions of methods and arguments appear in the IntelliSense menu.

You can add these descriptions to your own classes by using XML summaries. You'll create some of these in this lesson.

1 Open *My Project* from your sample files folder.

2 Open *CalculatorFunctions.cs*.

3 Examine a summary from the .NET library.

1. Add a new line to one of the methods.

2. On the new line, type: **Math.Round**

The IntelliSense menu appears.

```
decimal Math.Round(decimal d, int decimals, MidpointRounding mode)  (+ 7 overload(s))
Rounds a decimal value to a specified number of fractional digits. A parameter specifies how to round the value if it is midway
between two other numbers.
```

You can see that the description of the *Math.Round* method is: *Rounds a decimal value to a specified number of fractional digits...*

3. Type an opening bracket: **(**

This should cause the IntelliSense menu to change to show the description of the method's arguments. If it doesn't, delete what you've typed and retype:

Math.Round(

```
▲ 1 of 8 ▼  decimal Math.Round(decimal d)
            Rounds a decimal value to the nearest integral value.
            d: A decimal number to be rounded.
```

The method has a *decimal* argument called *d*, which has the description: *A decimal number to be rounded*.

You can use the black arrows or arrow keys on your keyboard to see the different groups of arguments that this method is able to process.

4. Delete the *Math.Round* line of code.

4 Add an XML summary to the RoundNumber method.

1. Add a new line before the *RoundNumber* method.

2. Type three forward slashes: **///**

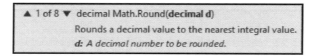

```
///
private static double RoundNumber(double Number)
```

As soon as you type the last forward slash, the framework for an XML summary is created automatically.

```
/// <summary>
///
/// </summary>
/// <param name="Number"></param>
/// <returns></returns>
private static double RoundNumber(double Number)
```

5   Add a description of the method.

1. Type the following on the blank line between the *<summary>* tags:

   Rounds a number to two decimal places.

   ```
   /// <summary>
   /// Rounds a number to two decimal places.
   /// </summary>
   ```

2. Add a new line to the *Add* method.

3. On the new line, type: **RoundNumber**

   The IntelliSense menu appears, and you can see that your method now has a description just like the ones from the .NET framework.

   ```
   double CalculatorFunctions.RoundNumber(double Number)
   Rounds a number to two decimal places.
   ```

4. Remove the *RoundNumber* code from the *Add* method.

6   Add a description for the *Number* argument.

1. Add the following inside the *<param>* tags in the summary:

   Number to be rounded.

   ```
   /// <summary>
   /// Rounds a number to two decimal places.
   /// </summary>
   /// <param name="Number">Number to be rounded.</param>
   /// <returns></returns>
   ```

2. Add a new line to the *Add* method.

3. On the new line, type: **RoundNumber(**

   The bracket is needed to open the description of the method's arguments.

   The *Number* argument is now described at the bottom of the summary.

   ```
   double CalculatorFunctions.RoundNumber(double Number)
   Rounds a number to two decimal places.
   Number: Number to be rounded.
   ```

4. Remove the *RoundNumber* code from the *Add* method.

   ```
   public static double Add(double FirstNumber, double SecondNumber)
   {
       return RoundNumber(FirstNumber + SecondNumber); //Add FirstNu
   }
   ```

   By using summaries, you can make your code even easier for other developers to use and maintain. They are extremely useful when working in a team environment.

7   Close Visual Studio.

Session 7: Exercise

1   Open the *Spark* sample project and open *viewtransactions.aspx* in *Design* view.

2   Add a *SelectedIndexChanged* event handler to the *DropDownListSelectedPeriod* control.

3   Add an *if* statement to the event handler that checks whether the value of the *DropDownListSelectPeriod* control's *SelectedValue* property is equal to: **"2010"**

4   If the value of the property is **"2010"**, make your *if* statement change the *Panel2010.Visible* property to **true** and the *Panel2011.Visible* property to **false.**

5   Use *else if* to check whether the value of *DropDownListSelectPeriod.SelectedValue* is **"2011"**. If it is, set the *Panel2011.Visible* property to **true** and the *Panel2010.Visible* property to **false.**

6   View *viewtransactions.aspx* in your browser and test your code.

7   Close your browser and open the code-behind file of *newtransaction.aspx*.

8   Add an *if* statement to the start of the *ButtonSubmit_Click* event handler to check whether the value of the *DropDownListCustomer* control's *SelectedValue* property is **"6"**, **"9"** or **"11"**. If so, set the *Text* property of the *LabelError* control to:
That customer is currently out of use

9   Add an *else* statement to the *ButtonSubmit_Click* event handler which will run if the value of the property is not **"6"**, **"9"** or **"11"**.

10   Add *try* and *catch* statements to the *ButtonSubmit_Click* event handler and place any error messages in the *Text* property of the *LabelError* control.

11   Add a comment to the *CalculateVAT* method to explain what it does. (VAT or Value Added Tax is a sales tax levied in Europe).

12   Add a summary to the *CalculateVAT* method and populate it with useful descriptions.

Spark - start

Spark - end

If you need help slide the page to the left

Session 7: Exercise Answers

These are the four questions that students find the most difficult to answer:

Q 10	Q 9	Q 8	Q 4

Add the code:
 	
try
{
 	
...at the very beginning of the event handler.
 	
At the very end of the event handler, add:
 	
}
catch (Exception Ex)
{
   LabelError.Text =
   Ex.Message;
}
 	
This was covered in: *Lesson 7-6: Use try and catch to handle errors.*
	After the end of your last *if* statement, add the code:
	
	else
	{
	
	}
	
	This was covered in: *Lesson 7-2: Use else and else if.*
		Use the following lines of code:
		
		string CustomerID = DropDownListCustomer .SelectedValue;
		if (CustomerID == "6"
		|| CustomerID == "9"
		|| CustomerID == "11")
		{
		   LabelError.Text =
		   "That customer is
		   currently out of use.";
		}
		
		This was covered in: *Lesson 7-3: Use basic logical operators.*
			Use the following lines of code:
			
			if
			(DropDownListSelectPeriod .SelectedValue == "2010")
			{
			   Panel2010.Visible = true;
			   Panel2011.Visible = false;
			}
			
			This was covered in: *Lesson 7-1: Use the if statement.*

If you have difficulty with the other questions, here are the lessons that cover the relevant skills:

1   Refer to: Lesson 1-7: Manage a project with the Solution Explorer.

2   Refer to: Lesson 3-2: Add event handlers to controls.

3   Refer to: Lesson 7-1: Use the if statement.

5   Refer to: Lesson 7-2: Use else and else if.

6   Refer to: Lesson 1-8: Add and remove files from a project.

7   Refer to: Lesson 1-7: Manage a project with the Solution Explorer.

11   Refer to: Lesson 7-7: Use comments.

12   Refer to: Lesson 7-8: Use summaries.

Session Eight: C# Collections and Loops

> My mind seems to have become a kind of machine for grinding general laws out of large collections of facts.
>
> *Charles Darwin, English naturalist (1809 – 1882)*

Believe it or not, you now know almost all of the basic principles of writing C# code!

After this session, you'll be spending the rest of the book applying what you've learned to access databases and create useful dynamic web sites.

In this session, the last on C# code, you'll learn how to deal with collections of objects and iterate through them.

Session Objectives

By the end of this session you will be able to:

- Create an array
- Create a collection
- Iterate through a collection using a foreach loop
- Iterate through a collection using a for loop
- Iterate through a collection using a while loop
- Use break and return

Lesson 8-1: Create an array

Arrays allow you to store multiple values in a single variable. Arrays are the simplest type of collection in C#, but they are also the most limited.

1   Open *Spark* from your sample files folder.

2   Open *Utilities.cs*.

This is a static class. As you may remember from *Lesson 6-9: Create a static method,* this means that it can be used without creating an instance of the class.

3   Add a public method to the class.

Use the following code:

public static string GetBlockedCustomers()
{
}

```
public static class Utilities
{
    public static string GetBlockedCustomers()
    {
    }
```

When complete, this method will return a list of blocked customer ID numbers as an array.

4   Create a string array in the new method.

Create an array using the following code:

string[] Customers = new string[3];

```
public static string GetBlockedCustomers()
{
    string[] Customers = new string[3];
}
```

string[] defines a new array of *string* variables. You can place square brackets *[]* after any type of variable to create an array of that type.

The *[3]* means that the new *Customers* array will be able to contain three strings.

5   Populate the array with the values 6, 9 and 11.

It's easy to set the values in an array:

1.   Add the following code to set the value of the first element in the array: **Customers[0] = "6";**

2.   Add the following code to set the second value in the array: **Customers[1] = "9";**

3.   Set the third value using similar code: **Customers[2] = "11";**

```
public static string GetBlockedCustomers()
{
    string[] Customers = new string[3];
    Customers[0] = "6";
    Customers[1] = "9";
    Customers[2] = "11";
}
```

tip

Dynamic arrays

Although you can't change the size of an array without recreating it, a new array will automatically size itself if you specify its contents when you create it.

Using this syntax uses less code, so it can be ideal for short arrays such as the one you create in this lesson.

You could create this lesson's array in a single line of code, as follows:

string[] Customers =
new string[]{"6","9","11"};

If you are not completing the course incrementally use the sample file: **Lesson 8-1** to begin this lesson.

Sample files with the starting point for each lesson are also provided for all of the other lessons in this session.

Your array will now contain the values *6, 9* and *11*.

You might think that you should be assigning a value to *Customers[3]* but, as you can see, the first element's index number is *[0]*.

When you created a *string[3]* array, you created a string array with 3 elements: [0], [1] and [2]. That's because all collections in C# are zero based. This was discussed in: *Lesson 4-7: Use the DropDownList control (zero-based indexing sidebar)*.

note

Multidimensional arrays

The array that you create in this lesson has a single dimension, but it's possible to create multidimensional arrays with elements such as *string[1,7]*. These are useful for situations where you have a grid of data.

Multidimensional arrays are covered in depth in the Expert Skills course in this series.

6   Make the method return the array.

1.   Change the line that starts the method to:

public static **string[]** *GetBlockedCustomers()*

The *string[]* return value is needed to tell the method that it will return an array rather than a single string.

2.   Add the following line at the end of the method:

return Customers;

```
public static string[] GetBlockedCustomers()
{
    string[] Customers = new string[3];
    Customers[0] = "6";
    Customers[1] = "9";
    Customers[2] = "11";
    return Customers;
}
```

This method will now return the *Customers* array when it is called.

7   Test the array on the *newtransaction.aspx* page.

1.   Open the code-behind file of *newtransaction.aspx*.

2.   Find the line that checks *CustomerID* numbers.

```
if (DropDownListCustomer.SelectedValue == "6" || DropDownListCus
{
    LabelError.Text = "That customer is currently out of use";
}
```

You created this line in the session 7 exercise so it may not be identical to the above example.

3.   Change the *if* statement's code to:

**if(Utilities.GetBlockedCustomers().
Contains(DropDownListCustomer.SelectedValue))**

```
if (Utilities.GetBlockedCustomers().Contains(DropDownListCustomer.SelectedValue))
{
    LabelError.Text = "That customer is currently out of use";
}
```

By using the *Contains* method of the array, you have simplified the *if* statement considerably. If you had 50 customers that you wanted to block this would almost be a necessity, although you would normally use a database to store a list that long.

By using an array, you have centralized your list of blocked customers and made it much easier to work with.

Lesson 8-2: Create a collection

Collections provide a more advanced way of storing multiple values inside a single object. Unlike arrays, which have a fixed size once they are created, you can add and remove items from collections. For most purposes collections are more convenient to work with than arrays.

In this lesson you'll create a *List* collection and add some items to it.

1 Open *Spark* from your sample files folder.

2 Open *Utilities.cs*.

3 Remove the contents of the *GetBlockedCustomers* method.

4 Create a *List* collection.

Add the following code to the *GetBlockedCustomers* method:

List<string> BlockedCustomers = new List<string>();

```
public static string GetBlockedCustomers()
{
    List<string> BlockedCustomers = new List<string>();
}
```

This code creates a new *List* collection that can contain only *string* variables.

You can put any data type between the < > marks to create a list of that type. For example, *List<int>* would create a list of *int* variables.

If you wanted a *List* to contain more than one type of variable, you would have to use a *List<object>*, but you would then have to convert the objects back to their original types when you retrieved them from the collection.

5 Add items to the *List* collection.

1. Add the following code to add a value to the *List* collection.

    BlockedCustomers.Add("6");

    ```
    public static string GetBlockedCustomers()
    {
        List<string> BlockedCustomers = new List<string>();
        BlockedCustomers.Add("6");
    }
    ```

    As you can see, it's very easy to add a value to a list.

2. Add the following code to add the other two values to the list:

    BlockedCustomers.Add("9");
    BlockedCustomers.Add("11");

    ```
    public static string GetBlockedCustomers()
    {
        List<string> BlockedCustomers = new List<string>();
        BlockedCustomers.Add("6");
        BlockedCustomers.Add("9");
        BlockedCustomers.Add("11");
    }
    ```

You now have a *List* collection containing the three strings that you previously stored in an array in: *Lesson 8-1: Create an array*.

tip

Quick lists

Just like with arrays, you can populate a *List* collection with a single line of code.

You could have created the *List* used in this lesson by simply typing:

List<string> BlockedCustomers = new List<string>()
{ "6", "9", "11" };

Of course, the huge advantage of lists is their ability to add and remove items.

note

Other types of collection

If you look at the *using* lines at the top of the class, you'll see *System.Collections.Generic*. This is where the *List* class is defined, and it contains other types of collection too.

Try typing the following code into any event handler:

System.Collections.Generic.

...and you'll see a list of collection types in the IntelliSense menu.

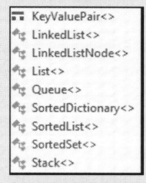

Two of the most useful are:

Dictionary
Works the same way as a *List*, but allows you to give each value a *Key*, which you can use to retrieve the value. This is very similar to the way that *ViewState* and *Session* work, as you may recall from: *Lesson 3-11: Send data between pages.*

SortedList
Very similar to a *List*, but has methods to easily sort the contents.

For most purposes the *List* collection is the best choice.

6 **Remove an item from the *List* collection.**

You can remove an item from a list by using the *Remove* method. Add the following code to the end of the method:

BlockedCustomers.Remove("11");

```
BlockedCustomers.Add("11");
BlockedCustomers.Remove("11");
```

7 **Retrieve a single item from the *List* collection.**

Lists have zero-based index numbers just like arrays. Retrieve the second item from the list and place its value into a *string* variable with the following code:

string SecondCustomer = BlockedCustomers[1];

```
BlockedCustomers.Remove("11");
string SecondCustomer = BlockedCustomers[1];
```

8 **Make the method return the *List* collection.**

You learned how to return values from methods in: *Lesson 6-7: Create methods that return a value.*

1. Change the line that defines the method to:

    public static **List<string>** *GetBlockedCustomers()*

    Unsurprisingly, you need to set the return value of the *GetBlockedCustomers* method to *List<string>* in order to return the *List* collection from the method.

2. Add the following line at the end of the method:

    return BlockedCustomers;

    ```
    public static List<string> GetBlockedCustomers()
    {
        List<string> BlockedCustomers = new List<string>();
        BlockedCustomers.Add("6");
        BlockedCustomers.Add("9");
        BlockedCustomers.Add("11");
        BlockedCustomers.Remove("11");
        string SecondCustomer = BlockedCustomers[1];
        return BlockedCustomers;
    }
    ```

    This will return the *List* collection when the method is called.

9 **Use the *List* collection in your code.**

1. Open the code-behind file of *newtransaction.aspx*.

2. Find the line:

    *if (Utilities.GetBlockedCustomers()
    .Contains(DropDownListCustomer.SelectedValue))*

```
if (Utilities.GetBlockedCustomers().Contains(DropDownListCustomer.SelectedValue))
{
    LabelError.Text = "That customer is currently out of use";
}
```

You'll notice that there are no errors appearing. The *List* collection has a *Contains* method just like an array so there's no need to change the code here at all!

Lesson 8-3: Iterate through a collection using foreach

One of the most common things you'll need to do with collections is to iterate through each item in the collection. Iterating through a collection is a little like flicking through the pages in a book.

If you knew the number of items in a collection, you could directly address them using *Collection[0], Collection[1],* etc. but most of the time you won't know in advance how many items your collection has.

In this lesson you will use a *foreach* loop to iterate through each item in a collection.

1   Open *My Project* from your sample files folder.

2   Open *CalculatorFunctions.cs.*

3   Add a method to total all of the numbers in a list of *int* variables.

You should be quite familiar with creating methods by now. Use the following code:

public static int TotalNumbers(List<int> ListToTotal)
{
}

```
public static int TotalNumbers(List<int> ListToTotal)
{

}
```

This method accepts a *List<int>* collection as an argument and returns an *int* value. When this method is complete it will add up the values of each element in the *ListToTotal* collection and then return the total.

This method is *static,* so you won't need to create an instance of the *CalculatorFunctions* class to call the method.

4   Create an *int* variable called: **Total**

To return the total as an *int* value, you'll need to create an *int* variable to return. Create one in the *TotalNumbers* method using the following code:

int Total = 0;

```
public static int TotalNumbers(List<int> ListToTotal)
{
    int Total = 0;
}
```

The *Total* variable is assigned a value of *0.* You'll add the value of each element in the *ListToTotal* collection to the *Total* variable as you iterate through them.

5   Iterate through each item in *ListToTotal* using a *foreach* loop.

Add the following code to the *TotalNumbers* method:

foreach (int NumberToTotal in ListToTotal) { }

```
int Total = 0;
foreach (int NumberToTotal in ListToTotal)
{
}
```

The *NumberToTotal* variable is called the *iteration variable*. The code will loop through all of the items in the *ListToTotal* collection. Each time the code loops, the value of the current item will be placed in the *NumberToTotal* iteration variable.

<table>
<tr><td>

note

Using var iteration variables with foreach loops is bad practice

You learned about the *var* variable type in: *Lesson 5-13: Use object and var variables.*

If you use a *var* iteration variable in a *foreach* statement, it will automatically assume the same variable type as the items in the collection.

If, in this example, you'd used:

foreach (var NumberToTotal in ListToTotal)

...the code would have worked in exactly the same way.

It is best practice to avoid using *var* variables, as it makes the code harder to understand.

This is a common "bad" programming practice. I've included this information because you may see this practice in other people's code.

</td></tr>
</table>

6 Add code to sum the total in the *Total* variable.

Add the following code inside the curly brackets following the *foreach* statement:

Total = Total + NumberToTotal;

As the *foreach* statement iterates through each item in the *ListToTotal* collection, their values will be added to the *Total* variable.

7 Add code to return the total value.

At the end of the method, you'll need to return the *Total* variable using: **return Total;**

```
int Total = 0;
foreach (int NumberToTotal in ListToTotal)
{
    Total = Total + NumberToTotal;
}
return Total;
```

8 Test the method on the *calculator.aspx* page.

1. Open the code-behind file of *calculator.aspx*.

2. Remove all code from the *ButtonCalculate2_Click* event handler.

3. Add code to the event handler to create a *List* of *int* variables, containing some values:

   List<int> ListToTotal = new List<int>() { 12, 17, 135 };

   This *List* collection contains the integer values 12, 17 and 135. Therefore its total should come to 164.

4. Add code to call the *TotalNumbers* method from the *CalculatorFunctions* class and display the result:

   int Total = CalculatorFunctions.TotalNumbers(ListToTotal);
   Response.Write(Total);

```
protected void ButtonCalculate2_Click(object sender, EventArgs e)
{
    List<int> ListToTotal = new List<int>() { 12, 17, 135 };
    int Total = CalculatorFunctions.TotalNumbers(ListToTotal);
    Response.Write(Total);
}
```

5. View *calculator.aspx* in your browser and click the second button (named *Button*).

   The number *164* is displayed, showing that your method totaled the numbers correctly!

Lesson 8-4: Iterate through a collection using a for loop

foreach is a really easy way to iterate through each item in a collection, but it has a major limitation. You can't modify the value in the iteration variable.

Another way to loop through all of the items in a collection is to use a *for* loop. *for* loops don't have to be used with collections, they can be used for any piece of code that you want to run several times.

1   Open *My Project* from your sample files folder.

2   Open *CalculatorFunctions.cs*.

3   Create a new method called: **AddToNumbers**

Your new method is going to take a *List* collection containing *int* variables and add an *int* value to each item in the collection.

Use the following code:

public static void AddToNumbers(int AmountToAdd, List<int> Numbers)
{
}

```
public static void AddToNumbers(int AmountToAdd, List<int> Numbers)
{

}
```

4   Create a *for* loop to iterate through the *List* collection.

1.   Store the number of items in the *List* collection in a variable using the following code:

int NumberOfNumbers = Numbers.Count;

This isn't strictly necessary, but it will make the next step easier to understand.

2.   Add the following code:

for (int Counter = 0; Counter < NumberOfNumbers;
Counter++)
{ }

```
public static void AddToNumbers(int AmountToAdd, List<int> Numbers)
{
    int NumberOfNumbers = Numbers.Count;
    for (int Counter = 0; Counter < NumberOfNumbers; Counter++)
    {

    }
}
```

This is the *for* loop. If you look at each part of it in turn it is easier to understand:

int Counter = 0
This creates a new *int* variable called *Counter* with a value of zero that will identify the current iteration in the loop.

Counter < NumberOfNumbers

This logical test determines when the loop will end. In this case, the loop will run as long as the value of *Counter* is less than the value of *NumberOfNumbers*.

Counter++

This code runs at the end of each iteration. In this case, it adds one to the value of the *Counter* variable (You learned about ++ in: *Lesson 5-10: Perform basic mathematical operations*).

Any code placed between the curly brackets will now run as many times as there are items in the *Numbers* collection.

5   Add code to add a value to each item in the collection.

Add the following code inside the *for* loop:

Numbers[Counter] = Numbers[Counter] + AmountToAdd;

```
public static void AddToNumbers(int AmountToAdd, List<int> Numbers)
{
    int NumberOfNumbers = Numbers.Count;
    for (int Counter = 0; Counter < NumberOfNumbers; Counter++)
    {
        Numbers[Counter] = Numbers[Counter] + AmountToAdd;
    }
}
```

By using the *Counter* variable, you can access each item in the *Numbers* collection by its index, just as you did with arrays in: *Lesson 8-1: Create an array*.

Here, you're adding the value of the *AmountToAdd* variable onto the value of each item in the *Numbers* collection as you iterate through the collection.

6   Test the method on the *calculator.aspx* page.

1.   Open the code-behind file of *calculator.aspx*.

2.   Add a new line after the *List<int> ListToTotal…* line.

3.   Call the *AddToNumbers* method on the new line, using the following code:

CalculatorFunctions.AddToNumbers(10, ListToTotal);

```
protected void ButtonCalculate2_Click(object sender, EventArgs e)
{
    List<int> ListToTotal = new List<int>() { 12, 17, 135 };
    CalculatorFunctions.AddToNumbers(10, ListToTotal);
    int Total = CalculatorFunctions.TotalNumbers(ListToTotal);
    Response.Write(Total);
}
```

This code calls your method, which will add 10 to each of the numbers in the *ListToTotal* collection. If it works correctly, you can expect the total to be *194* (12 + 10 + 17 + 10 + 135 + 10).

4.   View *calculator.aspx* in your browser and click the second button (named *Button*).

The number *194* is displayed, indicating that your method worked correctly!

© 2014 The Smart Method Ltd   **241**

note

Passing arguments by reference and by value

All of the simple variable types (such as *int, string, bool* and *double*) are, by default, sent to methods *by value* when used as arguments.

Some variable types (such as *List* collections) are sent to methods *by reference* when used as arguments.

The reason that the *AddToNumbers* method was able to permanently change the values in the *ListToTotal* collection was because the collection was sent *by reference*.

You'll learn more about sending variables *by reference* and *by value* in the Expert Skills book in this series.

For the moment, all you need to know is that methods can only permanently change the values of arguments when they are passed by reference.

Lesson 8-5: Iterate through a collection using a while loop

The last type of loop that is recognized by C# is the *while* loop. *while* loops are very similar to *for* loops, but use a slightly different syntax.

while syntax can be easier to understand than *for* syntax in some cases, but *while* loops are more prone to errors due to their more permissive syntax.

You'll create a *while* loop in this lesson and see the difference between the two.

1   Open *My Project* from your sample files folder.

2   Open *CalculatorFunctions.cs*.

3   Modify the *AddToNumbers* method to use a *while* loop instead of a *for* loop.

    1.   Remove all code from the *AddToNumbers* method.

```
public static void AddToNumbers(int AmountToAdd,
{

}
```

    2.   Add the following code:

       int NumberOfNumbers = Numbers.Count;

```
public static void AddToNumbers(int AmountToAdd,
{
    int NumberOfNumbers = Numbers.Count;
}
```

    This is the same code that you used for your *for* loop. You need to know how many items are in the collection to know how many times you will need to loop.

    3.   Add the following code on the next line:

       int Counter = 0;

```
public static void AddToNumbers(int AmountToAdd,
{
    int NumberOfNumbers = Numbers.Count;
    int Counter = 0;
}
```

    You're going to use *Counter* as the iteration variable for your *while* loop. Unlike the *for* loop, you need to define the iteration variable for a *while* loop on a separate line.

    This makes *while* loops more appropriate if you already have a variable defined that you would like to use as the iteration variable.

    4.   Add the following code on the next line:

       while (Counter < NumberOfNumbers)
       {
       }

```
public static void AddToNumbers(int AmountToAdd,
{
    int NumberOfNumbers = Numbers.Count;
    int Counter = 0;
    while (Counter < NumberOfNumbers)
    {

    }
}
```

This code defines the *while* loop and specifies that it will loop as long as the value of *Counter* is less than the value of *NumberOfNumbers*.

5. Add the following code inside the *while* loop:

Numbers[Counter] = Numbers[Counter] + AmountToAdd;

```
while (Counter < NumberOfNumbers)
{
    Numbers[Counter] = Numbers[Counter] + AmountToAdd;
}
```

This is the same code that you used in your *for* loop in: *Lesson 8-4: Iterate through a collection using a for loop*. It will add the value of *AmountToAdd* to each item in the *Numbers* collection.

If you didn't add any more code this loop would run forever, because the value of *Counter* will never increase. The loop would eventually crash when the value of the first item in the *Numbers* collection exceeded the limitations of the *int* type.

To complete this code, you need to add some code that will increase the value of *Counter* by one at the end of every loop.

6. Add the following code on the next line inside the *while* loop:

Counter++;

```
public static void AddToNumbers(int AmountToAdd, List<int> Numbers)
{
    int NumberOfNumbers = Numbers.Count;
    int Counter = 0;
    while (Counter < NumberOfNumbers)
    {
        Numbers[Counter] = Numbers[Counter] + AmountToAdd;
        Counter++;
    }
}
```

Your *while* loop is now complete. The *while* loop requires more code and has more scope for error than the *for* loop, but is also easier to integrate with existing variables and can be easier to understand.

The *for* loop is almost always best when looping through collections, but the *while* loop can be better for other code that you need to loop through several times.

4   Test your code on the *calculator.aspx* page.

View *calculator.aspx* in your browser and click the second button (named *Button*).

The correct result of *194* is displayed, proving that your *while* loop is working in exactly the same way as the *for* loop that you used in: *Lesson 8-4: Iterate through a collection using a for loop*.

Lesson 8-6: Use break and return

important

Avoid using break and return

It is best practice to avoid using *break* and *return* in loops wherever possible.

Instead of using *break* in this example, it would have been better to use a simple *if* statement.

The reason that this is best practice is because methods are expected to run from beginning to end through a logical process. Exiting in the middle of that process makes your code harder to understand.

It's still important to recognize *break* and *return*, since not all programmers will stick to that standard.

You've already used *return* to return a value from a method, but *return* and the similar *break* can also be used to escape from loops (although this is poor programming practice – see sidebar).

In this lesson you'll use *break* and *return* to escape from a loop.

1   Open *My Project* from your sample files folder.

2   Open *CalculatorFunctions.cs*.

3   Use *break* to make the *AddToNumbers* method stop iterating when it encounters a value of 17.

Using *break*, you can exit out of a loop without exiting the method.

1.   Add the following code immediately after the first curly bracket of the *while* loop:

   if (Numbers[Counter] == 17)
   {
      break;
   }

```
public static void AddToNumbers(int AmountToAdd, List<int> Numbers)
{
    int NumberOfNumbers = Numbers.Count;
    int Counter = 0;
    while (Counter < NumberOfNumbers)
    {
        if (Numbers[Counter] == 17)
        {
            break;
        }
        Numbers[Counter] = Numbers[Counter] + AmountToAdd;
        Counter++;
    }
}
```

   This is a simple *if* statement that checks whether the current item in the *Numbers* collection has a value of *17*. When this value is encountered it exits the *while* loop using *break*.

2.   View *calculator.aspx* in your browser and click the *Button* button.

   This time a total of *174* is displayed rather than the *194* you were expecting. This is because your loop stopped when it encountered a value of *17*, so instead of:

   (12 + 10) + (17 + 10) + (135 + 10) = 194

   …you're seeing:

   (12 + 10) + 17+ 135 = 174

3.   Close your browser.

4 Make the *AddToNumbers* method perform an operation after exiting the loop.

1. Add the following code to the end of the *AddToNumbers* method, outside the *while* loop's curly brackets:

Numbers[0] = Numbers[0] + 999;

```
public static void AddToNumbers(int AmountToAdd, List<int> Numbers)
{
    int NumberOfNumbers = Numbers.Count;
    int Counter = 0;
    while (Counter < NumberOfNumbers)
    {
        if (Numbers[Counter] == 17)
        {
            break;
        }
        Numbers[Counter] = Numbers[Counter] + AmountToAdd;
        Counter++;
    }
    Numbers[0] = Numbers[0] + 999;
}
```

2. View *calculator.aspx* in your browser and click *Button* again.

1173

This time the total comes to *1173*. Your calculation is now:

(12 + 10) + 17+ 135 + 999 = 1173

Although your *break* exited from the *while* loop, it didn't exit the method. This meant that the code following the closing curly bracket of the loop was executed.

3. Close your browser.

5 Change *break* to *return*.

As you might have guessed, *return* will exit the entire method rather than just exiting the loop.

1. Change your *break* to: **return**

```
if (Numbers[Counter] == 17)
{
    return;
}
```

2. View *calculator.aspx* in your browser and click *Button*.

174

The total is now *174*, as it was earlier in this lesson. The method terminated when *return* was encountered in your code so the line that adds *999* to the total was never reached.

This behavior isn't exclusive to *while* loops. *break* and *return* can be used in exactly the same way in *foreach* and *for* loops.

Session 8: Exercise

1   Open the *My Project* sample project and create a new class called: **MyData.cs**

2   Add a new public method called **GetNumbers**, which returns an array of *int* variables.

       (You'll see an error at this stage as you have not yet created code that returns a value).

3   Create an array of *int* variables called **Numbers** in the *GetNumbers* method containing the numbers: **1, 1, 3, 5, 8** and make the method return the array.

       (The previously flagged error should disappear as soon as you specify the return value).

4   Add a new public method called **GetNames**, which returns a *List* of *string* variables.

       (You'll see an error at this stage as you have not yet created code that returns a value).

5   Create a *List* of *string* variables called **Names** in the *GetNames* method containing the names: "**Mike**", "**Simon**", "**Emily**" and make the method return it.

       (The previously flagged error should disappear as soon as you specify the return value).

6   Add a new public method called **ProcessNames**, which doesn't return a value.

7   Create a *List* of *string* variables called **NamesToProcess** in the *ProcessNames* method and populate it with the *List* collection returned by the *GetNames()* method.

8   Use a *for* loop to loop through the list of names and make each one upper case using the *ToUpper* method of the *string* variable type.

9   Add a new public method called **AppendNames** which returns a *string* value.

       (You'll see an error at this stage as you have not yet created code that returns a value).

10   In the new method, add a *foreach* loop which loops through the names returned by the *GetNames* method and appends them all to a single *string* variable. Make the method return the *string*.

11   Add a new page called **test.aspx** and use the *Page_Load* event handler to call the *AppendNames* method of the *MyData* class and display the return value at the top of the web page.

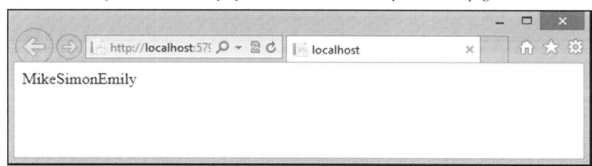

Session 8: Exercise Answers

These are the four questions that students find the most difficult to answer:

Q 10	Q 8	Q 5	Q 3

Use the following code:
 	
public string AppendNames()
{
   string AppendedNames = "";
   foreach (string Name in GetNames())
   {
      AppendedNames = AppendedNames + Name;
   }
   return AppendedNames;
}
 	
This was covered in: *Lesson 8-3: Iterate through a collection using foreach.*
	Use the following code:
	
	public void ProcessNames()
	{
	   List<string> NamesToProcess = GetNames();
	   for (int Counter = 0; Counter < NamesToProcess.Count; Counter++)
	   {
	      NamesToProcess [Counter] = NamesToProcess [Counter].ToUpper();
	   }
	}
	
	This was covered in: *Lesson 8-4: Iterate through a collection using a for loop.*
		Use the following code:
		
		public List<string> GetNames()
		{
		   List<string> Names = new List<string>();
		   Names.Add("Mike");
		   Names.Add("Simon");
		   Names.Add("Emily");
		   return Names;
		}
		
		It is also possible to do this using less code.
		
		This was covered in: *Lesson 8-2: Create a collection.*
			Use the following code:
			
			public int[] GetNumbers()
			{
			   int[] Numbers = new int[5];
			   Numbers[0] = 1;
			   Numbers[1] = 1;
			   Numbers[2] = 3;
			   Numbers[3] = 5;
			   Numbers[4] = 8;
			   return Numbers;
			}
			
			It is also possible to do this using less code.
			
			Both this and the alternative technique were covered in: *Lesson 8-1: Create an array.*

If you have difficulty with the other questions, here are the lessons that cover the relevant skills:

1   **Refer to: Lesson 6-1: Create a class.**

2   **Refer to: Lesson 6-7: Create methods that return a value, Lesson 8-1: Create an array.**

4   **Refer to: Lesson 6-7: Create methods that return a value, Lesson 8-2: Create a collection.**

6   **Refer to: Lesson 6-5: Create and use methods.**

7   **Refer to: Lesson 8-2: Create a collection.**

9   **Refer to: Lesson 6-7: Create methods that return a value.**

11   **Refer to: Lesson 1-7: Manage a project with the Solution Explorer, Lesson 6-2: Create an instance of a class, Lesson 3-7: Understand Request and Response.**

Session Nine: Authentication

Even paranoids have real enemies.

Delmore Schwartz, American poet and writer (1913 – 1966)

One of the most common requirements for a dynamic web application is the ability for your users to create accounts and log in to a member's area. This process is called *authentication*.

Creating a login system was a very complicated process in the early days of the web, but ASP.NET makes it surprisingly easy to create a secure login system without writing any C# code.

In this session you'll learn everything that you need to set up a web site with user accounts and a member's area.

Session Objectives

By the end of this session you will be able to:

- Use .NET's built-in security features
- Manage a site with ASP.NET Configuration
- Change authentication types
- Use the Login control
- Customize the Login control
- Use the CreateUserWizard control
- Use other login controls
- Add folder-level security
- Set up roles
- Use C# to limit access
- Use the security wizard

Lesson 9-1: Use .NET's built-in security features

Back in *Lesson 1-5: Create an ASP.NET Web Forms Application project*, you created a standard Web Forms Application project. The default project already contains a login system of its own! If you don't need anything more advanced, you can simply customize the pages that are created for you.

In this lesson, you'll look at the pages that are created automatically and see how they can be used.

1   Open Visual Studio.

2   Create a new *ASP.NET Web Forms Application* project called **MyMembership** in your sample files folder.

> You first learned how to do this in: *Lesson 1-5: Create an ASP.NET Web Forms Application project*.

3   Create a new account.

1. View *Register.aspx* in your browser.

   You will find it in the *Account* folder. See sidebar if an error message appears.

2. Complete the form using the password **learnasp**. Make a careful note of your chosen *User Name* as you will need it later.

3. Click *Register*.

   You have now created a user account and will be automatically logged in.

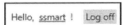

4   Log out of the site.

To log out, simply click the *Log off* button in the top-right corner of the page.

note

If an error message appears on Register.aspx

It's possible that an error message will appear when you view *Register.aspx*. This may happen because the project is new and has not yet been built (or *compiled*).

To solve this problem, click Build→Build Solution and try again.

Alternatively, simply start the project in Debug mode by clicking Debug→Start Debugging.

Starting the project in debug mode automatically builds the project.

note

Sample files all have the password: learnasp

If you are using the incremental sample files for this course, you will find that the User Name will be exactly as shown in the relevant lesson screenshot. (In this lesson the User Name is *ssmart*).

Later in this session you'll create other user accounts with different user names but the password in the sample files is always the same (*learnasp*).

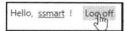

Alternatively, close the window and reopen it from *Visual Studio*.

5 **Log into the site with your new username and password.**

1. Close your browser window if it is open.

2. View *Login.aspx* in your browser.

   Login.aspx can be found in the *Account* folder.

3. Enter your username and password.

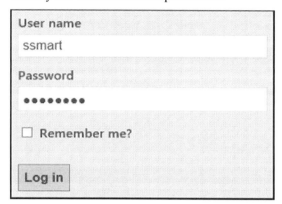

   Enter the username and password for the account that you created earlier in this lesson.

4. Click *Log In*.

   You are once again logged into the site.

   As you can see, it's very easy to create a site with login capabilities by simply customizing the automatically-generated pages.

   You'll learn more about customizing the default ASP.NET application in: *Lesson 12-1: Use master pages.*

   In the rest of this session you'll learn more about how the ASP.NET authentication system works and learn how to create similar pages yourself.

6 **Close your web browser and close Visual Studio.**

Lesson 9-2: Manage a site with ASP.NET Configuration

In the previous lesson you saw how easily you can set up a site to allow registration and membership, but you might be wondering how you can manage your members and change security settings.

You can do this very easily using the *ASP.NET Configuration* utility.

1   Open *MyMembership* from your sample files folder.

2   Open the *ASP.NET Configuration* utility.

　　1.　Open *Default.aspx* in *Source* view.

　　　　You need to have a page open in order for the *Project* menu to display the *ASP.NET Configuration* option.

　　2.　Click Project→ASP.NET Configuration.

　　　　The *ASP.NET Configuration* utility starts in a new browser window (see sidebar if an error occurs).

note

The Provider tab

As you'll see later in this session, ASP.NET has many controls that can be dropped onto the page to automatically interface with the membership database.

The provider is a class that provides all of the services that these controls need to function.

If you had very specialized membership requirements you could write your own provider class, but this isn't usually necessary.

The provider tab allows you to specify an alternate custom provider in these rare cases.

3   View a list of existing users.

　　1.　Click *Security*, either at the top of the page or in the table.

　　　　The security tab opens.

　　2.　Click *Manage Users*.

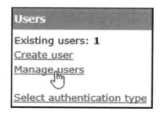

　　　　As you can see, you could create a user here by using the *Create user* option, but you could just as easily use the *Register.aspx* page on your site.

A list of existing users is displayed. At the moment there is only one user, which you created in: *Lesson 9-1: Use .NET's built-in security features*. As you can see, you could easily edit or delete the user from here.

Active	User name			
☑	ssmart	Edit user	Delete user	Edit roles

You will learn about roles in: *Lesson 9-9: Set up roles*.

4   Define email settings.

note

Taking your application offline

You might have noticed the *Take offline* option on the ASP.NET Configuration utility's *Application* tab.

If you click this option, your site will be taken offline. When the site is offline, none of the pages or files in the site will be accessible.

note

Configuring your provider

The *ASP.NET Configuration* utility is unfortunately limited in some areas. There are a number of important settings that can only be changed by editing the *Web.config* file.

If you open the *Web.config* file and look for the *DefaultMembershipProvider* element, you will see that it has settings such as *minRequiredPasswordLength*, which determines how long a user's password must be.

The only way to change these settings is to change them manually in *Web.config*.

note

Debugging and Tracing

The last set of options on the *Application* page allows you to define a default error page and to configure debugging and tracing.

Defining a default error page simply allows you to specify a page that will be shown whenever an error occurs.

Tracing is covered in the Expert Skills course in this series.

To enable your application to send email, you need to configure its email settings. You can do that easily using the *ASP.NET Configuration* utility.

1. Click the *Application* tab at the top of the screen.

   The settings on this page come from your *Web.config* file. You learned about *Web.config* settings in: *Lesson 3-13: Edit the Web.config file.*

   Most of the options on this page are quite self-explanatory. *Application Settings* are your own custom application properties. You won't use them in this book but they are covered in the Expert Skills book in this series.

2. Click *Configure SMTP e-mail settings*.

3. Complete the form with valid e-mail settings.

   Valid email settings aren't essential for any of the lessons in this book, so you can skip this step if you don't have access to a mail server.

   If you'd like to set up email anyway, you can use google's free email service by signing up for a *GMail* account at *http://www.gmail.com.*

   If you are using *GMail*, the following settings were correct in May 2013 (but as with all things on the web they may change):

Server Name:	**smtp.gmail.com**
Server Port:	**587**
From:	**[Your gmail address]**
Authentication:	**Basic**
Sender's user name:	**[Your gmail address]**
Sender's password:	**[Your gmail password]**

4. Click *Save*.

Email settings are important if you want to use security features that send emails to the user, such as when the user forgets their password.

5. Close your browser and close Visual Studio.

Lesson 9-3: Change authentication types

In *Lesson 9-1: Use .NET's built-in security features,* you created a web site where users can log in with a username and password. This is called *Forms* authentication.

Forms authentication is perfect for web sites on the Internet, but it can be cumbersome if you're making a site that is only going to be used on an internal network (known as an *intranet* site).

You can use *Windows* authentication to allow your site to recognize users by their Windows username and password when used on an internal network (saving them the bother of remembering multiple usernames and passwords).

1   Open *MyMembership* from your sample files folder.

2   Open the *ASP.NET Configuration* utility.

3   Switch the authentication type to *Windows*.

    1.   Click *Security,* either at the top of the page or in the table.

    2.   Click *Select Authentication Type.*

    A page appears, prompting you to choose between *From the Internet* and *From a local network.*

    3.   Click *From a local network.*

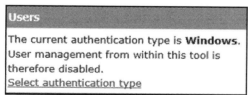

    This is the *Windows* authentication setting.

    4.   Click *Done.*

    The button is in the bottom-right corner.

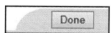

    Because you are now using Windows authentication, you will no longer be able to manage users using the *ASP.NET Configuration* utility. You can't use both *Windows* and *Forms* authentication at the same time.

    Note that you will no longer be able to log in using the user name and password that you created earlier.

Users

The current authentication type is **Windows**. User management from within this tool is therefore disabled.

Select authentication type

note

Windows authentication on the Internet

Although *Forms* authentication is the preferred form of authentication on the Internet, it's still possible to use *Windows* authentication on Internet sites.

If you use *Windows* authentication on an Internet site (as opposed to intranet), visitors will be prompted to log in when they first attempt to access any page on the site.

A visitor to a site using *Windows* authentication will have to provide a valid Windows username and password for the network that the site is hosted on (not the user's own computer).

Using Windows authentication on the Internet is generally not a good idea.

5. Close the *ASP.NET Configuration* utility.

4 **Test Windows authentication.**

1. View *Manage.aspx* (from the *Account* folder) in your browser.

An error message may appear. By default, Visual Studio 2012 is configured to disable Windows Authentication.

If no error message appears, you can skip to step 6.

2. Close your browser.

5 **Enable Windows authentication.**

1. Click *MyMembership* in the *Solution Explorer* window.

2. In the *Properties* window, set the *Windows Authentication* property to: **Enabled**

Unless you set this property, Windows authentication will always be disabled in Visual Studio 2012.

6 **Test Windows authentication.**

1. View *Manage.aspx* (from the *Account* folder) in your browser.

You may be prompted to enter your Windows username and password. If so, enter your login details and click *OK*.

Your windows username appears in the top-right corner.

Unfortunately, it's likely that this didn't happen automatically. See sidebar for an explanation of this.

3. Close your browser.

7 **Switch back to *Forms* authentication.**

1. Open the *ASP.NET Configuration* utility.

2. Click the *Security* tab.

3. Click *Select Authentication Type*.

4. Click *From the Internet*.

5. Click *Done*.

The options to create and manage your *Forms* users become available again and the existing user re-appears.

Users
Existing users: **1**
Create user
Manage users

6. Close the *ASP.NET Configuration* utility.

8 **Close Visual Studio.**

Lesson 9-4: Use the Login control

So far, you've used only automatically-generated pages to log in and register accounts. By using the controls from the *Login* category of the *Toolbox* you can easily add these features to pages of your own.

1   Open *MyMembership* from your sample files folder.

2   Create a new page named: **mylogin.aspx**

You first did this in: *Lesson 1-7: Manage a project with the Solution Explorer.*

3   Open *mylogin.aspx* in *Design* view.

4   Add a *Login* control to the page.

1. Drag the *Login* control from the *Toolbox* onto the page.

You will find it under the *Login* category of the *Toolbox*.

2. Set the *ID* property of the new *Login* control to: **LoginMyPage**

5   Make the *Login* control redirect when the user logs in successfully.

The *Login* control would already allow a user to log in without any problems, but since there are no links on this page it would be better if it redirected the user to another web page after they log in. Fortunately, it's easy to do so by using the *LoggedIn* event.

1. Add a *LoggedIn* event handler to the *LoginMyPage* control.

You first added event handlers to controls in: *Lesson 3-2: Add event handlers to controls.*

2. Add the following code to the new event handler:

Response.Redirect("Default.aspx");

note

Logging in with C#

As well as using the *Login* control, you can use the *System.Web.Security* namespace of the .NET library to log in using C#.

Assuming your username and password were in text boxes called *TextBoxUsername* and *TextBoxPassword*, you could use the following code:

*System.Web.Security.Membership
.ValidateUser
(TextBoxUsername.Text,
TextBoxPassword.Text);*

This method returns *true* and logs the user in if the username and password are correct and returns *false* if not.

```
protected void LoginMyPage_LoggedIn(object sender, EventArgs e)
{
    Response.Redirect("Default.aspx");
}
```

note

Returning to a page using a ReturnUrl query string value

Often you'll want to make a Log In page available from many pages on your web site.

When this is the case you'll often want your user to return to the previous page after logging in.

You can do this by calling your login page with a *ReturnUrl* query string value. For example:

<a href= "mylogin.aspx?ReturnUrl= about.aspx"> Log In</a>

The above HTML code would create a hyperlink with the text *Log In*. After logging in, the user would be returned to the *about.aspx* web page.

Youcan use this technique with any page that contains a *Login* control.

You learned about query strings in: *Lesson 3-11: Send data between pages.*

6   Test your *Login* control.

1.   View *mylogin.aspx* in your browser.

2.   Enter the login details of the user that you created earlier, but deliberately enter the wrong password.

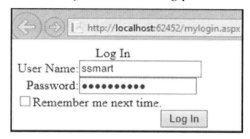

3.   Click *Log In*.

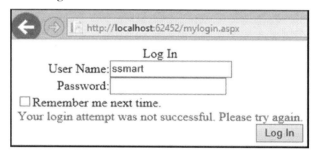

An error message is displayed. You entered the wrong password and weren't able to log in, so the *LoggedIn* event didn't fire.

You could customize this error message by changing the *FailureText* property of the *Login* control.

4.   Enter the correct login details and then click *Log In* again.

If you're using the incremental sample files, the username is *ssmart* and the password is *learnasp*.

This time you are logged in and sent to the *Default.aspx* page by the code you added. If you look in the top-right corner of the page, you'll see confirmation that you are logged in.

5.   Close your browser.

7   Close Visual Studio.

Lesson 9-5: Customize the Login control

The *Login* control can be customized using properties in the same way as every other control, but you can convert it into a *template* in order to customize it further.

Converting a control into a template splits the control into several individual elements, allowing you to customize the layout and style of the control even further.

The *Login* control is an excellent example of this, but there are several other controls that you can convert into templates using the same techniques that you'll use in this lesson.

1   Open *MyMembership* from your sample files folder.

2   Open *mylogin.aspx* in *Source* view.

```
<asp:Login ID="LoginMyPage" runat="server" onloggedin="LoginMyPage_LoggedIn">
</asp:Login>
```

You can see that the *Login* control is defined by a single pair of tags. This is fine if you're happy to customize it using its properties, but it won't allow you to change the layout of the control.

3   Convert the *Login* control into templates.

1.   Switch to *Design* view.

2.   Choose *Convert to Template* from the *QuickTasks* menu of the *LoginMyPage* control. You learned about the *QuickTasks* menu in: *Lesson 1-16: Use the QuickTasks menu.*

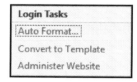

3.   Switch back to *Source* view.

```
<asp:Login ID="LoginMyPage" runat="server" OnLoggedIn="LoginMyPage_LoggedIn">
    <LayoutTemplate>
        <table cellpadding="1" cellspacing="0" style="border-collapse: collap
            <tr>
                <td>
                    <table cellpadding="0">
                        <tr>
                            <td align="center" colspan="2">
                                Log In
                            </td>
                        </tr>
                        <tr>
                            <td align="right">
                                <asp:Label ID="UserNameLabel" runat="server"
                            </td>
```

The *Login* control has been converted into an HTML table which you can fully customize.

Note that controls will only be recognized as part of the *Login* control if they are inside the *LayoutTemplate* tags, and their *ID* properties must not be changed from the automatically generated values.

4 Customize the *Login* control.

1. Select the *User Name:* label in *Design* view.

2. Set the *Text* property of the *Label* control to: **UID:**

You wouldn't have been able to change this text without converting the *Login* control into a template.

3. Change the *Text* property of the *Password:* label to: **PWD:**

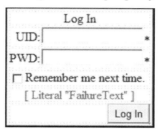

5 Replace the *Log In* button with a *LinkButton* control.

CommandName	Login
Enabled	True
EnableTheming	True
EnableViewState	True
OnClientClick	
PostBackUrl	
SkinID	
ToolTip	
UseSubmitBehavior	True
ValidateRequestMode	Inherit
ValidationGroup	LoginMyPage

1. Select the *LoginButton* control and view its properties.

The *CommandName* property contains the *Login* keyword. This tells the *Login* control to log the user in when the button is clicked.

2. Delete the *Log In* button.

3. Add a *LinkButton* control to the previous location of the *Log In* button.

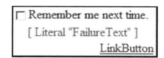

If you're having trouble getting the *LinkButton* control to appear in the right place, click in the table cell first and then add the *LinkButton* control.

4. Set the *ID* property of the new *LinkButton* control to: **LinkButtonLogin**

5. Set the *Text* property of the *LinkButton* control to: **Log In**

6. Set the *CommandName* property to the keyword: **Login**

6 Test your customized *Login* control.

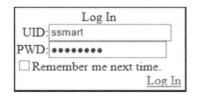

1. View *mylogin.aspx* in your browser.

2. Fill in the correct login details and click *Log In*.

You are logged in successfully.

7 Close your browser and close Visual Studio.

Lesson 9-6: Use the CreateUserWizard control

The *CreateUserWizard* control is used on the automatically-generated *Register.aspx* page that you saw in: *Lesson 9-1: Use .NET's built-in security features*.

In this lesson, you'll add a *CreateUserWizard* control to a page of your own and use it to create a new user.

1 Open *MyMembership* from your sample files folder.

2 Create a new page called: **myregister.aspx**

3 Add a *CreateUserWizard* control to the page.

  1. Open *myregister.aspx* in *Design* view.

  2. Add a *CreateUserWizard* control from the *Login* category of the *Toolbox*.

  This creates a standard form for registering a new account.

4 Customize the *CreateUserWizard* control.

  1. Set the *ID* property of the *CreateUserWizard* control to: **CreateUserWizardMyPage**

  2. Use *Auto Format* from the *QuickTasks* menu to apply the *Professional* format to the control. You learned about the *QuickTasks* menu in: *Lesson 1-16: Use the QuickTasks menu*.

5 Create a user with your new page.

  1. View *myregister.aspx* in your browser.

  2. Complete the form using the password: **learnasp**

This part of the process is called the *Create User* step.

You'll notice that the *Security Question* and *Security Answer* fields aren't appearing on the page. This is because of the settings in the *Web.config* file (see sidebar).

3. Click *Create User*.

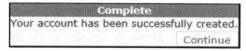

This part of the login process is called the *Complete* step.

The new user account has been created.

4. Close your web browser.

6 Convert the *CreateUserWizard* control into a template.

Just like the *Login* control, you can customize either, or both, steps of the *CreateUserWizard* control by converting them into templates.

You first encountered the concept of customizing controls with templates in: *Lesson 9-5: Customize the Login control.*

1. Open *myregister.aspx* in *Design* view.

2. Choose *Customize Complete Step* from the *QuickTasks* menu of the *CreateUserWizard* control.

The *Complete* step is converted into a template and made editable.

3. Change the *Your account has been successfully created* text to:

Thank you for registering an account!
Click Continue to proceed!

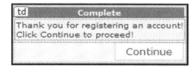

By using the customization options in the *QuickTasks* menu, you can fully customize each step of the *CreateUserWizard* control.

If your registration process has many special requirements it may be easier to create your own registration form and then use the *System.Web.Security.Membership.CreateUser* method to create users (see sidebar).

7 Close Visual Studio.

Lesson 9-7: Use other login controls

In this lesson you will learn how to use the other controls in the *Login* category of the *Toolbox*.

1   Open *MyMembership* from your sample files folder.

2   Add a new page to the project called: **mylogin2.aspx**

3   Open *mylogin2.aspx* in *Design* view.

4   Add a *Login* control to the page.

1.   Drag a *Login* control onto the page from the *Login* category of the *ToolBox*.

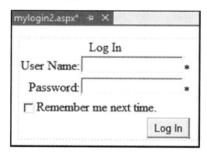

2.   Set the *ID* property of the *Login* control to: **LoginMyPage**

3.   Use *Auto Format* from the *QuickTasks* menu to set the new *Login* control to the *Professional* format.

You first used *Auto Format* in: *Lesson 1-16: Use the QuickTasks menu*.

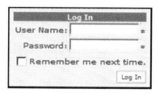

5   Add a *LoginName* control to the page.

The *LoginName* control displays the username of the logged-in user. You've seen it in the top-right corner of the automatically-generated pages.

It will be blank unless the user is logged in.

1.   Drag a *LoginName* control onto the page from the *Login* category of the *Toolbox*.

Place the new control below the *LoginMyPage* control.

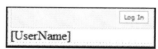

2.   Set the *ID* property of the new control to: **LoginNameMyPage**

3.   View *mylogin2.aspx* in your browser.

note

Other login controls

As well as the controls covered in this lesson, ASP.NET has the *ChangePassword* and *PasswordRecovery* controls, which are self-explanatory.

There is also the *LoginView* control, which allows you to create an area of the page which appears differently to logged-in users than to logged-out users.

An alternative approach would be to create two or more *Panel* controls and to set their *Visible* properties according to whether the user is logged in or not. You would use this approach if you wanted to base the visibility of the panels on more complex criteria than simply whether the user was logged in or not.

The *PasswordRecovery* control uses the email settings that you learned about in *Lesson 9-2: Manage a site with ASP.NET Configuration* to send a new password to the user's email address.

4. Log in using the username and password that you created earlier.

If you are not completing this course incrementally, the login details in the sample file will be:

Username: **ssmart**
Password: **learnasp**

After logging in, the *LoginName* control displays your username.

5. Close your browser.

6 Add a *LoginStatus* control to the page.

The *LoginStatus* control shows either a *Login* or *Logout* hyperlink, depending on whether or not a user is logged in. Clicking *Login* will send the user to the login page, clicking *Logout* will log them out, and all without writing any code at all!

1. Drag a *LoginStatus* control onto your page from the *Login* category of the *Toolbox*.

Place it just after your *LoginName* control.

2. Set the *ID* property of the new control to: **LoginStatusMyPage**

3. View *mylogin2.aspx* in your browser.

The *LoginStatus* control is currently displaying a *Login* link, since you are not currently logged in.

4. Log in using the same username and password that you used earlier in this lesson.

After logging in, the *LoginStatus* control shows a *Logout* link.

5. Click the *Logout* link.

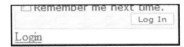

You are logged out.

6. Click the *Login* link.

You are redirected to *Login.aspx*. This is because it has been defined as the *loginUrl* in *Web.config* (see sidebar).

7 Close your web browser and Visual Studio.

Lesson 9-8: Add folder-level security

You will sometimes want to have pages that are accessible only to certain users. For example you might have an administration page which you want only system administrators to be able to access.

Fortunately, ASP.NET gives you a very easy way to set up page security, although it is limited to securing the contents of folders rather than individual pages.

1 Open *MyMembership* from your sample files folder.

2 Create an admin page.

    1. Add a new folder to the project called: **Admin**

       You learned how to add new folders in: *Lesson 1-7: Manage a project with the Solution Explorer*.

    2. Add a new page to the *Admin* folder called: **default.aspx**

       Because it is named *default.aspx*, if a user navigates to *www.[yoursite].com/Admin* the page will be automatically displayed.

3 Create a new access rule.

    1. Open the *ASP.NET Configuration* utility.

       You learned how to do this in: *Lesson 9-2: Manage a site with ASP.NET Configuration.*

    2. Click the *Security* tab.

    3. Click *Create access rules*.

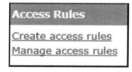

    4. Click the *Admin* folder on the left.

    5. Click *Anonymous Users*.

    Anonymous users are users who have not logged in.

    6. Click *Deny* on the right (if it's not selected already).

---

7. Click *OK* in the bottom-right corner of the screen.

8. Close the *ASP.NET Configuration* utility.

You have just created a rule that will make sure that only users who have logged in will be able to access pages in the *Admin* folder.

4 Try out your access rule.

1. View *default.aspx* (from the *Admin* folder) in your browser.

    Since you are not logged in by default, you are denied access and are automatically redirected to the login page.

2. Log in with your username (the one you created in: *Lesson 9-1: Use .NET's built-in security features*).

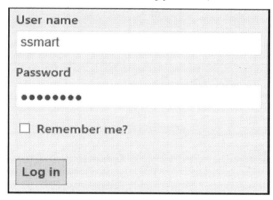

    If you're using the incremental sample files, the username is *ssmart* and the password is *learnasp*.

    After logging in, you are automatically redirected to *default.aspx* in the *admin* folder.

    Since the page is blank you won't actually see anything on the page, but before you logged in you were unable to access it at all.

    Using access rules in this way makes it easy to create areas that only registered users can access.

3. Close your browser.

5 Close Visual Studio.

Lesson 9-9: Set up roles

If you have a lot of users, it's useful to be able to group them together into roles. All members sharing the same role can then be given the same access rights.

By using roles, you can make your access rules much simpler and make your site's security easier to manage.

1   Open *MyMembership* from your sample files folder.

2   Create a role called: **Normal User**

   1.   Open the *ASP.NET Configuration* utility.

   2.   Click the *Security* tab.

   3.   Click *Enable Roles*.

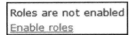

Roles are not enabled
Enable roles

     By default, roles are disabled. You have to enable them in order to use them.

   4.   Click *Create or Manage roles*.

Roles

Existing roles: **0**
Disable Roles
Create or Manage roles

   5.   Enter **Normal User** into the text box.

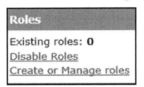

Create New Role

New role name: Normal User   Add Role

   6.   Click *Add Role*.

     You have just created a role.

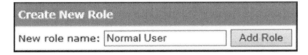

Role Name	Add/Remove Users
Normal User	Manage

3   Assign a user to the role.

   1.   Click the *Manage* button next to the *Normal User* role.

   2.   Use the search functions to find the first user you created.

     Either enter the username into the text box and click *Find User* or click on the letter of the alphabet that your username begins with.

A B C D E F G H I J K L M N O P Q R S T U V W X Y Z All

User name	User Is In Role
ssmart	☑

   3.   Tick the *User Is In Role* box.

Your user account is now part of the *Normal User* group.

4. Click *Back* in the bottom-right corner of the screen.

4 Add an access rule for the *Normal User* role.

1. Click the *Security* tab at the top of the page to return to the main *Security* page.

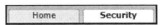

2. Click *Manage access rules*.

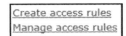

3. Click the *Admin* folder on the left.

4. Click *Add New Access Rule*.

The rule automatically applies to the *Normal User* role by default as this is the only role that currently exists.

5. Click *Deny* (if it isn't selected already).

6. Click *OK* in the bottom-right corner of the screen.

Your permissions now deny both members of the *Normal User* role and people who have not logged in from accessing the *Admin* folder.

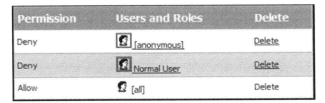

By combining roles and access rules, you can easily control which users are allowed to access which folders.

5 Close your browser and close Visual Studio.

Lesson 9-10: Use C# to limit access

As well as using the options in the *ASP.NET Configuration* utility, you can use certain C# methods and properties to check whether a user is logged in and redirect them accordingly.

1 Open *MyMembership* from your sample files folder.

1 Open the code-behind file of *About.aspx*.

2 Make the page only available to logged-in users using C#.

1. Add the following code to the *Page_Load* event handler:

if (!Page.User.Identity.IsAuthenticated)
{
 Response.Redirect("~/Account/Login.aspx");
}

```
protected void Page_Load(object sender, EventArgs e)
{
    if (!Page.User.Identity.IsAuthenticated)
    {
        Response.Redirect("~/Account/Login.aspx");
    }
}
```

The *Page.User.Identity.IsAuthenticated* property returns *true* if the user is logged in and *false* if they are not.

You learned about using the tilde (~) within paths in: *Lesson 4-2: Use the Button* control *(sidebar).* You learned about the NOT operator (!) in: *Lesson 7-3: Use basic logical operators.*

2. View *Default.aspx* in your browser.

3. Click the *About* link.

You are redirected to *Login.aspx* by the code you added because you are not logged in.

4. Log in with a valid username and password.

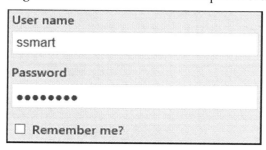

If you are not working through this course sequentially, the sample file for this lesson uses Username: **ssmart**, Password: **learnasp**.

You are logged in and your username appears in the top-right corner of the screen.

note

Page.User.Identity .Name

In this lesson you use the *Page.User.Identity .IsAuthenticated* property to check whether the user is logged in.

The *Page.User.Identity.Name* property will contain the username of the logged-in user if the user is logged in.

Hello, ssmart ! Log off

About. Your app description page.

Use this area to provide additional information.

Use this area to provide additional information.

Use this area to provide additional information.

5. Click the *About* link.

   This time you are able to access the page because you are logged in.

3   **Make the page only available to the *Normal User* role.**

1. Close your browser and return to the code-behind file of *About.aspx*.

2. Change the *if* statement in the *Page_Load* event handler to:

   if (!Page.User.IsInRole("Normal User"))

   ```
   protected void Page_Load(object sender, EventArgs e)
   {
       if (!Page.User.IsInRole("Normal User"))
       {
           Response.Redirect("~/Account/Login.aspx");
       }
   }
   ```

   This code will redirect the user if they are not assigned to the *Normal User* role.

3. View *Default.aspx* in your browser.

4. Click the *About* link.

   Because you're not logged in, you are once again redirected to the login page. This happens because *IsInRole* returns *false* for users that are not logged in, as well as for logged in users that are not members of the *Normal User* group.

5. Log in again as the user that you assigned to the *Normal User* role in: *Lesson 9-10: Use C# to limit access*. In the sample file for this lesson this is username: **ssmart**, password **learnasp**.

6. Click the *About* link.

   This time you are able to access the page because you are logged in as a user that has the *Normal User* role.

7. Log out by clicking *Log off* in the top-right corner.

   Hello, ssmart !   Log off

8. Log in as your second user (the one that you created in: *Lesson 9-6: Use the CreateUserWizard control*). In the sample file for this lesson this is username: **ssmart2**, password **learnasp**.

   This user doesn't have the *Normal User* role.

9. Try to access the *About* page.

   You are redirected to the login page. This user doesn't have the *Normal User* role so the user doesn't pass the *IsInRole* check.

10. Close your web browser.

Note that in a real-world application this implementation could confuse your users. See sidebar for details of how you could make this application friendlier.

Lesson 9-11: Use the security wizard

As well as using the individual security configuration pages in the *ASP.NET Configuration* utility, you can use the security wizard to set up your site's security on a step-by-step basis.

1 Open *MyMembership* from your sample files folder.

2 Open the *ASP.NET Configuration* utility.

3 Click the *Security* tab.

4 Start the security wizard.

   1. Click
      Use the security Setup Wizard to configure security step by step.

      The first page of the security wizard appears. This page gives a brief explanation of what the security wizard does.

   2. Click *Next* at the bottom-right of the screen.

5 Select the authentication method.

   The next page is almost identical to the one that you used to set the authentication method in: *Lesson 9-3: Change authentication types*.

   1. Click *From the Internet* (if it isn't selected already).

   2. Click *Next* in the bottom-right corner of the screen.

6 See provider information.

   The page you're on now is only useful if you're using a custom provider. Providers were explained in: *Lesson 9-2: Manage a site with ASP.NET Configuration (sidebar)*.

   Click *Next* in the bottom-right corner of the screen.

7 Enable or disable roles.

   The next step allows you to enable or disable roles.

   ☑ Enable roles for this Web site.

   Leave roles enabled and click *Next* in the bottom-right corner.

8 Add a role called: **Manager**

   This page allows you to add roles, just as you did in: *Lesson 9-9: Set up roles*.

   1. Enter *Manager* into the *New Role Name* text box.

2. Click *Add Role*.

The *Manager* role appears in the *Existing Roles* list, along with the *Normal User* role that you created earlier.

3. Click *Next* in the bottom-right corner of the screen.

9 Examine the *Create User* page.

This page allows you to create new users. It uses the *CreateUserWizard* control that you learned about in: *Lesson 9-6: Use the CreateUserWizard control.*

Click *Next* in the bottom-right corner of the screen.

10 Add an access rule.

The next page allows you to add access rules, just as you did in *Lesson 9-8: Add folder-level security.*

1. Expand the folder on the left by clicking the + sign.

A list of all of the folders in your site appears.

2. Click the *Admin* folder on the left.

The rules that you created earlier are displayed.

3. Select the *Manager* role from the dropdown menu.

4. Click *Allow*.

5. Click *Add This Rule*.

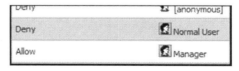

A new rule appears, allowing users with the *Manager* role to access all files in the *Admin* folder.

11 Complete the wizard.

Click the *Finish* button to close the wizard. Note that you could have clicked *Finish* at any time if you wanted to end the wizard early.

It's up to you whether you prefer to use the wizard to set up ASP.NET security settings or to use the individual pages. They both do exactly the same thing.

Session 9: Exercise

1   Create a new *ASP.NET Web Forms Application* project in your sample files folder, named: **Session9**

2   Start the project in *Debug* mode, view its pages and then close your web browser.

(This is necessary because the project must be built before the *ASP.NET Configuration* utility will work properly. Starting debugging causes the project to be built).

3   Open the *ASP.NET Configuration* utility for your new project.

4   Enable roles for the application.

5   Add a new role called: **Moderator**

6   Add a new folder to the project called: **Moderate**

7   Add a new *aspx* page to the *Moderate* folder called: **default.aspx**

8   Add a *Calendar* control to your new page.

9   Use the *ASP.NET Configuration* utility to add access rules to allow only users with the *Moderator* role to access the *Moderate* folder.

10   Create a new user account and assign it to the *Moderator* role.

11   Attempt to view the new *default.aspx* page in the *Moderate* folder in your browser.

12   Log in when prompted using the user account that you created in step 10.

If all of the above questions were completed correctly you will now see the new *default.aspx* file in the *Moderate* folder.

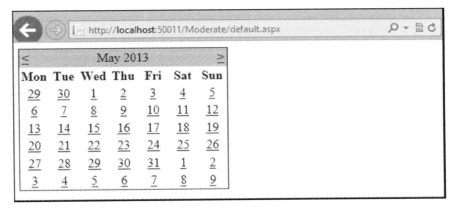

Session9 - end

If you need help slide the page to the left

Session 9: Exercise Answers

These are the four questions that students find the most difficult to answer:

Q 10	Q 9	Q 5	Q 3
1. Open the *ASP.NET Configuration* utility (if it isn't open already). 2. Click the *Security* tab. 3. Click *Create user*. 4. Complete the form. 5. Check the *Moderator* box. 6. Click *Create User*. This was covered in: *Lesson 9-1: Use .NET's built-in security features.*	1. Open the *ASP.NET Configuration* utility. 2. Click the *Security* tab. 3. Click *Manage Access Rules*. 4. Click the *Moderate* folder on the left. 5. Click *Add new access rule*. 6. Click *Allow*. 7. Click *OK*. 8. Click *Add new access rule*. 9. Click *Anonymous Users*. 10. Click Deny. 11. Click *OK*. This was covered in: *Lesson 9-8: Add folder-level security.*	1. Open the *ASP.NET Configuration* utility. 2. Click the *Security* tab. 3. Click *Create or Manage roles*. 4. Type **Moderator** into the *New role name* text box. 5. Click *Add Role*. This was covered in: *Lesson 9-9: Set up roles.*	Click Project→ ASP.NET Configuration. This was covered in: *Lesson 9-2: Manage a site with ASP.NET Configuration.*

If you have difficulty with the other questions, here are the lessons that cover the relevant skills:

1   Refer to: Lesson 1-5: Create an ASP.NET Web Forms Application project.

2   Refer to: Lesson 1-9: Run a project in debug mode.

4   Refer to: Lesson 9-9: Set up roles.

6   Refer to: Lesson 1-8: Add and remove files from a project.

7   Refer to: Lesson 1-7: Manage a project with the Solution Explorer.

8   Refer to: Lesson 1-15: Add controls to a page with the Toolbox.

11   Refer to: Lesson 9-1: Use .NET's built-in security features.

12   Refer to: Lesson 9-1: Use .NET's built-in security features.

Session Ten: Accessing Data

As a general rule, the most successful man in life is the man who has the best information.

Benjamin Disraeli, British Prime Minister (1804 – 1881)

Almost every ASP.NET web site has a database of some kind. For example, online shops have databases filled with products, customer details and orders.

Being able to interact with a database is almost always required when writing interactive web sites.

In this session you'll learn how to use Microsoft's new LINQ technology to allow your website to interact with a database by creating web pages that are able to read, write and edit data.

Session Objectives

By the end of this session you will be able to:

- Work with SQL databases in Visual Studio
- Add LINQ data classes to a project
- Retrieve a single row of data using LINQ
- Retrieve multiple rows of data using LINQ
- Sort results and call Stored Procedures using LINQ
- Check whether a record exists using LINQ
- Update database records using LINQ
- Insert database records using LINQ
- Delete database records using LINQ
- Use LINQ with collections

note

Database types

Visual Studio is capable of working with any type of SQL-compliant database.

Visual Studio works best with Microsoft's SQL Server database product, but it is entirely possible to use other database types such as Access, Oracle and MySQL.

The free Express version of SQL Server was automatically installed on your machine when you installed Visual Studio.

note

The App_Data folder

The *App_Data* folder is a special folder which ASP.NET assumes will contain any databases used by a web site.

If you right-click on the first item displayed in the *Solution Explorer* and then click *Add→Add ASP.NET Folder*, you will see that there are a number of other 'special' ASP.NET folders which are expected to contain certain things.

For now, the *App_Data* folder is the only one that is important.

If you are not completing the course incrementally use the sample file: **Lesson 10-1** to begin this lesson.

Sample files with the starting point for each lesson are also provided for all of the other lessons in this session.

Lesson 10-1: Work with SQL databases in Visual Studio

SQL (Structured Query Language) is a query language that allows computer applications to add, edit and delete data from a database.

Whenever your application interacts with a database it does so by constructing an SQL query.

You don't need to learn SQL to access data in your projects because ASP.NET provides classes which generate SQL code for you.

1   Open *My Project* from your sample files folder.

2   Add a new SQL database to the project called: **MyDatabase.mdf**

   1.   Right-click on *My Project* in the *Solution Explorer* and click Add→New Item… from the shortcut menu.

   2.   Click *Data* in the panel on the left.

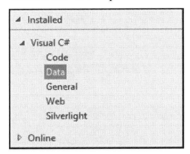

   3.   Click *SQL Server Database* in the center panel.

   4.   Type **MyDatabase.mdf** into the *Name* text box.

   5.   Click *Add*.

   You are prompted to place the new database in the *App_Data* folder of the site, rather than the main folder (see sidebar).

   6.   Click *Yes*.

   You have just added a new database to your project. Of course, it is completely empty.

In a typical work environment database design is done by a specialized team member called a DBA (database administrator).

Most ASP.NET programmers do not have database design skills, but have the skills needed to access data from a database designed by a DBA. If you are interested in database design there are many books on this subject.

You don't need any database design skills to complete this course as sample databases are provided to work with.

3   Open *Spark* from your sample files folder.

The *Spark* project already has its own database, named *Spark.mdf*.

4   View the *Spark.mdf* database.

1.   Expand the *App_Data* folder in the *Solution Explorer*.

2.   Double-click *Spark.mdf*.

After a short delay, you are transferred to the *Database Explorer* window.

The *Database Explorer* appears in the same area as the *Solution Explorer*. You can switch back to the *Solution Explorer* by clicking on the *Solution Explorer* tab at the bottom of the window.

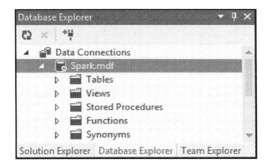

5.   Expand the *Tables* folder in the *Database Explorer*.

You can see that the *Spark* database contains the *Customer* and *Invoice* tables.

Tables are the containers that databases store their data in. Database tables are similar to spreadsheets as they contain tables of information divided into rows and columns.

5   View the contents of the *Customer* table.

Right click the *Customer* table and click *Show Table Data* from the shortcut menu. After a few seconds, the contents of the table appear in the central panel of Visual Studio.

	CustomerID	CustomerName
▶	1	Bottom-Dollar Markets
	2	Romero y tomillo
	3	Ana Trujillo Emparedados y helados

You are able to edit the data in the table by changing the values in the cells.

Lesson 10-2: Add LINQ data classes to a project

LINQ, which stands for Language Integrated Query, is a relatively new addition to .NET which makes working with databases much easier.

Before LINQ, programmers would usually create their own set of classes to generate the SQL code that is needed to interact with a database. This took a lot of time and effort.

ASP.NET's LINQ classes automatically create the SQL code needed to interact with your data, making it unnecessary to learn SQL. LINQ also streamlines the development process by removing the need to create your own data access classes.

1   Open *Spark* from your sample files folder.

2   Add LINQ data classes to the project.

1.   Right-click on *Spark* in the *Solution Explorer* and click Add→New Item... from the shortcut menu.

2.   Click *Data* in the left panel.

3.   Click *LINQ to SQL Classes* in the center panel.

4.   Type **Spark.dbml** into the *Name* text box.

5.   Click *Add*.

The *dbml* file is added and automatically opened, displaying what it calls the *Object Relational Designer*.

The Object Relational Designer allows you to visualize data classes in your code.

Create data classes by dragging items from **Database Explorer** or **Toolbox** onto this design surface.

Although your LINQ data class file has been created, you now need to create classes for the objects in your database by using this designer.

3   Add a table to your LINQ classes.

1.   Open the *Database Explorer* by clicking its tab underneath the *Solution Explorer*.

2.   Expand the *Spark.mdf* database.

3.   Expand the *Tables* folder.

4.   Click and drag the *Customer* table from the *Tables* folder onto the *Object Relational Designer* in the central panel.

The table appears in the LINQ designer panel.

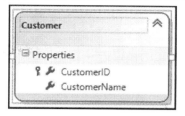

Your LINQ file now contains a class for the *Customer* table, which allows you to easily search and update the table using the C# code that you'll learn later in this session.

4 Add the *Invoice* table to your LINQ classes.

In the same way as you did with the *Customer* table, drag the *Invoice* table onto the LINQ designer.

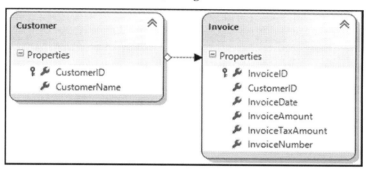

The *Invoice* table is now available to your LINQ classes.

You'll notice the arrow between the two tables. This indicates the presence of a *relationship* between the tables.

The line and arrow tell you that each customer may have many invoices.

Your LINQ classes will allow you to very easily find all of the invoices for any customer and to find the customer for any invoice. You'll see this in action in: *Lesson 10-4: Retrieve multiple rows of data using LINQ.*

5 Add a stored procedure to your LINQ classes.

Stored procedures are similar to methods, but are stored inside the database. Stored procedures contain SQL code that can manipulate data in ways that would be difficult using C# code. In a team environment, stored procedures are usually written by the DBA.

The stored procedure in this example finds the highest invoice number in the *Invoice* table.

1. Expand the *Stored Procedures* folder in the *Database Explorer.*

2. Drag the *SpGetLastInvoiceNumber* procedure onto the LINQ designer.

The stored procedure appears in the right panel of the *Linq Designer.*

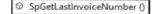

Now that the stored procedure is part of the LINQ data class, you can call it just like any other C# method. You'll do this in: *Lesson 10-5: Sort results and call stored procedures using LINQ.*

Lesson 10-3: Retrieve a single row of data using LINQ

In this lesson, you'll see how easily you can extract any data you want from a database using LINQ.

1   Open *Spark* from your sample files folder.

2   Open the code-behind file of *reports.aspx*.

3   Create an instance of your LINQ data class.

Create an instance of your data class with the *using* statement. This causes the class to automatically dispose of itself (see sidebar).

Add the following code to the *Page_Load* event handler:

using (SparkDataContext Data = new SparkDataContext())
{
}

```
protected void Page_Load(object sender, EventArgs e)
{
    using (SparkDataContext Data = new SparkDataContext())
    {
    }
}
```

The LINQ data class always appends *DataContext* to the name of the *dbml* file. You provided the name *Spark.dbml*, so the class is called *SparkDataContext*. You've just created an instance of the class called *Data*.

4   Use the data class to retrieve a customer record from the database.

When you added the *Customer* table to the LINQ classes in the last lesson, a *Customer* class was automatically created. The *Customer* class is used to represent rows of data in the *Customer* table.

1. Add the following code inside the *using* statement:

   Customer MyCustomer = Data.Customers.First();

   ```
   using (SparkDataContext Data = new SparkDataContext())
   {
       Customer MyCustomer = Data.Customers.First();
   }
   ```

   This code gets the first row from the *Customers* table and places it in an object called *MyCustomer*, which is an instance of the *Customer* class.

2. On the next line (inside the *using* statement), type:

   MyCustomer.

   The IntelliSense menu appears for *MyCustomer*. As you can see, it has *CustomerID* and *CustomerName* as properties.

   The *CustomerID* property is an *int* and the *CustomerName* property is a *string*. You already know how to work with these types.

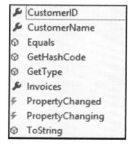

You'll also notice the *Invoices* property. Using *Invoices*, you can extract all of the invoices that belong to the customer that is stored in the *MyCustomer* object.

3. Delete the *MyCustomer.* text you just added.

5 Display the customer name on the page.

1. Type the following code on the next line:

LabelReport.Text = MyCustomer.CustomerName;

```
using (SparkDataContext Data = new SparkDataContext())
{
    Customer MyCustomer = Data.Customers.First();
    LabelReport.Text = MyCustomer.CustomerName;
}
```

The *CustomerName* property is a string, so you can display it in the *Label* control on the page.

2. View *reports.aspx* in your browser.

> Bottom-Dollar Markets

Bottom Dollar Markets appears on the page: the first customer in the *Customers* table.

3. Close your browser.

6 Retrieve a specific customer record from the database.

1. Change the *Customer MyCustomer...* line to:

Customer MyCustomer = Data.Customers
.Single(Customer => Customer.CustomerID == 5);

```
using (SparkDataContext Data = new SparkDataContext())
{
    Customer MyCustomer = Data.Customers
            .Single(Customer => Customer.CustomerID == 5);
    LabelReport.Text = MyCustomer.CustomerName;
}
```

This code will search the *Customer* table for a customer record with a *CustomerID* of 5 and return the record as an instance of the *Customer* class.

The code inside the *Single* method looks a little strange. It's what's called a *Lambda Expression*. All you need to understand about a lambda expression is that the part before the => is an alias that is used to represent the database table.

In this example you used *Customer* as an alias to avoid confusion. It is possible to use any combination of letters as an alias.

2. View *reports.aspx* in your browser.

> Lehmanns Marktstand

This time *Lehmanns Marktstand* appears on the page.

If you compared this with the data in the database table by using the *Database Explorer*, you'd see that *Lehmanns Marktstand* has a *CustomerID* of 5.

note

LINQ Query and Lambda syntax

There are two ways to use LINQ. You can use the lambda expressions that you see in this lesson or a 'query' syntax which looks more like SQL code.

Unless you're familiar with SQL the lambda syntax is easier to understand, so all examples in this book use that approach.

Here's what this lesson's code would look like using the 'query' approach:

Customer MyCustomer =
(from Customer in
Data.Customers
where Customer.CustomerID == 5
select Customer).Single();

note

Extracting data without using LINQ

Before LINQ, databases were usually accessed using the *System.Data.SqlClient* namespace of the .NET library.

System.Data.SqlClient is still available, but it requires a lot more code to use. This method also requires you to either use stored procedures or SQL code.

LINQ has made this approach obsolete but you may still see it used in older projects.

Lesson 10-4: Retrieve multiple rows of data using LINQ

In the previous lesson, you retrieved a single row of data from a database and stored it in an object. LINQ can also retrieve multiple rows and place them into a collection of objects.

1 Open *Spark* from your sample files folder.

2 Open the code-behind file of *reports.aspx*.

3 Remove the code inside the *using* statement.

You're going to create a new LINQ query, so remove the old one.

```
protected void Page_Load(object sender, EventArgs e)
{
    using (SparkDataContext Data = new SparkDataContext())
    {

    }
}
```

note

LINQ collections and var

As you may recall from *Lesson 5-13: Use object and var variables,* using the *var* variable type is usually bad practice.

When working with LINQ, the *var* variable type is actually the preferred type since, in some cases, you will not know in advance the type of object that LINQ will return.

It is also possible to convert the LINQ output into a *List* collection by using the *ToList* method.

For example:

List<Invoice> Invoices = Data.Invoices.Where (Invoice => Invoice.InvoiceAmount > 990) .ToList();

You learned about *List* collections in: *Lesson 8-2: Create a collection.*

The 'real' type that will be returned by LINQ is *IEnumerable<Invoice>. IEnumerable* is an *interface.*

You'll learn about interfaces in the Expert Skills course in this series.

4 Use your LINQ data class to retrieve multiple rows.

In *Lesson 10-3: Retrieve a single row of data using LINQ,* you retrieved a single customer from the *Customer* table in the database. This time you're going to retrieve several records from the *Invoice* table.

Add the following code inside the *using* statement:

var Invoices = Data.Invoices
.Where(Invoice => Invoice.InvoiceAmount > 990);

```
using (SparkDataContext Data = new SparkDataContext())
{
    var Invoices = Data.Invoices
        .Where(Invoice => Invoice.InvoiceAmount > 990);
}
```

This code retrieves a collection of *Invoice* objects from the *Invoice* table of the database with *InvoiceAmount* values greater than 990.

See the sidebar for more information about why you're using the *var* type instead of a *List* collection for this.

5 Display the list of invoices on the page.

Because *Invoices* is a collection, you'll need to use *foreach* to iterate through the collection in order to display its contents on the screen.

You learned about *foreach* in: *Lesson 8-3: Iterate through a collection using foreach.*

1. Add a *string* variable on the next line to contain the HTML code that will be displayed on the page:

   string Output = "";

2. Add a *foreach* loop to iterate through the *Invoices* collection:

   foreach (Invoice InvoiceToOutput in Invoices)
   {
   }

note

LINQ criteria

In both of the examples that you've worked with so far, your LINQ queries have used only a single criteria (in this example: InvoiceAmount > 990)

You can use any of C#'s logical operators to build your criteria expression.

(For more on logical operators see: *Lesson 7-3: Use basic logical operators*).

For example, to get all invoices that have either an *InvoiceAmount* greater than 900 or a *CustomerID* of 5 you could use the following LINQ code:

Data.Invoices.Where
(Invoice =>
Invoice.InvoiceAmount > 900
|| Invoice.CustomerID == 5);

3. Make the *foreach* loop add the *InvoiceNumber* property from each *Invoice* object to the *Output* string variable:

Output += InvoiceToOutput.InvoiceNumber;
Output += "<br />";

4. Place the value of *Output* on the page (outside the *foreach* loop):

LabelReport.Text = Output;

```
var Invoices = Data.Invoices
    .Where(Invoice => Invoice.InvoiceAmount > 990);
string Output = "";
foreach (Invoice InvoiceToOutput in Invoices)
{
    Output += InvoiceToOutput.InvoiceNumber;
    Output += "<br />";
}
LabelReport.Text = Output;
```

6 View *reports.aspx* in your browser.

The invoice numbers of all invoices with values above 990 are displayed.

Home	New Invoice
9654	
6700	
9728	

7 Use LINQ to 'drill-down' through relationships.

In *Lesson 10-2: Add LINQ data classes to a project*, you saw that the *Customer* and *Invoice* tables were linked by a line with an arrow, indicating a relationship between the two tables.

Because there is a relationship, you can very easily 'drill-down' from your *Invoice* objects to the *Customer* objects they belong to.

1. Close your browser if it is open.

2. Add the following code at the beginning of your *foreach* statement:

Output += InvoiceToOutput.Customer.CustomerName;
Output += " - ";

```
foreach (Invoice InvoiceToOutput in Invoices)
{
    Output += InvoiceToOutput.Customer.CustomerName;
    Output += " - ";
    Output += InvoiceToOutput.InvoiceNumber;
    Output += "<br />";
}
```

As you can see, you can access the properties of the *Customer* associated with each *Invoice* by simply using its *Customer* property. This works with any table that has a relationship.

A correctly designed database will always have relationships defined.

3. View *reports.aspx* in your browser.

Because of the code you added, the *CustomerName* now appears next to each *InvoiceNumber* in the browser window.

4. Close your browser.

Lehmanns Marktstand - 5016
Lehmanns Marktstand - 6540
Hanari Carnes - 9728
Lehmanns Marktstand - 8289
Hanari Carnes - 4498

Lesson 10-5: Sort results and call stored procedures using LINQ

You now know the basics of querying a database using LINQ, but LINQ offers many more methods to accomplish some more advanced queries.

1 Open *Spark* from your sample files folder.

2 Open the code-behind file of *reports.aspx*.

3 Sort the LINQ results.

At the moment, the results of your query are being returned in no particular order.

You can use the *OrderBy* method to sort your results.

note

Other LINQ methods

You can do even more advanced queries in LINQ using methods such as *Sum, Average* and *Count*.

These are explored in more depth in the Expert Skills course in this series.

1. Remove the semicolon from the end of the *var Invoices…* code line and append the following code:

    .OrderBy(Invoice => Invoice.InvoiceNumber);

    ```
    var Invoices = Data.Invoices
        .Where(Invoice => Invoice.InvoiceAmount > 990)
        .OrderBy(Invoice=>Invoice.InvoiceNumber);
    ```

2. View *reports.aspx* in your web browser.

    As you might have guessed, your results are now sorted by *InvoiceNumber*, from lowest to highest.

    ```
    Lehmanns Marktstand - 1266
    Lehmanns Marktstand - 1579
    B's Beverages - 3122
    ```

3. Close your browser.

4. Change *.OrderBy* to: **.OrderByDescending**

    ```
    var Invoices = Data.Invoices
        .Where(Invoice => Invoice.InvoiceAmount > 990)
        .OrderByDescending(Invoice=>Invoice.InvoiceNumber);
    ```

5. View *reports.aspx* in your web browser.

    Now your results are sorted from the highest *InvoiceNumber* to the lowest.

    ```
    Hanari Carnes - 9728
    B's Beverages - 9726
    Island Trading - 9654
    ```

6. Close your browser.

4 Get only the top 5 results from the database.

By using the *Take* method, you can return only the number of results you want.

1. Remove the semicolon from the end of the *var Invoices…* code line and append the following code:

    .Take(5);

```
var Invoices = Data.Invoices
    .Where(Invoice => Invoice.InvoiceAmount > 990)
    .OrderByDescending(Invoice => Invoice.InvoiceNumber)
    .Take(5);
```

2. View *reports.aspx* in your browser.

```
Hanari Carnes - 9728
B's Beverages - 9726
Island Trading - 9654
Ana Trujillo Emparedados y helados - 8869
Hanari Carnes - 7615
```

Only the top 5 invoice numbers are displayed.

3. Close your browser.

By using the *OrderBy* and *Take* methods together, you can retrieve the top or bottom values from any database table.

5 Call a stored procedure using LINQ.

In *Lesson 10-2: Add LINQ data classes to a project*, you added a stored procedure to your LINQ data classes.

Stored procedures can do pretty much anything with a database, and LINQ makes it very easy to call them.

1. Remove all of the code inside your *using* statement.

2. Add the following code inside the *using* statement:

int LastInvoice = Data.SpGetLastInvoiceNumber();

```
using (SparkDataContext Data = new SparkDataContext())
{
    int LastInvoice = Data.SpGetLastInvoiceNumber();
}
```

This code calls the *SpGetLastInvoiceNumber* stored procedure and puts its return value into an *int* variable called *LastInvoice*.

Stored procedures can be called anything, but I always prefix them with *Sp* to make them easier to find in the IntelliSense list.

3. Add the following code inside the *using* statement:

LabelReport.Text = LastInvoice.ToString();

```
using (SparkDataContext Data = new SparkDataContext())
{
    int LastInvoice = Data.SpGetLastInvoiceNumber();
    LabelReport.Text = LastInvoice.ToString();
}
```

This code will output the last invoice number onto the page.

4. View *reports.aspx* in your browser.

```
9987
```

The number *9987* appears. This is the highest invoice number in the *Invoices* table.

6 Close your browser and close Visual Studio.

---

note

Stored procedure methods

In this example, the stored procedure doesn't need any arguments and simply returns an *int* value, but stored procedures can have arguments and return values, just like any other method.

You can use the IntelliSense description of stored procedure methods to check which arguments the method requires and the type of value it returns.

note

LINQ or Stored Procedures?

Stored procedures can do everything that LINQ can do and will usually be faster and more efficient.

Using stored procedures for everything seems ideal, but having hundreds of stored procedures in a database often becomes unmanageable and difficult to maintain.

I recommend using LINQ for simple, everyday queries and stored procedures for anything more complicated, or if you see performance issues.

Lesson 10-6: Check whether a record exists using LINQ

There will be times when you'll need to run a LINQ query without being sure whether it will find any records in the database. When returning multiple records using the *Where* method this will simply return an empty collection, but when using the *Single* method it will cause an exception.

In this lesson you'll write LINQ code that will check whether a single record exists and only return a result if so.

1   Open *Spark* from your sample files folder.

2   Open the code-behind file of *reports.aspx*.

3   Write code to return a single record.

In *Lesson 10-3: Retrieve a single row of data using LINQ,* you used the *Single* method to return a single row of data. If the row of data hadn't existed it would have caused an exception.

1. Remove all code from the *using* statement.

2. Add the following code inside the *using* statement:

   Customer CheckCustomer = Data.Customers
   .Single(Customer => Customer.CustomerID == 99);

   ```
   using (SparkDataContext Data = new SparkDataContext())
   {
       Customer CheckCustomer = Data.Customers
           .Single(Customer => Customer.CustomerID == 99);
   }
   ```

3. Add the following code on the next line:

   LabelReport.Text = CheckCustomer.CustomerName;

   ```
   using (SparkDataContext Data = new SparkDataContext())
   {
       Customer CheckCustomer = Data.Customers
           .Single(Customer => Customer.CustomerID == 99);
       LabelReport.Text = CheckCustomer.CustomerName;
   }
   ```

4. View *reports.aspx* in your browser.

   ## Server Error in '/' Application.

   Sequence contains no elements

   An error message appears. This happened because there is no record in the database for customer ID 99 so the *Single* method generated an exception.

   You could use *try* and *catch* to work around this, but it's better to avoid that approach because you can make your code work without causing an exception.

   You learned about *try* and *catch* in: *Lesson 7-6: Use try and catch to handle errors.*

note

FirstOrDefault

The *FirstOrDefault* method works in a similar way to the *SingleOrDefault* method.

FirstOrDefault returns the first record in a database table or returns *null* if the table is empty.

The *First* method would cause an exception if the table was empty.

5. Close your browser.

4 Add code to check whether the record exists.

1. Change the *Single* method to: **SingleOrDefault**

    The *SingleOrDefault* method works in exactly the same way as *Single*, but it will return *null* if the record doesn't exist instead of causing an exception.

    ```
    Customer CheckCustomer = Data.Customers
        .SingleOrDefault(Customer => Customer.CustomerID == 99);
    LabelReport.Text = CheckCustomer.CustomerName;
    ```

2. View *reports.aspx* in your browser.

    ## Server Error in '/' Application.

    Object reference not set to an instance of an object.

    A different error appears. This time it's because the *CheckCustomer* object is *null*, so the code can't set *LabelReport.Text* to the value of its *CustomerName* property.

    You can fix this with a simple *if* statement.

3. Close your browser.

4. Change the *LabelReport.Text...* line to:

    if (CheckCustomer == null)
    {
        LabelReport.Text = "Customer does not exist!";
    }
    else
    {
        LabelReport.Text = CheckCustomer.CustomerName;
    }

    ```
    using (SparkDataContext Data = new SparkDataContext())
    {
        Customer CheckCustomer = Data.Customers
            .SingleOrDefault(C => C.CustomerID == 99);
        if (CheckCustomer == null)
        {
            LabelReport.Text = "Customer does not exist!";
        }
        else
        {
            LabelReport.Text = CheckCustomer.CustomerName;
        }
    }
    ```

    This code checks whether the returned *Customer* object is *null*. If the return value is *null*, the text *Customer does not exist!* is displayed instead of the return value.

5. View *reports.aspx* in your browser.

    Customer does not exist!

    This time your code does not cause an exception and instead shows that customer ID 99 does not exist.

6. Close your browser.

Lesson 10-7: Update database records using LINQ

You're not limited to simply retrieving and displaying data from your database, you can very easily update it too.

In this lesson you'll update some rows in your database using LINQ.

1   Open *Spark* from your sample files folder.

2   Open the code-behind file of *reports.aspx*.

3   Retrieve an invoice from the database.

1.   Remove all code from the *using* statement.

2.   Add code to retrieve a single invoice record from the database:

Invoice MyInvoice = Data.Invoices.Single
(Invoice => Invoice.InvoiceID == 1882);

3.   Add code to display the invoice's details on the page:

LabelReport.Text = MyInvoice.InvoiceNumber;
LabelReport.Text += "<br />";
LabelReport.Text += MyInvoice.InvoiceAmount.ToString();

```
using (SparkDataContext Data = new SparkDataContext())
{
    Invoice MyInvoice = Data.Invoices.Single
        (Invoice => Invoice.InvoiceID == 1882);
    LabelReport.Text = MyInvoice.InvoiceNumber;
    LabelReport.Text += "<br />";
    LabelReport.Text += MyInvoice.InvoiceAmount.ToString();
}
```

4.   View *reports.aspx* in your browser.

```
2431
526.1200
```

The *InvoiceNumber* and *InvoiceAmount* of the invoice are displayed.

4   Add a Button control to update the invoice.

1.   Close your browser and open *reports.aspx* in *Design* view.

2.   Add a *Button* control to the page.

Place the *Button* control after the *LabelReport* control.

3.   Name the *Button*: **ButtonUpdateInvoice**

4.   Set the *Text* property of the *Button* to: **Update Invoice**

5.   Add a *Click* event handler to the *Button*.

5   Add code to update the invoice record.

1.   Copy and paste the code from your *Page_Load* event handler into your *ButtonUpdateInvoice_Click* event handler.

note

The SubmitChanges method

The *SubmitChanges* method will commit any changes you have made to your database.

If you have a large collection of data that you want to update, you still only need to call the *SubmitChanges* method once.

LINQ will keep track of any changes made prior to committing them to the database.

note

Keeping the page up to date

In this lesson you update the invoice that is displayed on the page, but the page doesn't immediately display the changes you made.

Ideally, you would store the code that retrieves and displays the invoice details in a separate method that is called by both the *Page_Load* and *ButtonUpdateInvoice_Click* event handlers.

Of course this approach wouldn't be very efficient as the method would be called twice when the button was clicked.

You'll discover a more efficient solution in: *Lesson 12-10: Create a Checkout page.*

2. Remove the three lines of code that set the value of *LabelReport.Text* from your *ButtonUpdateInvoice_Click* event handler.

```
protected void ButtonUpdateInvoice_Click(object sender, EventArgs e)
{
    using (SparkDataContext Data = new SparkDataContext())
    {
        Invoice MyInvoice = Data.Invoices.Single
            (Invoice => Invoice.InvoiceID == 1882);
    }
}
```

3. Add code to change the *InvoiceAmount* property of the invoice:

MyInvoice.InvoiceAmount = 123;

```
Invoice MyInvoice = Data.Invoices.Single
    (Invoice => Invoice.InvoiceID == 1882);
MyInvoice.InvoiceAmount = 123;
```

4. View *reports.aspx* in your browser and click *Update Invoice*.

Nothing happens. LINQ never updates the database unless you specifically tell it to.

5. Close your browser.

6. Add the following code to the *using* statement in the *ButtonUpdateInvoice_Click* event handler:

Data.SubmitChanges();

```
Invoice MyInvoice = Data.Invoices.Single
    (Invoice => Invoice.InvoiceID == 1882);
MyInvoice.InvoiceAmount = 123;
Data.SubmitChanges();
```

This code tells LINQ to update the database with any changes that you have made.

7. View *reports.aspx* in your browser and click *Update Invoice* again.

The value did update, but this isn't apparent as the updated value isn't displayed on the screen. That is because the code in the *Page_Load* event handler is executed before the code in the *Click* event handler (see: *Lesson 3-2: Add event handlers to controls).*

Your *Page_Load* event handler will have to run again in order to retrieve and display the updated value.

(See sidebar for a discussion of a solution to this problem).

8. Using your browser's refresh button, refresh the page.

Now you can see the updated value (*123*).

As you can see, simply changing the properties of your LINQ objects and then calling the *SubmitChanges* method allows you to update any of the values stored in your database.

You can also do this with collections of data by using a *foreach* loop and calling the *SubmitChanges* method once it has finished (see sidebar).

Lesson 10-8: Insert database records using LINQ

As well as retrieving and updating database records, you can use LINQ to add new records using a similar technique.

In this lesson you'll use LINQ to make the *New Invoice* page functional.

1   Open *Spark* from your sample files folder.

2   View *newtransaction.aspx* in Design view.

This web page is not yet functional. Eventually you'll be able to choose a customer from the drop-down list and add a new customer invoice.

3   Open the code-behind file of *newtransaction.aspx*.

4   Create a new instance of your *DataContext* class.

Add a new *using* statement inside the *else* statement to create a new instance of the *SparkDataContext* class:

using (SparkDataContext Data = new SparkDataContext())
{
}

5   Create a new instance of the *Invoice* class.

In previous lessons, you've retrieved an *Invoice* object from the database by using the *SparkDataContext* class. In this lesson you want to add a new invoice, so you need to create a new instance of the *Invoice* class.

Add the following code inside the *using* statement:

Invoice NewInvoice = new Invoice();

```
else
{
    using (SparkDataContext Data = new SparkDataContext())
    {
        Invoice NewInvoice = new Invoice();
```

As you'll recall from *Lesson 6-10: Create and dispose of instances*, this code creates a new instance of the *Invoice* class called *NewInvoice*.

6   Set the new invoice's properties.

1.   Add the following code after the line that creates the *NewInvoice* object:

NewInvoice.CustomerID = 5;

```
Invoice NewInvoice = new Invoice();
NewInvoice.CustomerID = 5;
```

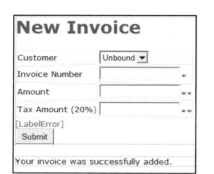

New Invoice

Customer	Unbound ▾
Invoice Number	*
Amount	**
Tax Amount (20%)	**

[LabelError]
Submit

Your invoice was successfully added.

note

Naming of controls

If you look at the page in *Design* view, you'll notice that the names of the controls on the page closely match the names of the properties in the database.

This is best practice. If a control is used to display or set a value in a database, its name should match the name of the database field it displays or sets.

note

InvoiceID

When setting the properties of the *Invoice* object, you might have noticed that there's an *InvoiceID* property that you don't set.

InvoiceID is the table's unique *primary key*, which is automatically maintained by the database.

In most well-designed databases, the primary key is automatically maintained.

tip

Inserting a collection

As well as inserting a single *Invoice* object using the *InsertOnSubmit* method, you can insert a collection of *Invoice* objects (such as a *List<Invoice>*) by using the *InsertAllOnSubmit* method.

```
Data.SubmitChanges();
PanelAddInvoice.Visible = false;
PanelConfirmAdded.Visible = true;
```

Your invoice was successfully added.

The *Customer* dropdown isn't functional yet, so you're setting the *CustomerID* manually for now to test the page.

In *Lesson 11-2: Attach a data source to a control*, you'll configure the *Customer* dropdown to automatically retrieve every customer from the database.

2. Add code to set the other properties according to the values placed in the controls on the page:

NewInvoice.InvoiceNumber = TextBoxInvoiceNumber.Text;
NewInvoice.InvoiceAmount =
Convert.ToDecimal(TextBoxAmount.Text);
NewInvoice.InvoiceTaxAmount =
Convert.ToDecimal(TextBoxTaxAmount.Text);

3. Add code to set the date and time:

NewInvoice.InvoiceDate = DateTime.Now;

```
NewInvoice.CustomerID = 5;
NewInvoice.InvoiceNumber = TextBoxInvoiceNumber.Text;
NewInvoice.InvoiceAmount =
    Convert.ToDecimal(TextBoxAmount.Text);
NewInvoice.InvoiceTaxAmount =
    Convert.ToDecimal(TextBoxTaxAmount.Text);
NewInvoice.InvoiceDate = DateTime.Now;
```

7 **Tell LINQ to send the data to the database.**

Just creating an *Invoice* object and calling the *SubmitChanges* method isn't enough. You need to specifically tell LINQ to insert the record.

1. Tell LINQ which record needs to be inserted into the *Invoice* table with the following code:

Data.Invoices.InsertOnSubmit(NewInvoice);

2. Call the *SubmitChanges* method to insert the record.

Data.SubmitChanges();

```
NewInvoice.InvoiceTaxAmount =
    Convert.ToDecimal(TextBoxTaxAmount.Text);
NewInvoice.InvoiceDate = DateTime.Now;
Data.Invoices.InsertOnSubmit(NewInvoice);
Data.SubmitChanges();
```

8 **Add code to inform the user that the invoice was added successfully.**

Add the following code after the *SubmitChanges* line:

PanelAddInvoice.Visible = false;
PanelConfirmAdded.Visible = true;

This code will hide the panel containing the new invoice details and show a panel that contains some confirmation text.

9 **Test *newtransaction.aspx*.**

1. View *newtransaction.aspx* in your browser and complete the form (you don't need to select a *Customer*).

2. Click *Submit*.

The confirmation text appears on the page.

note

Deleting records

It is best practice never to delete records from databases.

In the old days of computing disk space was at a premium so old records were physically deleted.

These days disk storage space is very cheap so it is useful to keep deleted records in case the user needs to recall them later.

Ideally, instead of deleting a record, you should update it with a property to indicate that the record should be treated as if it did not exist.

note

Database permissions

If you are working with a remote database server, you will need to be given a username and password that has permission to access it.

The database administrator can allow or disallow a user to view, update, insert or delete records.

If you don't have permission to carry out an action on the database, an exception will be generated.

Lesson 10-9: Delete database records using LINQ

You can now retrieve, update and insert database records using LINQ. The only common database operation that you haven't covered is deleting.

1 Open *Spark* from your sample files folder.

2 Open the code-behind file of *reports.aspx*.

3 Remove the *ButtonUpdateInvoice* control and its code.

   1. Remove the *ButtonUpdateInvoice_Click* event handler.

   2. Open *reports.aspx* in *Design* view.

   3. Delete the *ButtonUpdateInvoice* control.

4 Add a new button control.

   1. Add a new *Button* control where the *ButtonUpdateInvoice* control used to be.

   2. Name the new button: **ButtonDeleteInvoice**

   3. Set the *Text* property of the button to: **Delete Invoice**

   4. Add a new *Click* event handler to the *ButtonDeleteInvoice* control.

   [LabelReport] [Delete Invoice]

5 Create a new instance of your LINQ *DataContext* class in the new event handler.

using (SparkDataContext Data = new SparkDataContext())
{
}

```
protected void ButtonDeleteInvoice_Click(object sender, Ev
{
    using (SparkDataContext Data = new SparkDataContext())
    {

    }
}
```

6 Retrieve an *Invoice* object for the invoice currently displayed on the page.

Before you can delete an invoice, you need to retrieve an *Invoice* object that matches the invoice record that you want to delete.

Copy the code that retrieves the invoice currently displayed from the *Page_Load* event handler and paste it into your *ButtonDeleteInvoice_Click* event handler (inside the *using* statement):

Invoice MyInvoice = Data.Invoices
.Single(Invoice => Invoice.InvoiceID == 1882);

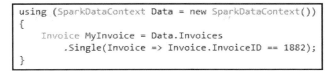

```
using (SparkDataContext Data = new SparkDataContext())
{
    Invoice MyInvoice = Data.Invoices
        .Single(Invoice => Invoice.InvoiceID == 1882);
}
```

You now have an *Invoice* object which represents the record that you're going to delete from the database.

7   Add code to tell LINQ to delete the invoice.

Deleting a record is very similar to inserting one:

1.   Tell LINQ which record needs to be deleted from the *Invoice* table with the following code:

Data.Invoices.DeleteOnSubmit(MyInvoice);

2.   Call the *SubmitChanges* method to delete the record:

Data.SubmitChanges();

```
using (SparkDataContext Data = new SparkDataContext())
{
    Invoice MyInvoice = Data.Invoices
        .Single(Invoice => Invoice.InvoiceID == 1882);
    Data.Invoices.DeleteOnSubmit(MyInvoice);
    Data.SubmitChanges();
}
```

8   Test your code.

1.   View *reports.aspx* in your browser.

The page still retrieves the details of the invoice with the InvoiceID of *1882*.

2.   Click the *Delete Invoice* button.

3.   Refresh the page.

An error message appears. Your code successfully deleted the record from the database, but this has introduced an error.

The error ocurred because your *Page_Load* event handler is trying to use the *Single* method to retrieve invoice ID 1882 which no longer exists because you have deleted it.

9   Fix the error.

1.   Close your browser and return to the code-behind file of *reports.aspx*.

2.   In the *Page_Load* event handler, change *1882* to: **1883**

```
Invoice MyInvoice = Data.Invoices
    .Single(I => I.InvoiceID == 1883);
```

3.   View *reports.aspx* in your browser.

There is no longer an error: your code was able to find invoice ID *1883*.

You could also have fixed the error by changing the *Page_Load* event handler to use the *SingleOrDefault* method instead of the *Single* method and then handling the possibility of a *null* value. You did this in: *Lesson 10-6: Check whether a record exists using LINQ*.

note

Deleting a collection

In the same way that you can insert a collection of database records using the *InsertAllOnSubmit* method, you can delete a collection of database records using the *DeleteAllOnSubmit* method.

Server Error in '/' Application.

Sequence contains no elements

Lesson 10-10: Use LINQ with collections

The LINQ code that you've used in this session doesn't just work with databases; you can use it on any collection!

1   Open *Spark* from your sample files folder.

2   Open the code-behind file of *reports.aspx*.

3   Remove all code from the *Page_Load* event handler.

4   Remove the *ButtonDeleteInvoice_Click* event handler.

5   Remove the *ButtonDeleteInvoice* control from the page.

6   Retrieve the customer collection from the *Utilities* class.

In the *Page_Load* event handler, call the *Utilities.GetBlockedCustomers* method to get back the collection of *string* variables that you created in *Lesson 8-2: Create a collection* and place it in a new *List<string>* collection named: **BlockedCustomers**

List<string> BlockedCustomers =
Utilities.GetBlockedCustomers();

```
protected void Page_Load(object sender, EventArgs e)
{
    List<string> BlockedCustomers = Utilities.GetBlockedCustomers();
}
```

7   Retrieve a single item using the *Single* method.

In exactly the same way as you did in *Lesson 10-3: Retrieve a single row of data using LINQ,* you can use LINQ to retrieve a single item from any collection. Of course, this time it will be a *string* value instead of a *Customer* object.

Add the following code to the *Page_Load* event handler:

string SingleCustomer = BlockedCustomers
.Single(CustomerID => CustomerID == "6");

```
List<string> BlockedCustomers = Utilities.GetBlockedCustomers();
string SingleCustomer = BlockedCustomers
    .Single(CustomerID => CustomerID == "6");
```

Because the items in the *BlockedCustomers* collection don't have any properties, you can use the alias (*CustomerID*) on its own to represent the values in the collection.

8   Test your code.

1.   Add the following code to display the value of the *SingleCustomer* string variable in the label on the page:

LabelReport.Text = SingleCustomer;

```
List<string> BlockedCustomers = Utilities.GetBlockedCustomers();
string SingleCustomer = BlockedCustomers
    .Single(CustomerID => CustomerID == "6");
LabelReport.Text = SingleCustomer;
```

6

2. View *reports.aspx* in your browser.

   The number 6 appears on the page. It was found in the collection and output by your code.

3. Close your browser.

9 Retrieve multiple items from the BlockedCustomers collection using LINQ's *Where* method.

You can do this in exactly the same way as you did in: *Lesson 10-4: Retrieve multiple rows of data using LINQ.*

1. Remove code, so that you are left with just the line beginning: *List<string> BlockedCustomers…*

```
protected void Page_Load(object sender, EventArgs e)
{
    List<string> BlockedCustomers = Utilities.GetBlockedCustomers();
}
```

2. Use the *Where* LINQ method to return a sub-set of items from the list collection.

   var SubList = BlockedCustomers
     .Where(CustomerID => CustomerID == "6"
     || CustomerID == "9" || CustomerID == "99");

```
List<string> BlockedCustomers = Utilities.GetBlockedCustomers()
var SubList = BlockedCustomers
    .Where(CustomerID =>
            CustomerID == "6"
        || CustomerID == "9"
        || CustomerID == "99");
```

This code will search the *BlockedCustomers* collection for items with the values *6, 9* or *99* and put the results into a new collection called *SubList*.

10 Output the list to the page.

Use a *foreach* loop to display the resulting values in the *LabelReport* control.

foreach (string CustomerID in SubList)
{
  LabelReport.Text += CustomerID;
  LabelReport.Text += "<br />";
}

```
foreach (string CustomerID in SubList)
{
    LabelReport.Text += CustomerID;
    LabelReport.Text += "<br />";
}
```

11 Test your code.

View *reports.aspx* in your browser.

The numbers *6* and *9* appear, but *99* does not. That is because it wasn't found in the collection.

LINQ can make working with collections very easy, but you should be careful not to let it impact performance (see sidebar).

6
9

---

note

LINQ and performance

When you use LINQ on a database, it creates SQL code which is used by the database to retrieve your information.

Databases don't have to look through every record in the database to find the one you need. They use indexes to speed up searching.

When you use LINQ with collections, it actually does the equivalent of a *foreach* loop, looking through every value in the collection in order to find the ones you want. With large collections, this can be a slow process that is demanding on the computer running it.

Be aware of this when using LINQ with collections.

Session 10: Exercise

1   Open the *Session10* project from your sample files folder.

2   Add *LINQ to SQL Classes* to the project. Call the file: **Session10.dbml**

3   Add the *Customer* table from the *Spark* database to the *LINQ to SQL Classes*.

4   Add the *SpGetLastInvoiceNumber* stored procedure from the *Spark* database to the *LINQ to SQL Classes*.

5   Open the code-behind file of *Default.aspx*.

6   Add code to the *Page_Load* event handler to retrieve a *Customer* object with the *CustomerID* of 7 and display the object's *CustomerName* property in the *TextBoxEditCustomerName* control.

7   Add *Click* event handlers to the *ButtonAddCustomer* and *ButtonSaveCustomer* controls on the page.

8   Add code to the *ButtonSaveCustomer_Click* event handler to retrieve the customer with the *CustomerID* of 7 and set its *CustomerName* property to the value entered in the *TextBoxEditCustomer* control.

9   Add code to the *ButtonSaveCustomer_Click* event handler to commit the changes to the *CustomerName* property to the database by calling the *SubmitChanges* method.

10   Add code to the *ButtonAddCustomer_Click* event handler to add a new record to the *Customer* table in the database.

           Set the new record's *CustomerName* property to the value of the *TextBoxNewCustomerName.Text* property.

           (Remember to use the *InsertOnSubmit* method before the *SubmitChanges* method).

11   Add *try* and *catch* code to all three event handlers and put the *Message* property of any exceptions into the *LabelError.Text* property.

12   View and test the *Default.aspx* page in your browser.

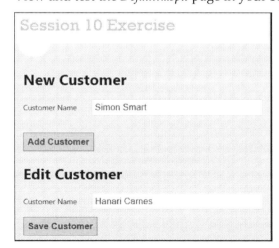

Session10 - start   Session10 - end

If you need help slide the page to the left

Session 10: Exercise Answers

These are the four questions that students find the most difficult to answer:

Q 11	Q 10	Q 8	Q 6

1. Enclose your code in the following:
 	
try
{
    [Code]
}
 	
2. Add the following:
 	
catch (Exception Ex)
{
    LabelError .Text = Ex .Message;
}
 	
This was covered in: *Lesson 7-6: Use try and catch to handle errors.*
	Use the following code:
	
	using (Session10DataContext Data = new Session10DataContext())
	{
	    Customer NewCustomer = new Customer(); NewCustomer .CustomerName = TextBoxNewCustomer Name.Text; Data.Customers .InsertOnSubmit (NewCustomer); Data.SubmitChanges();
	}
	
	This was covered in: *Lesson 10-8: Insert database records using LINQ.*
		Use the following code:
		
		using (Session10DataContext Data = new Session10DataContext())
		
		{
		    Customer MyCustomer = Data.Customers.Single (Customer => Customer.CustomerID = 7); MyCustomer .CustomerName = TextBoxEditCustomer Name.Text;
		}
		
		This was covered in: *Lesson 10-7: Update database records using LINQ.*
			Use the following code:
			
			if (!Page.IsPostBack)
			{
			    using (Session10DataContext Data = new Session10DataContext())
			    {
			        Customer MyCustomer = Data.Customers .Single (Customer => Customer .CustomerID = 7); TextBoxEditCustomer Name.Text = MyCustomer .CustomerName;
			    }
			}
			
			This was covered in: *Lesson 10-3: Retrieve a single row of data using LINQ.*

If you have difficulty with the other questions, here are the lessons that cover the relevant skills:

1   Refer to: Lesson 1-7: Manage a project with the Solution Explorer.

2   Refer to: Lesson 10-2: Add LINQ data classes to a project.

3   Refer to: Lesson 10-2: Add LINQ data classes to a project.

4   Refer to: Lesson 10-2: Add LINQ data classes to a project.

5   Refer to: Lesson 1-7: Manage a project with the Solution Explorer.

7   Refer to: Lesson 3-2: Add event handlers to controls.

9   Refer to: Lesson 10-7: Update database records using LINQ.

12   Refer to: Lesson 1-9: Run a project in debug mode.

Session Eleven: Using data controls

> Errors using inadequate data are much less than those using no data at all.
>
> *Charles Babbage, English mathematician (1792 – 1871)*

Using the code that you learned in the last session along with your knowledge of ASP.NET controls and HTML, you can already create web applications that read and write data to a database.

However, ASP.NET comes with several controls that can do a lot of the work for you, making creating data-centric web pages even easier.

In this session, you'll work with some of these controls and see how you can easily interact with databases without needing to write any code at all!

Session Objectives

By the end of this session you will be able to:

- Use the LinqDataSource control
- Attach a data source to a control
- Use the GridView control
- Add sorting and paging to a GridView
- Add editing features to a GridView
- Use the DetailsView control
- Use the SqlDataSource control
- Bind data to a control using C# code

Lesson 11-1: Use the LinqDataSource control

The easiest way to bind data to a control on a page is to use a data source control. There are a few of these in the *Data* category of the *Toolbox*, but in this lesson you're going to use the *LinqDataSource* control.

The *LinqDataSource* control retrieves data using *LINQ to SQL Classes*.

1   Open *Spark* from your sample files folder.

2   Open *newtransaction.aspx* in *Design* view.

3   Add a *LinqDataSource* control to the page.

Drag a *LinqDataSource* control from the *Data* category of the *Toolbox* onto the page. Place it just before the *Customer* drop down.

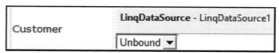

note

Placing data sources

In this lesson you place the *LinqDataSource* control near the *DropDownList* control that it is going to populate, but the placement of a data source control doesn't matter.

Data sources aren't visible to people visiting the page, so you can place them wherever seems most logical.

4   Configure the *LinqDataSource* control.

1. Set the *ID* property of the new *LinqDataSource* control to: **LinqDataSourceCustomer**

2. Click *Configure Data Source…* from the *QuickTasks* menu of the *LinqDataSource* control.

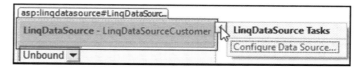

A configuration dialog appears.

3. Make sure that *Spark.SparkDataContext* is selected.

In the first step of configuration, you must select which LINQ data context (ie dbml file) to use.

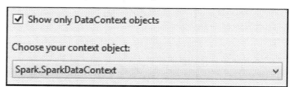

Since you only have one (*SparkDataContext*), it should already be selected. If it isn't, select it.

4. Click *Next*.

5. Select the *Customers* table to retrieve data from that table.

This data source control is going to retrieve a list of customers for the *DropDownListCustomer* control to use, so select the *Customers* table from the *Table* dropdown.

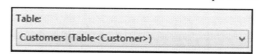

6. Click *OrderBy…*

If you are not completing the course incrementally use the sample file: **Lesson 11-1** to begin this lesson.

Sample files with the starting point for each lesson are also provided for all of the other lessons in this session.

A dialog opens, allowing you to configure sorting. Sorting works in exactly the same way as using the *OrderBy* and *OrderByDescending* methods in LINQ (see: *Lesson 10-5: Sort results and call stored procedures using LINQ*).

7. Select *CustomerName* and *Ascending*.

8. Click *OK*.

9. Click *Where…*

A dialog opens, allowing you to configure query criteria, which work the same way as the *Single* and *Where* methods in LINQ (see: *Lesson 10-3: Retrieve a single row of data using LINQ*).

10. Select *CustomerID* from the *Column* drop-down.

This tells the *LinqDataSource* control that *CustomerID* is the database column that you want to use for your criteria.

11. Select *!=* from the *Operator* drop-down.

This is the 'does not equal' operator. You learned about it in: *Lesson 7-3: Use basic logical operators*.

12. Select *None* from the *Source* drop-down.

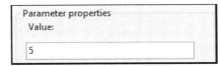

The *Source* drop-down allows you to tell your data source to retrieve a value from several different sources (see sidebar).

In this case, you want a value that doesn't change. *None* allows you to type in the value that you want to use.

13. Enter **5** into the Parameter Properties *Value* text box.

This data source will

14. Click *Add*.

Your new parameter has been added. This data source will now retrieve everything from the *Customer* table except for *CustomerID* 5.

15. Click *OK*.

16. Click *Finish*.

note

Other Source options

In this lesson, you use the *None* source to specify your own value for a parameter, but you can choose between several sources.

Control
Retrieve a value from a control on the page.

Cookie
Retrieve a value from a cookie.

Form
Retrieve a value from:
Page.Request.Form

Profile
Retrieve a value from a user profile.

QueryString
Retrieve a value from:
Page.Request.QueryString

Session
Retrieve a value from a *Session* variable.

Route
Retrieve a value from a URL.

Lesson 11-2: Attach a data source to a control

In this lesson, you'll attach the *LinqDataSource* control that you created in *Lesson 11-1: Use the LinqDataSource control* to a *DropDownList* control, allowing the *DropDownList* to be automatically populated with data.

1   Open *Spark* from your sample files folder.

2   Open *newtransaction.aspx* in *Design* view.

3   Set the data source of the *DropDownListCustomer* control to *LinqDataSourceCustomer*.

    1. Click *Choose Data Source…* from the *QuickTasks* menu of the *DropDownListCustomer* control.

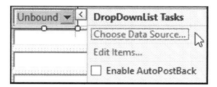

    2. Select the *LinqDataSourceCustomer* control from the first drop-down menu.

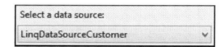

       This is the *LinqDataSource* control that you created in: *Lesson 11-1: Use the LinqDataSource control.*

    3. Select *CustomerName* from the second drop-down menu.

       This tells the *DropDownList* control to display *CustomerName*. This is the value that will be shown on the page and will be stored in the *DropDownListCustomer.SelectedItem.Text* property.

    4. Select *CustomerID* from the third drop-down menu.

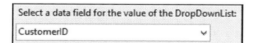

       This determines the hidden value that will accompany each item in the *DropDownList* control. The value will be stored in the *DropDownListCustomer.SelectedValue* property.

    5. Click *OK*.

       Your data source is now linked to your control. When the page is viewed, the list of customers will be automatically displayed in your *DropDownList* control.

4   View *newtransaction.aspx* in your browser.

You can see that the drop-down list has been populated with customers from the project's database.

Ana Trujillo Emparedados y helados
Bottom-Dollar Markets
B's Beverages
Cactus Comidas para llevar
Frankenversand
Hanari Carnes
Island Trading
La maison d'Asie
Magazzini Alimentari Riuniti
Morgenstern Gesundkost
QUICK-Stop
Romero y tomillo

note

Other controls that can be attached to data sources

You can attach a data source to the *BulletedList, CheckBoxList, ListBox* and *RadioButtonList* controls in exactly the same way as you attach one to a *DropDownList* control.

There are also more advanced data controls in the *Data* category such as the *GridView* control, which you'll use in: *Lesson 11-3: Use the GridView control.*

5   Inspect the properties of the *DropDownListCustomer* control.

The *QuickTasks* menu makes things easier in this case, but it doesn't do anything that can't be done by manually setting the properties of the *DropDownList* control.

1. Close your browser and return to Visual Studio.

2. In the *Properties* window, examine the *DataSourceID* property of the *DropDownListCustomer* control.

DataSourceID	LinqDataSourceCustomer

   This property determines which data source control the *DropDownList* control uses. As you can see, it's currently set to *LinqDataSourceCustomer*.

   You could change the data source by changing this property.

3. Examine the *DataTextField* property.

DataTextField	CustomerName

   This is the field that is displayed in the *DropDownList* control. It is currently set to *CustomerName*.

4. Examine the *DataValueField* property.

DataValueField	CustomerID

   This is the field that is stored in the hidden value of each item in the drop-down list. It is currently set to *CustomerID*.

   Whether you prefer to use the *QuickTasks* dialog or set these properties manually is up to you.

6   Add an item to the *DropDownList* control control manually.

1. Use the *Edit Items… QuickTasks* dialog to add a new item to the *DropDownListCustomer* control with the *Text*:
   -- Select Customer --

   You first did this in: *Lesson 1-16: Use the QuickTasks menu.*

2. View *newtransaction.aspx* in your browser.

   Your item isn't displayed. That's because it was overwritten by the items from the database. Fortunately this is easy to fix.

3. Close your browser and set the *AppendDataBoundItems* property of the *DropDownListCustomer* control to: **True**

   Setting this property to *True* specifies that items from the database should be added to the *DropDownList* control's list of items instead of overwriting any existing items.

4. View *newtransaction.aspx* in your browser.

   This time your manually-added item stays where it is.

-- Select Customer --
Ana Trujillo Emparedados y helados
Bottom-Dollar Markets
B's Beverages
Cactus Comidas para llevar
Frankenversand
Hanari Carnes
Island Trading
La maison d'Asie
Magazzini Alimentari Riuniti
Morgenstern Gesundkost
QUICK-Stop
Romero y tomillo

Lesson 11-3: Use the GridView control

The *GridView* control is an extremely flexible control that allows you to retrieve and display data in an automatically-generated table.

In this lesson you'll create a basic *GridView* control that displays invoices in order of date.

1 Open *Spark* from your sample files folder.

2 Open the code-behind file of *reports.aspx*.

3 Remove all existing code from the *Page_Load* event handler.

4 Add a *LinqDataSource* control to the page.

    1. Open *reports.aspx* in *Design* view.

    2. Add a new *LinqDataSource* control after the *LabelReport* control.

    3. Name the new control: **LinqDataSourceInvoice**

    4. Configure the data source to retrieve records from the *Invoice* table, sorted by *InvoiceDate* in ascending order.

       You learned how to do this in: *Lesson 11-1: Use the LinqDataSource control.*

5 Add a *GridView* control to the page.

    1. Add a *GridView* control from the *Data* category of the *Toolbox*.

       Place it after the *LinqDataSourceInvoice* control.

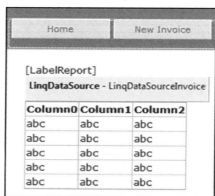

    2. Set the *ID* property of the *GridView* control to: **GridViewInvoice**

    3. Set the *EnableViewState* property of the *GridView* control to **False** (see sidebar).

6 Set the data source of the *GridView* control.

Choose *LinqDataSourceInvoice* from the *Choose Data Source* drop-down in the *QuickTasks* menu for the *GridView* control.

important

GridView controls and ViewState

You should almost always disable ViewState on the *GridView* control by setting its *EnableViewState* property to **False**.

If you leave ViewState enabled, the user's browser will send back the entire contents of the *GridView* control every time they post back the page.

The only time you might want to leave ViewState enabled is if you have a particularly slow query. In this case it might be faster for the user to keep sending back the data than it would be to re-run the query.

As a general rule, always disable ViewState on *GridView* and other data controls and only enable it again if it is absolutely necessary.

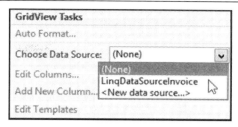

The columns from the database table are automatically added to the *GridView* control!

InvoiceID	CustomerID	InvoiceDate	InvoiceAmount	InvoiceTaxAmount	InvoiceNumber
0	0	14/05/2013 00:00:00	0	0	abc

7 Edit the *GridView* control's columns.

1. Click *Edit Columns…* from the *QuickTasks* menu of the *GridView* control.

    The *Fields* dialog appears.

2. Click *InvoiceID* in the *Selected Fields* list.

    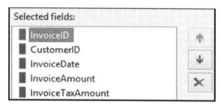

3. Click the *Delete* button to remove it. ☒

4. Delete the *CustomerID* field in the same way.

5. Click the *InvoiceDate* field.

    The field's properties are displayed in the *BoundField properties* panel.

6. Scroll down to the *DataFormatString* property and set it to: **{0:d}**

Data	
DataField	InvoiceDate
DataFormatString	{0:d}

    This is a data format string. It's different to the format strings that you can use in the *ToString* method (see sidebar).

7. Set the *DataFormatString* of the *InvoiceAmount* and *InvoiceTaxAmount* fields to: **{0:c}**

8. Click *OK*.

    The date and value fields are now much easier to read.

8 Format the *GridView* control.

The *GridView* control looks nicer now, but it's not as attractive as it could be. You can use *Auto Format* to change that very easily.

1. Click *Auto Format…* from the *QuickTasks* menu of the *GridView* control.

2. Choose the *Classic* format and then click *OK*.

Lesson 11-4: Add sorting and paging to a GridView

GridView controls are often used to display data for reporting purposes. For example, the *GridView* control that you created in *Lesson 11-3: Use the GridView control* shows a list of invoices.

Being able to sort data and break a long list into a number of shorter pages makes a report much easier for a user to work with. In this lesson, you'll add sorting and paging features to your *GridView* control.

1   Open *Spark* from your sample files folder.

2   Open *reports.aspx* in *Design* view.

3   Enable sorting and paging features.

1.   Set the *AllowPaging* property of the *GridViewInvoice* control to: **True**

Page number links appear at the bottom of the *GridView* control. You can further customize paging by using the other properties in the *Paging* category.

2.   Set the *AllowSorting* property of the *GridViewInvoice* control to: **True**

This allows the user to change the sort order of the *GridView* control by clicking on the column names at the top of the table.

You can also enable sorting and paging by using the *Enable Paging* and *Enable Sorting* check boxes in the *QuickTasks* menu.

4   Test your sorting and paging features.

1.   View *reports.aspx* in your browser.

2.   Click the *InvoiceNumber* heading on the *GridView* control.

InvoiceDate	InvoiceAmount	InvoiceTaxAmount	InvoiceNumber
6/30/2010	$264.03	$52.81	1000
7/29/2010	$199.27	$39.85	1002
1/20/2011	$904.50	$180.90	1002
1/21/2010	$52.88	$10.58	1007
1/18/2011	$871.90	$174.38	1008
10/21/2010	$287.35	$57.47	1012
3/6/2010	$587.79	$117.56	1013
8/4/2010	$38.16	$7.63	1013
3/16/2010	($82.46)	($16.49)	1018
5/23/2010	$80.62	$16.12	1023
12345678910...			

The data is now sorted by *InvoiceNumber*, from lowest to highest. The actual currency prefix that you will see ($ in the above example) may be different on your computer. That's because it reflects the locale of your computer.

note

Limitations of sorting and paging

ASP.NET's automatic sorting and paging functions are great for simple sorting and paging, but have some limitations.

Sorting can only support one sort at a time. For example you can't sort by both *InvoiceDate* and *InvoiceAmount* at the same time.

Sorting and paging can also be problematic when binding data to a *GridView* control using C# code, as you will see in: *Lesson 11-8: Bind data to a control using C#.*

3. Click the *InvoiceNumber* heading again.

InvoiceDate	InvoiceAmount	InvoiceTaxAmount	InvoiceNumber
8/6/2010	$117.51	$23.50	9987
7/4/2010	$421.15	$84.23	9974
9/18/2010	$856.01	$171.20	9974
10/18/2010	$158.21	$31.64	9970
4/27/2010	$116.45	$23.29	9966
9/22/2010	$453.62	$90.72	9962
2/14/2011	$128.65	$25.73	9958
4/25/2010	$303.52	$60.70	9954
5/20/2010	$371.63	$74.33	9951
2/9/2011	$892.76	$178.55	9947

1 2 3 4 5 6 7 8 9 10 ...

Now the data is sorted by *InvoiceNumber* from highest to lowest.

4. Click the number 5 from the page numbers at the bottom of the *GridView* control.

InvoiceDate	InvoiceAmount	InvoiceTaxAmount	InvoiceNumber
3/24/2010	($885.83)	($177.17)	9818
9/26/2010	$468.44	$93.69	9817
8/19/2010	$99.37	$19.87	9816
12/31/2010	$443.65	$88.73	9815
2/26/2010	$141.92	$28.38	9813
6/17/2010	$224.61	$44.92	9812
5/6/2010	$310.53	$62.11	9811
9/24/2010	$364.66	$72.93	9803
12/19/2010	$400.97	$80.19	9798
7/9/2010	$877.94	$175.59	9797

1 2 3 4 5 6 7 8 9 10 ...

You are taken to the fifth page of data.

5. Click the three dots ... after page number 10.

InvoiceDate	InvoiceAmount	InvoiceTaxAmount	InvoiceNumber
8/18/2010	$937.21	$187.44	9521
2/10/2010	$759.87	$151.97	9516
12/6/2010	$460.22	$92.04	9515
5/2/2010	$572.05	$114.41	9511
1/9/2010	$665.41	$133.08	9508
3/14/2010	$245.74	$49.15	9497
8/27/2010	$927.57	$185.51	9488
2/19/2011	$824.93	$164.99	9485
8/9/2010	$515.70	$103.14	9484
7/13/2010	$477.99	$95.60	9477

... 11 12 13 14 15 16 17 18 19 20 ...

You are taken to page number 11 and shown the next 10 page numbers.

As you can see, adding sorting and paging features to your *GridView* control is very easy indeed!

Lesson 11-5: Add editing features to a GridView

GridView controls can do more than just display information. By using some of their more advanced features, you can set them up to edit and delete records without needing to write any code!

1 Open *Spark* from your sample files folder.

2 Open *reports.aspx* in *Design* view.

3 Add editing buttons to the *GridView* control.

1. Click *Edit Columns…* from the *QuickTasks* menu of the *GridViewInvoice* control.

2. Expand *CommandField* in the *Available fields* list.

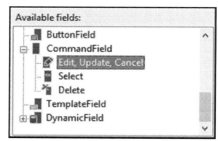

3. Click *Edit, Update, Cancel.*

4. Click *Add.*

5. Use the 'up' arrow to move your *Edit, Update, Cancel* field to the top of the list.

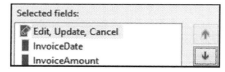

This will make your *Edit, Update* and *Cancel* buttons appear in the first column of the table.

6. Click *OK.*

Notice that *Edit* links have appeared on the left of the *GridView* control. The *Edit, Update* and *Cancel* links aren't very nice to look at by default. See the sidebar for information on customizing them.

4 Test your new editing features.

1. View *reports.aspx* in your browser.

2. Click one of the *Edit* links next to a record.

The fields change into text boxes, allowing you to edit their values.

3. Change the *InvoiceNumber* value to: **TSM-185**

note

Customizing the GridView control further

From this course, you've learned how to use ASP.NET's automatic features to easily create a *GridView* control that can access and edit data.

By using more advanced fields such as the *ButtonField* and *TemplateField*, you can customize the behavior of your *GridView* controls even further.

You'll learn more about this in: *Lesson 12-6: Create a Products page*.

InvoiceNumber
TSM-185

4. Click the *Update* link.

Server Error in '/' Application.
LinqDataSource 'LinqDataSourceInvoice' does not support

An error message appears. This is because the *LinqDataSource* control doesn't allow you to update records by default.

5. Close the browser window and return to Visual Studio.

6. Set the *EnableUpdate* property of the *LinqDataSourceInvoice* control to: **True**

(You can also enable updating by using the *QuickTasks* menu).

7. View *reports.aspx* in your browser and try changing an invoice number to **TSM-185** again.

InvoiceDate	InvoiceAmount	InvoiceTaxAmount	InvoiceNumber
Edit 1/1/2010	$970.88	$194.18	TSM-185

This time the record is updated successfully.

8. Close the browser window and return to Visual Studio.

5 Add delete buttons to the *GridView* control.

1. Return to the *Edit Columns* dialog of the *GridViewInvoice* control by using the *QuickTasks* menu.

2. Add a *Delete* field from the *CommandField* category.

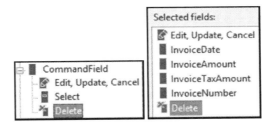

note

The Select CommandField

Along with *Edit, Update, Cancel* and *Delete*, you'll notice *Select*.

The *Select* field allows the user to select a row in the *GridView*, which will be highlighted and will be accessible to your C# code as: *GridView.SelectedRow*

The only reason to use a *Select* field is if you intend to use C# code to take an action depending upon the selected row.

When a *Select* field is clicked, the *SelectedIndexChanged* event of the *GridView* runs.

3. Click *OK*.

4. Set the *EnableDelete* property of the *LinqDataSourceInvoice* control to: **True**

In the same way that you needed to set the *EnableUpdate* property to *True* in order to update records, you must set the *EnableDelete* property to *True* in order to delete records.

As long as you don't set these properties to *True*, you can be assured that your *LinqDataSource* controls will never allow any database records to be updated or deleted.

5. View *reports.aspx* in your browser.

6. Try deleting a record by clicking one of the *Delete* buttons.

The record is deleted from the database.

Lesson 11-6: Use the DetailsView control

There are several other data controls, including *DataList, DetailsView, FormView, ListView* and *Repeater*. Of these, only the *DetailsView* control has the convenient *Edit Fields* dialog that the *GridView* control offers. The other controls use templates, which you may recall from: *Lesson 9-5: Customize the Login control*.

In this lesson, you'll work with the *DetailsView* control.

1 Open *Spark* from your sample files folder.

2 Open *reports.aspx* in *Design* view.

3 Add a *DetailsView* control to the page.

    1. Drag a *DetailsView* control from the *Data* category of the *Toolbox* onto the page.

    2. Set the *ID* property of the new *DetailsView* control to: **DetailsViewInvoice**

    3. Use the *Choose Data Source* drop-down in the *QuickTasks* menu of the *DetailsView* control to set its data source to *LinqDataSourceInvoice*.

    You did this in: *Lesson 11-2: Attach a data source to a control*.

    The fields from the *Invoice* table should appear in the *DetailsView* control. If they don't, click *Refresh Schema* from the *QuickTasks* menu and click *No* if prompted (see sidebar).

InvoiceID	0
CustomerID	0
InvoiceDate	14/05/2013 00:00:00
InvoiceAmount	0
InvoiceTaxAmount	0
InvoiceNumber	abc

    As you can see, a *DetailsView* control is very similar to a *GridView* control, but it only displays one record at a time and displays the data in rows instead of in columns.

4 Enable paging on the *DetailsView* control.

Enable paging on the *DetailsView* control in exactly the same way as you did with the *GridView* control in: *Lesson 11-4: Add sorting and paging to a GridView*.

This adds page numbers that allow you to move between records in the *DetailsView* control.

5 Add editing features to the *DetailsView* control.

    1. Tick the *Enable Editing* box in the *QuickTasks* menu of the *DetailsView* control.

    This does exactly the same thing as adding an *Edit, Update, Cancel* field manually (as you did in: *Lesson 11-5: Add editing features to a GridView*).

note

The DataList, FormView, ListView and Repeater controls

The *DataList, FormView, ListView* and *Repeater* controls all use templates rather than convenient dialog boxes.

This means that you have to customize them by working in *Source* view rather than simply changing properties and using *QuickTasks* dialogs.

DataList
Similar to *DetailsView*, but displays multiple records at once and can only be customized using templates.

FormView
Almost identical to *DetailsView*, but uses templates instead of the *Edit Columns* dialog.

ListView
An extremely flexible control with a dialog to customize it in various ways, but cannot be customized fully without editing the code manually in *Source* view.

Repeater
The control that the *ListView* control is based on. No dialogs of any kind: you have to configure this control manually in *Source* view.

You will learn more about working with templates and the *ListView* control in the Expert Skills course in this series.

2. View *reports.aspx* in your browser.

3. Click the *Edit* button in the *DetailsView* control.

4. Modify the values and click *Update*.

InvoiceID	2184	
CustomerID	5	
InvoiceDate	01/01/2010 00:00:00	
InvoiceAmount	444	
InvoiceTaxAmount	111	
InvoiceNumber	TSM-1	
Update Cancel		

Your updated record appears in the *GridView* control above, as well as in the *DetailsView* control.

5. Close the browser window and return to Visual Studio.

6 **Make the *DetailsView* control insert a record.**

One thing *DetailsView* controls can do that *GridView* controls can't is to automatically add new records to a database.

1. Use the *Edit Fields* dialog of the *DetailsView* control to add a *New, Insert, Cancel* field from the *CommandField* category.

2. Set the *EnableInsert* property of the *LinqDataSourceInvoice* control to: **True**

Just like *EnableUpdate* and *EnableDelete*, you need to set *EnableInsert* to *True* to allow records to be inserted through your *LinqDataSource* control.

3. View *reports.aspx* in your browser.

4. Click *New* in the *DetailsView* control.

5. Complete the *DetailsView* control's form to add an invoice for CustomerID 5 as shown.

CustomerID	5
InvoiceDate	01 Jan 1980
InvoiceAmount	9986
InvoiceTaxAmount	153
InvoiceNumber	TSM-2
Insert Cancel	

6. Click *Insert*.

7. Your new invoice appears in the *GridView* control as well as the *DetailsView* control.

	InvoiceDate	InvoiceAmount	InvoiceTaxAmount	InvoiceNumber	
Edit	01/01/1980	£9,986.00	£153.00	TSM-2	Delete

8. Close the browser window and return to Visual Studio.

7 **Delete the *DetailsViewInvoice* control.**

Lesson 11-7: Use the SqlDataSource control

For any new projects I would recommend that you always use the *LinqDataSource* control and not the *SqlDataSource* control.

LINQ is Microsoft's newer (and better) technology.

The reason I'm showing you how to use the *SqlDataSource* control is that you may work on older projects that were created before the LINQ technology became available.

The *SqlDataSource* control is very similar to the *LinqDataSource* control, but instead of accessing data via your LINQ classes, it interacts directly with the database.

1 Open *Spark* from your sample files folder.

2 Open *reports.aspx* in *Design* view.

3 Add a *SqlDataSource* control to the page.

  1. Add a *SqlDataSource* control just after the *LinqDataSource* control.

  2. Set the *ID* property of the *SqlDataSource* control to: **SqlDataSourceInvoice**

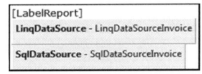

4 Configure the *SqlDataSource* control.

  1. Click *Configure Data Source* from the *QuickTasks* menu of the *SqlDataSourceInvoice* control.

    A dialog appears.

  2. Select *SparkConnectionString* from the drop-down menu.

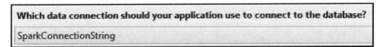

    The connection string tells the *SqlDataSource* control how to connect to your database. Visual Studio automatically added *SparkConnectionString* to the *Web.config* file when the database was added to the project.

  3. Click *Next*.

    A configuration dialog appears that is similar to the configuration dialog for the *LinqDataSource* control.

  4. Select *Invoice* from the *Name* drop-down.

Name:
Invoice ⌄

Some code appears in the *SELECT Statement* box. This is the automatically-generated SQL code that will be sent to the database.

5. Click *ORDER BY...*

   A sorting dialog appears that is almost identical to the one for the *LinqDataSource* control.

6. Set the *SqlDataSource* control to sort by *InvoiceDate*.

7. Click *OK*.

   You will notice that some more SQL code has been added to sort the results.

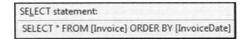

   This *SqlDataSource* control now does exactly the same thing as the *LinqDataSourceInvoice* control on this page.

8. Click *Next*.

9. Click *Finish*.

5   Use the new data source.

   1. Use the *QuickTasks* menu of the *GridView* control to set its data source to: **SqlDataSourceInvoice**. Click *No* when asked if you wish to refresh the fields and keys. If you were to click *Yes* you'd lose all of the formatting that you applied earlier in this session.

   2. View *reports.aspx* in your browser.

      The data is displayed without any problems.

   3. Click *Edit* and try to update one of the records.

      An error message appears.

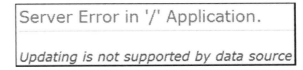

   SqlDataSource controls can't update records unless you manually add SQL code to the control's *UpdateQuery* property.

6   Switch back to the *LinqDataSource* control.

   1. Close your browser.

   2. Use the *QuickTasks* menu of the *GridView* control to change its data source back to: **LinqDataSourceInvoice**. Remember to click *No* when prompted.

   3. Delete the *SqlDataSourceInvoice* control.

Lesson 11-8: Bind data to a control using C# code

Although it's very easy to use the *LinqDataSource* control to connect controls to a database, you can also use the LINQ code you learned in *Lesson 10-3: Retrieve a single row of data using LINQ* to do the same thing.

Using C# code instead of data source controls is helpful when you need more flexibility on your pages. For example, you can use *if* statements to return different sets of data depending on different conditions. You'll see how useful this can be in: *Lesson 12-8: Create a Search page.*

1 Open *Spark* from your sample files folder.

2 Open *reports.aspx* in *Design* view.

3 Delete the *LinqDataSourceInvoice* control.

You're going to connect the database to the *GridView* control manually, so you don't need the *LinqDataSource* control anymore.

4 Remove the data source property from the *GridView* control.

Remove the text from the *DataSourceID* property of the *GridViewInvoice* control so that it is blank.

```
DataSourceID
```

Click *No* when prompted to refresh the *GridView* control's fields.

5 Add code to retrieve the data.

1. Open the code-behind file of *reports.aspx*.

2. Add the following code to the *Page_Load* event handler:

using (SparkDataContext Data = new SparkDataContext())
{
**   var Invoices = Data.Invoices**
**   .OrderBy(Invoice => Invoice.InvoiceDate);**
}

```
protected void Page_Load(object sender, EventArgs e)
{
    using (SparkDataContext Data = new SparkDataContext())
    {
        var Invoices = Data.Invoices
        .OrderBy(Invoice => Invoice.InvoiceDate);
    }
}
```

This code retrieves the contents of the *Invoices* table sorted by *InvoiceDate* and places it into a collection called *Invoices*.

6 Bind the data to the *GridView* control.

1. Add the following code to the *using* statement:

GridViewInvoice.DataSource = Invoices;

```
var Invoices = Data.Invoices
.OrderBy(Invoice => Invoice.InvoiceDate);
GridViewInvoice.DataSource = Invoices;
```

tip

Binding to other controls

You can bind data to any control that has a *DataSource* property by using the techniques learned in this lesson.

The data that you bind to your controls doesn't have to be created by LINQ; you can use any collection as a data source.

This code provides the *GridView* control with the data returned by *LINQ*. Since the *Invoice* objects all have names that correspond to the items in the table, the columns that were automatically generated by the *LinqDataSource* control earlier will continue to work without any problems.

If you were to use data from a different table, you would have to set up your *GridView* control's columns to match the new table.

2. Add the following code on the next line:

GridViewInvoice.DataBind();

```
var Invoices = Data.Invoices
.OrderBy(Invoice => Invoice.InvoiceDate);
GridViewInvoice.DataSource = Invoices;
GridViewInvoice.DataBind();
```

Without this line, the data will not appear in the control. Whenever you change a control's data source property, you must call the *DataBind* method before the new data will be displayed.

7 See the code in action.

1. View *reports.aspx* in your browser.

InvoiceDate	InvoiceAmount	InvoiceTaxAmount	InvoiceNumber
01/01/1980	9986.0000	153.0000	TSM-2
01/01/2010	444.0000	111.0000	TSM-1
01/01/2010	91.3500	18.2700	9557

2. Click *Edit, Delete* or one of the page numbers.

An error message is displayed. Without the *LinqDataSource* control to handle these events they will not work (see sidebar).

3. Close your browser.

8 Add a *PageIndexChanging* event to the *GridView* control.

You can create your own event handler to enable the *GridView* control to use paging.

1. Add a *PageIndexChanging* event handler to the *GridViewInvoice* control.

2. Add the following code to the new event handler:

GridViewInvoice.PageIndex = e.NewPageIndex;
GridViewInvoice.DataBind();

```
protected void GridViewInvoice_PageIndexChanging(obj
{
    GridViewInvoice.PageIndex = e.NewPageIndex;
    GridViewInvoice.DataBind();
}
```

This code will enable the paging features to work.

Note that an object called *e* is often passed into an event handler as an argument. In this case the *NewPageIndex* property of the *e* object must be provided to the *GridView* control in order for it to move to the next page.

note

Adding Edit and Delete functionality to your GridView control

The easiest way to allow editing and deleting of records in a *GridView* is to use a *LinqDataSource* control.

If you bind data to your control manually, you can still use the *GridView* control's automatic functions by adding *RowEditing* and *RowDeleting* event handlers.

You will learn more about this topic in the Expert Skills course in this series.

Server Error in '/' Application.

The GridView 'GridViewInvoice' fired event

note

Efficient querying

Since the LINQ code in this lesson is in the *Page_Load* event handler, the database will be queried every time the page posts back.

On this page that isn't a problem, but it's inefficient to re-query the database if the data hasn't changed.

You can make your queries more efficient by using an *if* statement along with the *Page.IsPostBack* property.

You'll make use of this technique in: *Lesson 12-10: Create a Checkout page.*

Session 11: Exercise

1 Open the *Spark* project from your sample files folder.

2 Open *customer.aspx* in *Design* view.

3 Add a *LinqDataSource* control and configure it to retrieve records from the *Customer* table, sorted by *CustomerName*. Name your new control: **LinqDataSourceCustomer**

4 Add a *GridView* control and attach it to the *LinqDataSource* control.

5 Enable sorting and paging for the *GridView* control.

6 Add *Command fields* to the *GridView* control to allow records to be edited and deleted.

7 Use *Auto Format* to make the *GridView* control more presentable.

8 Add a *DropDownList* control to the page. Name your new control: **DropDownListCustomer**

9 Add C# code to the *Page_Load* event handler of *customer.aspx* to retrieve the contents of the *Customer* table and place it in the *DropDownList* control.

10 Set the *DropDownList* control's *DataTextField* property to **CustomerName** and the *DataValueField* property to **CustomerID**.

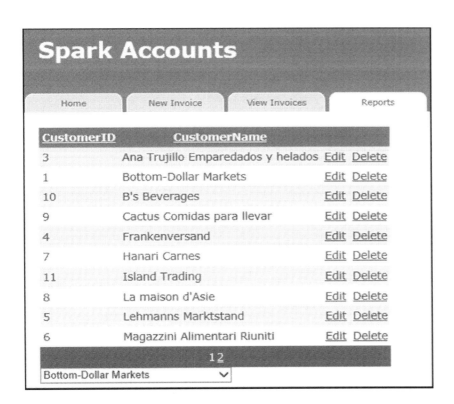

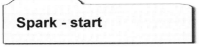

Spark - start

Spark - end

If you need help slide the page to the left

Session 11: Exercise Answers

These are the three questions that students find the most difficult to answer:

Q 9	Q 6	Q 3

Use the following code:
 	
using (SparkDataContext Data = new SparkDataContext())
{
   DropDownListCustomer
   .DataSource = Data.Customers;
   DropDownListCustomer
   .DataBind();
}
 	
This was covered in: *Lesson 11-8: Bind data to a control using C# code.*
	1. Click *Edit Columns…* in the QuickTasks menu of the *GridView* control.
	
	2. Expand the *CommandField* category in the *Available Fields* list.
	
	3. Click *Edit, Update, Cancel* from the *CommandField* category.
	
	4. Click *Add*.
	
	5. Click *Delete* from the *CommandField* category.
	
	6. Click *Add*.
	
	7. Click *OK*.
	
	This was covered in: *Lesson 11-5: Add editing features to a GridView.*
		1. Add a *LinqDataSource* control to the page.
		
		2. Set the *ID* property of the new control to: **LinqDataSourceCustomer**
		
		3. Click *Configure Data Source…* from the QuickTasks menu of the control.
		
		4. Ensure that *Spark.SparkDataContext* is selected and click *Next*.
		
		5. Ensure that *Customers(Table<Customer>)* is selected in the *Table* drop-down.
		
		6. Click *OrderBy…*
		
		7. Ensure that *CustomerName* is selected in the *Sort by* drop-down.
		
		8. Click *OK*.
		
		9. Click *Finish*.
		
		This was covered in: *Lesson 11-1: Use the LinqDataSource control.*

If you have difficulty with the other questions, here are the lessons that cover the relevant skills:

1   **Refer to: Lesson 1-7: Manage a project with the Solution Explorer.**

2   **Refer to: Lesson 1-7: Manage a project with the Solution Explorer.**

4   **Refer to: Lesson 11-3: Use the GridView control.**

5   **Refer to: Lesson 11-4: Add sorting and paging to a GridView.**

7   **Refer to: Lesson 1-16: Use the QuickTasks menu.**

8   **Refer to: Lesson 1-15: Add controls to a page with the Toolbox.**

Session Twelve: Build a complete ASP.NET site

> We have finished the job. What shall we do with the tools?
>
> *Haile Selassie, Ethiopian statesman (1892 – 1975)*

You've now mastered all of the essential skills needed to work with ASP.NET, C# and Visual Studio.

You've worked with all of the major ASP.NET controls, you've learned how to create all of the most important programming structures in C# and you've used the most important features of Visual Studio.

With the skills you've learned, you have a solid foundation upon which to further develop your C# code and Visual Studio skills.

In this session, you'll explore some of the new features of ASP.NET 4.5 and then put your skills to use by finishing the *SmartMethodStore* project, a simple e-commerce site with products, a shopping cart and many advanced features.

Session Objectives

By the end of this session you will be able to:

- Use master pages
- Handle errors with Global.asax
- Understand Web Optimization
- Understand FriendlyUrls
- Log errors to a database
- Create a Products page
- Create a Shopping Cart
- Create a Search page
- Add functionality to a Search page
- Create a Checkout page
- Create a Payment page
- Implement security
- Publish a site

note

Whether to use master pages

Master pages provide a convenient way to create multiple pages based on a single template. By using a master page, you can avoid having to manually update each page when a minor change is made to your site's layout.

The disadvantage of master pages if that you lose the ability to completely customize each page.

Whether you prefer to use master pages or not is up to you.

A good compromise between using master pages and having complete code on every page is *Web User Controls*. You can learn about them in the Expert Skills course.

note

The ScriptManager control

You'll notice that the automatically-generated master page contains a *ScriptManager* control, which you haven't yet used.

The *ScriptManager* control in *Site.Master* is used to include certain JavaScript files on every page that uses the master page.

You'll learn more about the *ScriptManager* control in the Expert Skills course in this series.

If you are not completing the course incrementally use the sample file: **Lesson 12-1** to begin this lesson.

Sample files with the starting point for each lesson are also provided for all of the other lessons in this session.

Lesson 12-1: Use master pages

Master pages offer a way to store your site's layout in a single file, which you can then assign to many pages. The automatically-generated site that is created when you create a new *ASP.NET Web Forms Application* includes a master page.

1   Open *SmartMethodStore* from your sample files folder.

2   Open *Site.Master* in *Design* view.

As you can see, a master page looks exactly the same as any other .aspx page.

3   Examine the *ContentPlaceHolder* control.

ContentPlaceHolder is a special control that's only available on master pages. It's used to define areas that can be edited on pages that use the master page.

The *ContentPlaceHolder* control appears in the *Standard* category of the *Toolbox*.

1.   Select the *MainContent* control.

   The easiest way to do this is to select *MainContent* from the drop-down menu at the top of the *Properties* window.

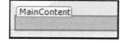

   This is a *ContentPlaceHolder* control. It doesn't have any interesting properties, but it will create an editable region for all pages that use this master page.

2.   Open *Default.aspx* in *Design* view.

   As you can see, *Default.aspx* uses the *Site.Master* master page.

3.   Select the *BodyContent* control.

   This is the *ContentPlaceHolder* control that you saw on the master page. You can edit only the contents of the *ContentPlaceHolders* on this page. Everything else is provided by the master page.

4.   Switch to *Source* view.

```
⊞<asp:Content ID="FeaturedContent" ...>...</asp:Content>
⊟<asp:Content runat="server" ID="BodyContent" ContentPlaceHolderID="MainContent">
⊟    <p>
         This is a very basic e-commerce site with a products database and shopping cart functionality.
     </p>
 </asp:Content>
```

As you can see, the only controls on this page are the, *FeaturedContent* and *BodyContent* controls. These controls are the local copies of the *FeaturedContent* and *MainContent* placeholders that were defined on the master page.

FeaturedContent links to the area within the blue box on the page and *MainContent* links to the page's main content area.

At the top of the page, you can see the master page referenced in the *MasterPageFile* property.

4 **Add a new page which uses a master page.**

1. Open the *New Item…* dialog from the *Solution Explorer*.

2. Choose *Web form using Master Page* from the *Web* category.

3. Name the new page: **products.aspx**

4. Click *Add*.

   You are prompted to select which master page to use.

   > Contents of folder:
   > ▢ Site.Master
   > ▢ Site.Mobile.Master

   The default site contains two master pages: *Site.Master* and *Site.Mobile.Master* (see sidebar).

5. Click *Site.Master*.

6. Click *OK*.

7. Switch to *Source* view, if you aren't already in that view.

   You can see that *Content* controls linked to the *ContentPlaceHolder* controls in the master page have been created automatically.

   ```
   <asp:Content ID="Content3" ContentPlaceHolderID="MainContent"
   </asp:Content>
   ```

8. Enter the following HTML code inside the *MainContent* placeholder:

   <h2>Products</h2>

   ```
   <asp:Content ID="Content2" ContentPlac
       <h2>Products</h2>
   </asp:Content>
   ```

9. View *products.aspx* in your browser.

   ASP.NET has used the master page to create an attractive web page that displays the content that you have added to the placeholder.

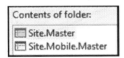

The Smart Method Store

Products

Lesson 12-2: Handle errors with Global.asax

The *Global.asax* file is automatically created when you create a new *ASP.NET Web Forms Application* project.

Global.asax contains event handlers that are related to your application and user sessions. *Global.asax* also contains an event handler that runs whenever an error happens anywhere in your application.

By using *Global.asax*, you can intercept every error that happens on your site. There are other event handlers in *Global.asax* that can also be useful (see sidebar).

1   Open *SmartMethodStore* from your sample files folder.

2   Open *Global.asax*.

```
public class Global : System.Web.HttpApplication
{
    void Application_Start(object sender, EventArgs e)...
```

You can see the automatically-created event handlers:

Application_Start
Runs when your site is started by the web server.

Application_End
Runs when your site is stopped by the web server.

Application_Error
Runs whenever an error occurs on your site.

You'll also notice that there is some code in the *Application_Start* event handler. This is automatically added to all new *ASP.NET Web Forms Application* projects.

```
void Application_Start(object sender, EventArgs e)
{
    // Code that runs on application startup
    BundleConfig.RegisterBundles(BundleTable.Bundles);
    AuthConfig.RegisterOpenAuth();
    RouteConfig.RegisterRoutes(RouteTable.Routes);
}
```

This code is used to implement some of the new features of ASP.NET 4.5.

BundleConfig.RegisterBundles runs some code that uses ASP.NET 4.5's new *Web Optimization* features. You'll learn about this in: *Lesson 12-3: Understand Web Optimization*.

AuthConfig.RegisterOpenAuth runs some code from the *AuthConfig.cs* file in the *App_Start* folder. The code is commented out by default, but can be uncommented to add support for the *OpenAuth* protocol that is used by Microsoft, Twitter and Facebook.

RouteConfig.RegisterRoutes runs some code that enables ASP.NET 4.5's new *FriendlyUrls* feature. You'll learn about this in: *Lesson 12-4: Understand FriendlyUrls*.

note

Other event handlers in Global.asax

As you can see in this lesson, the *Application_Start* event handler can be used to initialize some settings when your application starts. You'll learn more about this later in this session.

It's rare to use *Application_End* in ASP.NET, but it could be used for logging and testing purposes.

In addition to the event handlers that are automatically added to *Global.asax*, you can add several other event handlers.

The most useful 'hidden' events are *Session_Start* and *Session_End*, which run when a user's session begins or ends. The most likely use for these would be to log details of your site's users when they arrive at or leave your site.

3 Add an error page to your application.

The default error screen that appears in ASP.NET is not very nice to see. Creating a page to display in case of errors is good practice.

1. Add a new *Web Form using Master Page* named: **error.aspx**

2. Add the following HTML code to the *MainContent* area of *error.aspx*:

<h2>Something went wrong</h2>
<p>We're sorry, but something went wrong with your request. If you continue to have problems, please contact support.</p>

4 Add redirection code to the *Global.asax* file.

1. Open *Global.asax*.

2. Add the following code to the *Application_Error* event handler:

Response.Redirect("~/error.aspx");

```
void Application_Error(object sender, EventArgs e)
{
    // Code that runs when an unhandled error occurs
    Response.Redirect("~/error.aspx");
}
```

Note that you can also set the default error page in the *ASP.NET Configuration* utility. You may have noticed the option when you worked through: *Lesson 9-2: Manage a site with ASP.NET Configuration*.

Setting the error page in the *ASP.NET Configuration* utility is very easy and convenient, but *Global.asax* allows you to do more than just redirect the user, as you'll see in: *Lesson 12-5: Log errors to a database*.

5 Test your redirection code.

1. View *Default.aspx* in your browser.

2. Replace *Default.aspx* in the browser's web address bar with **qqqqqq.aspx** (a page that does not exist).

You are automatically redirected to your site's error page instead of being shown a standard error.

Something went wrong

We're sorry, but something went wrong with your request.

6 Close Visual Studio.

Lesson 12-3: Understand Web Optimization

ASP.NET 4.5 includes some new features in the *System.Web.Optimization* namespace that make your web applications faster and more efficient.

Web Optimization speeds up page loading by 'bundling' all of the page's CSS and JavaScript files into a single file. This allows your user's web browser to load all of a page's styles and scripts with a single request instead of having to send a separate request for each file.

As well as 'bundling' the files together, Web Optimization also 'minifies' the files by removing all line breaks and white space, making the files smaller.

note

JavaScript libraries that are included by default

Several JavaScript libraries are included with the default ASP.NET Web Forms Application project.

These include:

jquery
A library that provides many useful extended JavaScript features and enables compatibility with all major web browsers.

modernizr
A library that enables extended support for older web browsers that do not support modern features.

WebForms and *MsAjax*
These JavaScript libraries are used by the validation controls in ASP.NET 4.5 to enable the new "unobtrusive validation" features. JQuery is also needed for this.

1   Open *SmartMethodStore* from your sample files folder.

2   Open *Global.asax* and examine the *Application_Start* event handler.

```
void Application_Start(object sender, EventArgs e)
{
    // Code that runs on application startup
    BundleConfig.RegisterBundles(BundleTable.Bundles);
    AuthConfig.RegisterOpenAuth();
    RouteConfig.RegisterRoutes(RouteTable.Routes);
}
```

BundleConfig.RegisterBundles refers to some code in a file called *BundleConfig.cs* that is in the *App_Start* folder.

Note that the *App_Start* folder is <u>not</u> a 'special' ASP.NET folder like the *App_Data* folder. Items in the *App_Start* folder are not treated specially in any way.

3   Open *BundleConfig.cs* from the *App_Start* folder.

Here you can see the code that defines the bundles that are used by the default project.

```
bundles.Add(new ScriptBundle("~/bundles/WebFormsJs").Include(
    "~/Scripts/WebForms/WebForms.js",
    "~/Scripts/WebForms/WebUIValidation.js",
    "~/Scripts/WebForms/MenuStandards.js",
    "~/Scripts/WebForms/Focus.js",
    "~/Scripts/WebForms/GridView.js",
    "~/Scripts/WebForms/DetailsView.js",
    "~/Scripts/WebForms/TreeView.js",
    "~/Scripts/WebForms/WebParts.js"));

bundles.Add(new ScriptBundle("~/bundles/MsAjaxJs").Include(
    "~/Scripts/WebForms/MsAjax/MicrosoftAjax.js",
    "~/Scripts/WebForms/MsAjax/MicrosoftAjaxApplicationServices.js",
    "~/Scripts/WebForms/MsAjax/MicrosoftAjaxTimer.js",
    "~/Scripts/WebForms/MsAjax/MicrosoftAjaxWebForms.js"));

// Use the Development version of Modernizr to develop with and learn from. Then, when you're
// ready for production, use the build tool at http://modernizr.com to pick only the tests you need
bundles.Add(new ScriptBundle("~/bundles/modernizr").Include(
    "~/Scripts/modernizr-*"));
```

This code creates three *ScriptBundle* objects named *WebFormsJs*, *MsAjaxJs* and *modernizr*, each bundling together several JavaScript

note

The ScriptManager control

The default *Site.Master* page uses a *ScriptManager* control to include some additional bundles.

The bundles that are included using the *ScriptManager* control are specifically intended to enable AJAX functionality. AJAX is covered in the Expert Skills course in this series.

However, the names of the bundles do not match those that you saw defined in *BundleConfig.cs*.

The reason for this is that Microsoft have hard-coded these names into the *ScriptManager* control. For example, *MsAjaxBundle* will be read by the *ScriptManager* control and converted to refer to the *MsAjaxJs* bundle.

This is extremely confusing, and will hopefully be improved with future updates.

files. The *WebFormsJs* bundle, for example, could now be tested by navigating to *http://localhost/bundles/WebFormsJs*.

Because this code is called through *Global.asax*, it is slightly obfuscated that the bundles are being added using the *System.Web.Optimization.BundleTable.Bundles.Add* method.

4   Open *Bundle.config*.

Bundles can be registered using an XML file called *Bundle.config* instead of using the *System.Web.Optimization.BundleTable* class. In this file you can see two bundles that contain several CSS files.

```
<bundles version="1.0">
  <styleBundle path="~/Content/css">
    <include path="~/Content/Site.css" />
  </styleBundle>
  <styleBundle path="~/Content/themes/base/css">
    <include path="~/Content/themes/base/jquery.ui.core.css" />
    <include path="~/Content/themes/base/jquery.ui.resizable.css" />
```

Bundle.config is probably a better way to set up bundles, as this allows you to modify bundle settings without recompiling the entire project, although there is an even simpler solution (see sidebar).

I'd only recommend the approach that is used in *BundleConfig.cs* if you needed to use additional C# code to control the configuration of your bundles.

5   Open *Site.Master* in *Source* view.

At the top of the page, you can see the code:

<%: Scripts.Render("~/bundles/modernizr") %>

and:

<webopt:BundleReference runat="server" Path="~/Content/css" />

```
<asp:PlaceHolder runat="server">
    <%: Scripts.Render("~/bundles/modernizr") %>
</asp:PlaceHolder>
<webopt:BundleReference runat="server" Path="~/Content/css" />
```

Scripts.Render("~/bundles/modernizr") links this page to the *modernizr* bundle that you saw defined in *BundleConfig.cs*.

The *webopt:BundleReference* control bundles all of the CSS files from the *Content* folder into a single file and links them to this page.

To make things even more confusing, some bundles are also being added using a *ScriptManager* control a little further down the page (see sidebar for more on this).

As you've seen, the default project uses three different techniques to define bundles and another three techniques to include them on a page! This is extremely confusing even to an expert and underlines just how new this feature is.

In future versions of ASP.NET these features will probably be included much more gracefully.

Lesson 12-4: Understand FriendlyUrls

FriendlyUrls is a new feature of ASP.NET 4.5 that enables your sites to recognize addresses in more complex ways.

1   Open *SmartMethodStore* from your sample files folder.

2   Open *Global.asax* and examine the *Application_Start* event handler.

```
void Application_Start(object sender, EventArgs e)
{
    // Code that runs on application startup
    BundleConfig.RegisterBundles(BundleTable.Bundles);
    AuthConfig.RegisterOpenAuth();
    RouteConfig.RegisterRoutes(RouteTable.Routes);
}
```

RouteConfig.RegisterRoutes refers to some code in a file called *RouteConfig.cs* that is in the *App_Start* folder.

3   Open *RouteConfig.cs* from the *App_Start* folder.

The code in this file enables the *FriendlyUrls* feature.

```
public static void RegisterRoutes(RouteCollection routes)
{
    routes.EnableFriendlyUrls();
}
```

Without this code, none of the features of *FriendlyUrls* will work.

Because this code is called through *Global.asax,* it is slightly obfuscated that the method that is being called is: *System.Web.Routing.RouteTable.EnableFriendlyUrls*.

4   View *Default.aspx* using *FriendlyUrls*.

The first feature of *FriendlyUrls* is that it enables your pages to be accessed without needing the *.aspx* extension.

1.   View *Default.aspx* in your web browser.

2.   Using your web browser's address bar, change *Default.aspx* to **Default** and press **<Enter>**.

The page is displayed without any problems. This will work with any page as long as *FriendlyUrls* is enabled.

3.   Close your browser and return to Visual Studio.

5   Add code to extract extra segments from friendly URLs.

As well as allowing pages to be accessed without extensions, *FriendlyUrls* enables you to extract additional segments from a request for a page.

For example, if the user navigated to */Default/Test,* the *Default.aspx* page would still be displayed, but with an awareness that the user entered *Test*.

© 2014 The Smart Method Ltd

important

Real pages override FriendlyUrls

Imagine that you visit the following friendly URL:

Default/Test

This friendly URL recognizes the *Default.aspx* page and delivers the user to *Default.aspx* with the rest of the path being used for information purposes only.

However, if the project contained a *Default* folder with a page called *Test.aspx*, the user would be delivered to *Test.aspx* instead of *Default.aspx*.

The presence of a 'real' page always overrides friendly URLs.

note

FriendlyUrls for mobile devices

FriendlyUrls automatically checks whether the user is visiting your site on a mobile device (such as an iPad or Nexus tablet) and sends an alternative 'mobile' version of each page to the user if one exists.

To create an alternative page for mobile devices, simply add *Mobile* to its name. For example:

Default.Mobile.aspx

...would create a version of *Default.aspx* that is only displayed to mobile device users.

You'll notice that a *Site.Mobile.Master* master page already exists. This master page will be displayed to mobile users.

This was also mentioned in: *Lesson 12-1: Use master pages.*

1. Open the code-behind file of *Default.aspx*.

2. Add the following *using* line to the top of the page:

   using Microsoft.AspNet.FriendlyUrls;

   ```
   using System.Web.UI.WebControls;
   using Microsoft.AspNet.FriendlyUrls;
   ```

   You learned about *using* lines in: *Lesson 6-3: Use the .NET framework.*

3. Add the following code to the *Page_Load* event handler:

   foreach (string Segment in Page. Request.GetFriendlyUrlSegments())
   {
       Response.Write(Segment + "<br />");
   }

   ```
   protected void Page_Load(object sender, EventArgs e)
   {
       foreach (string Segment in Page.Request.GetFriendlyUrlSegments())
       {
           Response.Write(Segment + "<br />");
       }
   }
   ```

   This code extracts any additional information from the address that was requested and displays it.

4. View *Default.aspx* in your web browser.

5. Using your web browser's address bar, change *Default.aspx* to **Default/Test/Friendly/Urls**

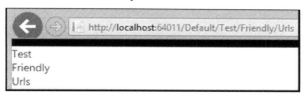

   Default.aspx is displayed and the additional parts of the address are extracted by your C# code. This feature allows you to easily create 'friendly' ways to access information.

   For example, you might have a *Customers.aspx* page that allows each customer to be accessed through a friendly URL such as */Customers/Customer1*. Earlier versions of ASP.NET required a huge amount of code to achieve this.

   There are some more advanced features of *FriendlyUrls* that allow you to define addresses without needing an underlying *aspx* page. These features are covered in the Expert Skills course in this series.

6   Close Visual Studio.

Lesson 12-5: Log errors to a database

By adding some LINQ database code to your *Global.asax* file, you can log any errors that happen on your site into a database.

Keeping a log of errors that happen on your site is good practice as it helps you to track down and fix any problems that occur, even if they are not reported by your users.

If you had several web applications (on a corporate intranet, for example), you could even use this technique to centralize your error logging into a single database, allowing you to see all application problems in one place.

1   Open *SmartMethodStore* from your sample files folder.

2   Open *Global.asax*.

3   Add code to log all errors to a database.

Although the error handling code that you added in *Lesson 12-2: Handle errors with Global.asax* is useful, you could have done the same thing using the *ASP.NET Configuration* utility (you learned how to use this in: *Lesson 9-2: Manage a site with ASP.NET Configuration*).

Manually adding code to *Global.asax* allows you to customize error handling to a far greater extent.

1.   Add *LINQ to SQL Classes,* naming the LINQ file: **Store.dbml**

You learned how to do this in *Lesson 10-2: Add LINQ data classes to a project*.

2.   Add all database tables from the *Store* database to your new LINQ classes.

You learned how to do this in *Lesson 10-2: Add LINQ data classes to a project*.

3.   Open *Global.asax*.

4.   Add the following code to the beginning of your *Application_Error* event handler:

```
using (StoreDataContext Data = new StoreDataContext())
{
   Exception ExceptionToLog = Server.GetLastError();
   Error NewError = new Error();
   NewError.ErrorMessage = ExceptionToLog.Message;
   NewError.ErrorStackTrace = ExceptionToLog.StackTrace;
   NewError.ErrorURL = Request.Url.ToString();
   NewError.ErrorDate = DateTime.Now;
   Data.Errors.InsertOnSubmit(NewError);
   Data.SubmitChanges();
}
```

This code uses the *Server.GetLastError* method to retrieve an *Exception* object (called *ExceptionToLog*) containing details of the last error that occurred on the web server. You learned about the *Exception* object in: *Lesson 3-5: Understand the Exception object*.

The code then needs to log the information in the *ExceptionToLog* object by adding a new row to the *Error* table in the *Store* database. It does this by creating a new *Error* object (representing a row in the *Error* table) called *NewError*.

The error details are then transferred from the *ExceptionToLog* object to the *NewError* object and inserted into the database.

This process is covered in more depth in: *Lesson 10-8: Insert database records using LINQ*.

```
void Application_Error(object sender, EventArgs e)
{
    // Code that runs when an unhandled error occurs
    using (StoreDataContext Data = new StoreDataContext())
    {
        Exception ExceptionToLog = Server.GetLastError();
        Error NewError = new Error();
        NewError.ErrorMessage = ExceptionToLog.Message;
        NewError.ErrorStackTrace = ExceptionToLog.StackTrace;
        NewError.ErrorURL = Request.Url.ToString();
        NewError.ErrorDate = DateTime.Now;
        Data.Errors.InsertOnSubmit(NewError);
        Data.SubmitChanges();
    }
    Response.Redirect("~/error.aspx");
}
```

4   Test your error logging.

1.   View the site in your browser.

2.   Attempt to navigate to a URL that doesn't exist.

http://localhost:64011/sdfdsf.aspx

You are redirected to the error page, just as you were in: *Lesson 12-2: Handle errors with Global.asax*.

Something went wrong

We're sorry, but something went wrong with your request.

This time, however, the error was also logged in the *Error* table of the *Store* database.

3.   Close your web browser.

4.   View the contents of the *Error* table using the *Database Explorer*.

You learned how to do this in: *Lesson 10-1: Work with SQL databases in Visual Studio*.

You can see that the details of the error have been logged in the table.

	ErrorID	ErrorURL	ErrorMessage
▶	1	http://localhost:64011/sdfdsf.aspx	The file '/sdfdsf.aspx' does not exist.
＊	NULL	NULL	NULL

5   Close Visual Studio.

Lesson 12-6: Create a Products page

1   Open *SmartMethodStore* from your sample files folder.

2   Open *products.aspx* in *Design* view.

3   Add a *LinqDataSource* control to the page called: **LinqDataSourceProduct**

4   Configure the *LinqDataSource* control to retrieve all records from the *Product* table and sort them by *ProductName* in ascending order.

You learned how to do this in: *Lesson 11-1: Use the LinqDataSource control.*

5   Add a *GridView* control to the page called: **GridViewProduct**

If the text in the new *GridView* control is very large, switch to *Source* view and make sure that it is not inside the *<h2>* tag.

6   Link the *GridViewProduct* control to *LinqDataSourceProduct*.

You learned how to do this in: *Lesson 11-3: Use the GridView control.*

7   Configure your *GridView* control.

1. Set the *ShowHeader* property of the *GridView* control to: **False**

2. Open the *Edit Columns…* dialog of the *GridViewProduct* control using the *QuickTasks* menu.

3. Remove the *ProductID* and *ProductImageUrl* fields from the *Selected fields* pane.

4. Add an *ImageField* to the *Selected fields* pane from the *Available fields* pane and set the *DataImageUrlField* property of the new *ImageField* to: **ProductImageUrl** (see sidebar).

5. Use the arrows to move the *ImageField* to the top of the *Selected fields* pane.

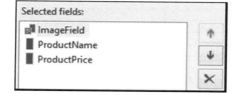

6. Set the *DataFormatString* of the *ProductPrice* column to: **{0:c}**

7. Click *OK*.

8. Use *Auto Format…* from the *GridView* control's *QuickTasks* menu to set the format to *Classic*.

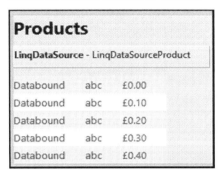

8 Create buttons to add products to the shopping cart.

The *ButtonField* causes a post-back when it is clicked, and fires the *RowCommand* event handler of the *GridView* control.

1. Open the *Edit Columns…* dialog of the *GridViewProduct* control.

2. Add a *ButtonField* to the *Selected fields* pane from the *Available fields* pane.

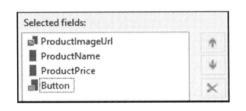

3. Set the *Text* property of the new *ButtonField* to: **Add to cart**

4. Set the *CommandName* property of the *ButtonField* to: **AddToCart**

   The *CommandName* property is used to determine which button field has been clicked.

5. Click *OK*.

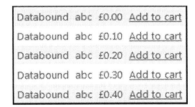

In *Lesson 12-7: Create a Shopping Cart*, you'll add code that will add the selected product from the *GridView* control to the shopping cart when the *ButtonField* is clicked.

9 Test *products.aspx* in your browser.

Lesson 12-7: Create a Shopping Cart

1 Open *SmartMethodStore* from your sample files folder.

2 Open *products.aspx* in *Design* view.

3 Add code to add the selected product to the shopping cart.

1. Add a *RowCommand* event handler to the *GridViewProduct* control.

    You learned to do this in: *Lesson 3-2: Add event handlers to controls.*

    The *RowCommand* event runs when the user clicks a *ButtonField.*

2. Add the following code to the *GridViewProduct_RowCommand* event handler:

    if (e.CommandName == "AddToCart")
    {
    }

    ```
    protected void GridViewProduct_RowCommand(
    {
        if (e.CommandName == "AddToCart")
        {
        }
    }
    ```

    This isn't strictly necessary, since you only have one *ButtonField.*

    If you had more than one, you could tell which *ButtonField* had been clicked by checking the *e.CommandName* property against the *CommandName* properties you gave to each *ButtonField.*

3. Add the following code inside the *if* statement:

    int RowClicked = Convert.ToInt32(e.CommandArgument);

    ```
    if (e.CommandName == "AddToCart")
    {
        int RowClicked = Convert.ToInt32(e.CommandArgument);
    }
    ```

    The *CommandArgument* property contains the index number of the row that was clicked. This will be used in the next step to retrieve the *ProductID.*

    You learned about the *e* object in: *Lesson 11-8: Bind data to a control using C#.*

4. Add the following code on the next line:

    int ProductID = Convert.ToInt32
    (GridViewProduct.DataKeys[RowClicked].Value);

    ```
    int RowClicked = Convert.ToInt32(e.CommandArgument);
    int ProductID = Convert.ToInt32
        (GridViewProduct.DataKeys[RowClicked].Value);
    ```

    The *Value* property of the *GridViewProduct.DataKeys* collection contains the *ProductID* of the row that was clicked (see sidebar for more on this).

5. Add the following code on the next line:

    List<int> ProductsInCart = (List<int>)Session["Cart"];

note

The DataKeys property

In this example, you extract a value from a specific row of a *GridView* control by using the *DataKeys* property.

Because you linked the *GridView* to a *LinqDataSource* control, it automatically populated the *DataKeys* property with the values from the *ProductID* column in the database.

The database values that are stored in the *DataKeys* property can be changed by altering the *DataKeys* property of the control with the *Properties* window while in Design view.

```
int RowClicked = Convert.ToInt32(e.CommandArgument);
int ProductID = Convert.ToInt32
    (GridViewProduct.DataKeys[RowClicked].Value);
List<int> ProductsInCart = (List<int>)Session["Cart"];
```

As you learned in: *Lesson 3-12: Use Session,* the *Session* object can contain a collection of objects of different types. These objects can be retrieved using a key (in this case you've decided to use *Cart* as the key).

It is common practice to implement a shopping cart by storing the cart items in a *Session* collection (but see sidebar for alternative techniques).

If the user hasn't added any items to their cart yet, the *Cart* collection will not exist and a *null* value will be returned.

Note that values stored in the *Session* object have a type of *object* (this was covered in *Lesson 5-13: Use object and var variables*). For this reason you need to cast the *object* into the correct type (in this case *List<int>*). You learned about casting in: *Lesson 5-9: Convert variables using cast and ToString.*

6. Add the following code on the next line:

if (ProductsInCart == null)
{
    ProductsInCart = new List<int>();
}

As discussed in the previous step, *ProductsInCart* will be null if the user hasn't added any products yet. In this case the above code creates a new *List* collection for the shopping cart.

You learned about creating *List* collections in: *Lesson 8-2: Create a collection.*

7. Add the following code on the next line:

ProductsInCart.Add(ProductID);

Now that the code has established that the *List* collection exists, it adds the *ProductID* to the collection.

8. Add the following code on the next line:

Session["Cart"] = ProductsInCart;

```
if (e.CommandName == "AddToCart")
{
    int RowClicked = Convert.ToInt32(e.CommandArgument);
    int ProductID = Convert.ToInt32
        (GridViewProduct.DataKeys[RowClicked].Value);
    List<int> ProductsInCart = (List<int>)Session["Cart"];
    if (ProductsInCart == null)
    {
        ProductsInCart = new List<int>();
    }
    ProductsInCart.Add(ProductID);
    Session["Cart"] = ProductsInCart;
}
```

Finally, the updated *List* collection (shopping cart) is stored in the *Session* collection.

You'll retrieve the shopping cart again on the checkout page that you create in: *Lesson 12-10: Create a Checkout page.*

Lesson 12-8: Create a Search page

Although the site doesn't currently have very many products, there may come a time when there are too many for users to easily scroll through.

In this lesson you'll add a search page to enable users to easily find products.

In this example the search functionality is only provided on a single page. You could use the same techniques to put search capabilities on your *Products* page, or even on the master page to make it available throughout the site.

In this lesson you'll create the user interface for the search page. In: *Lesson 12-9: Add functionality to a Search page* you'll add code to make the page functional.

1   Open *SmartMethodStore* from your sample files folder.

2   Open *search.aspx* in *Design* view.

3   Add an HTML table to the bottom of the page.

     1.   Click in the area below *Search*.

     2.   Click Table→Insert Table.

        The *Insert Table* dialog appears.

     3.   Uncheck *Specify Width*.

     4.   Click *OK*.

note

Formatting problems

You might find that the text that you type into the table is very large. If so, it's because you placed your table inside the *H2* tags containing the page title.

To correct this, you will have to go into *Source* view and move the *</h2>* tag so that it is just after the *Search* text.

4   Populate the table with text and controls.

     1.   Type **Product Name:** into the first cell.

     2.   Add a *TextBox* control to the second cell on the top row named: **TextBoxProductName**

     3.   Type **Price Below:** into the first cell on the next row.

     4.   Add a *TextBox* control to the last empty cell called: **TextBoxPriceBelow**

     5.   Add a third row to the table.

        You can do this by right-clicking on last row of the table and then clicking Insert→Row Below from the shortcut menu.

6. Add a *Button* control to the first cell of the new row named: **ButtonSearch**

7. Set the *Text* property of the *ButtonSearch* control to: **Search**

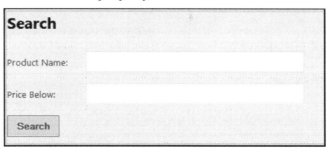

5 Copy the *GridView control* from the *products.aspx* page to the *search.aspx* page.

You'll need a *GridView* control to display the search results. Fortunately, you have already created one on the *Products* page that does everything you need.

1. Open *products.aspx* in *Design* view.

2. Copy the *GridViewProduct* control.

3. Return to *search.aspx* in *Design* view.

4. Paste the *GridView* onto the page.

    After pasting the *GridView* control, you might need to go into *Source* view to move it so that it is outside the table.

    ```
    </table>
    <asp:GridView ID="GridViewProduct" runat="server"
    ```

5. Clear the *DataSourceID* property of the *GridView* (click *No* when prompted).

6. Open the code-behind file of *products.aspx* and copy the entire *GridViewProduct_RowCommand* event handler.

7. Open the code-behind file of *search.aspx* and paste in the event handler just after the end of the *Page_Load* event handler.

    ```
    public partial class search : System.Web.UI.Page
    {
        protected void Page_Load(object sender, EventArgs e)
        {

        }
        protected void GridViewProduct_RowCommand(object sender, GridVie
        {
            if (e.CommandName == "AddToCart")
            {
                int RowClicked = Convert.ToInt32(e.CommandArgument);
                int ProductID = Convert.ToInt32
                    (GridViewProduct.DataKeys[RowClicked].Value);
                List<int> ProductsInCart = (List<int>)Session["Cart"];
                if (ProductsInCart == null)
                {
                    ProductsInCart = new List<int>();
                }
                ProductsInCart.Add(ProductID);
                Session["Cart"] = ProductsInCart;
            }
        }
    ```

Lesson 12-9: Add functionality to a Search page

1   Open *SmartMethodStore* from your sample files folder.

2   Open *search.aspx* in *Design* view.

3   Add code to search the database.

1. Add a *Click* event handler to the *ButtonSearch* control.

2. Add a *using* statement to the *ButtonSearch_Click* event handler:

    using (StoreDataContext Data = new StoreDataContext()) { }

    ```
    protected void ButtonSearch_Click(object sender, EventArgs e)
    {
        using (StoreDataContext Data = new StoreDataContext())
        {
        }
    }
    ```

3. Add the following code inside the *using* statement:

    string ProductName = TextBoxProductName.Text;

    ```
    using (StoreDataContext Data = new StoreDataContext())
    {
        string ProductName = TextBoxProductName.Text;
    }
    ```

    This code places the text entered into the *TextBoxProductName* control into a *string* variable called *ProductName*.

4. Add the following code inside the *using* statement:

    ```
    string ProductName = TextBoxProductName.Text;
    decimal? PriceBelow = null;
    ```

    decimal? PriceBelow = null;

    The question mark after *decimal* denotes a nullable *decimal* variable. You learned about nullable variables in: *Lesson 5-12: Understand null.*

    The code also initializes the variable with a value of *null*.

5. Add the following code inside the *using* statement:

    ```
    decimal? PriceBelow = null;
    if (TextBoxPriceBelow.Text.Length > 0)
    {
        PriceBelow =
        Convert.ToDecimal(TextBoxPriceBelow.Text);
    }
    ```

    if (TextBoxPriceBelow.Text.Length > 0)
    {
    **   PriceBelow =**
    **   Convert.ToDecimal(TextBoxPriceBelow.Text);**
    }

    This code converts the contents of the *TextBoxPriceBelow* control to *decimal* only if the text box is not empty.

    This means that the *PriceBelow* variable will remain *null* if the user has not entered any text into the textbox.

    Note that this will still cause an exception if the user enters non-numeric data into the textbox. You could fix this by using *try* and *catch* or by using a validation control to ensure that the value is a valid decimal.

6. Add the following LINQ code to the *ButtonSearch_Click* event handler (inside the *using* statement):

var SearchResults = Data.Products.Where
    (Product =>
    (Product.ProductName.Contains(ProductName)
    || ProductName.Length == 0)
    &&
    (Product.ProductPrice <= PriceBelow
    || PriceBelow == null));

```
var SearchResults = Data.Products.Where
    (Product =>
    (Product.ProductName.Contains(ProductName) || ProductName.Length == 0)
    &&
    (Product.ProductPrice <= PriceBelow || PriceBelow == null));
```

You learned about logical operators in: *Lesson 7-3: Use basic logical operators* and in *Lesson 7-4: Use advanced logic.*

You learned how to retrieve records using LINQ in*: Lesson 10-4: Retrieve multiple rows of data using LINQ.*

Product.ProductName.Contains(ProductName)

This expression returns products with a *ProductName* that contains the text that was entered into the search box.

|| ProductName.Length == 0

By using the OR operator, a blank search box will return all records (this is normally how search boxes are implemented).

(Product.ProductPrice <= PriceBelow
|| PriceBelow == null))

This code works in a similar way. If a *PriceBelow* has been entered by the user only products with prices below or equal to the entered price are returned.

7. Add the following code on the next line inside the *using* statement:

GridViewProduct.DataSource = SearchResults;
GridViewProduct.DataBind();

```
    (Product.ProductPrice <= PriceBelow || PriceBelow == null));
GridViewProduct.DataSource = SearchResults;
GridViewProduct.DataBind();
```

This code displays the search results in the *GridView* control.

Your search page is now fully functional!

4   Test your search page.

Lesson 12-10: Create a Checkout page

Earlier, you wrote code to allow users to add products to their shopping cart. Now you need a page where your users can view their shopping cart, remove items from it and go on to pay for the products that they want to buy.

1 Open *SmartMethodStore* from your sample files folder.

2 Open *checkout.aspx* in *Design* view.

3 Add a *GridView* control to display the shopping cart.

1. Copy and paste the *GridViewProduct* control from *search.aspx* to the bottom of *checkout.aspx*.

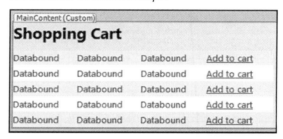

2. Open the *Edit Columns…* dialog from the *QuickTasks* menu of the *GridView* control.

3. Change the *Text* property of the *Add To Cart* field to: **Remove from cart**

4. Change the *CommandName* property to: **RemoveFromCart**

5. Click OK.

4 Add code to remove items from the shopping cart.

1. Add a *RowCommand* event handler to the *GridViewProduct* control.

2. Add the following code to the event handler:

```
if (e.CommandName == "RemoveFromCart")
{
    int RowClicked = Convert.ToInt32(e.CommandArgument);
    int ProductID = Convert.ToInt32
    (GridViewProduct.DataKeys[RowClicked].Value);
    List<int> ProductsInCart = (List<int>)Session["Cart"];
    ProductsInCart.Remove(ProductID);
    Session["Cart"] = ProductsInCart;
}
```

This is very similar to the code that you added in *Lesson 12-7: Create a Shopping Cart,* but it removes items from the shopping cart instead of adding them.

5 Add a method to retrieve the products from the database.

1. Add a new private method just after the *Page_Load* event handler:

note

Extending the page

This page works fine, but it doesn't have some of the features that you might have seen on other sites, such as product quantities and a total cost.

To add these features, you could create a new class with properties for both ProductID and quantity.

The Expert Skills course in this series will also teach you more skills to help you implement this and other features.

```
private void GetProductsFromCart()
{

}
```

2. Add the following code to the method:

```
if (Session["Cart"] != null)
{
    using (StoreDataContext Data = new StoreDataContext())
    {
        List<int> Cart = (List<int>)Session["Cart"];
        var Products = Data.Products.
        Where(Product => Cart.Contains(Product.ProductID));
        GridViewProduct.DataSource = Products;
        GridViewProduct.DataBind();
    }
}
```

This code retrieves records from the database that match the product ID numbers stored in the shopping cart collection and then displays them in the *GridViewProduct* control.

6   Add code to call the *GetProductsFromCart* method.

Before your page will retrieve any data, it will need to need to call your method.

1. Add the following code to the *Page_Load* event handler:

```
if (!Page.IsPostBack)
{
    GetProductsFromCart();
}
```

This code will call your method and retrieve the shopping cart when the user first loads the page.

2. Add the following code to the end of the *GridViewProduct_RowCommand* event handler:

GetProductsFromCart();

This code calls the method that refreshes the *GridView* control after an item has been removed from the shopping cart.

```
if (e.CommandName == "RemoveFromCart")
{
    int RowClicked = Convert.ToInt32(e
    int ProductID = Convert.ToInt32(Gr

    List<int> ProductsInCart = (List<i
    ProductsInCart.Remove(ProductID);
    Session["Cart"] = ProductsInCart;
    GetProductsFromCart();
}
```

7   Add a *Button* control to continue to payment.

1. Open *checkout.aspx* in *Design* view.

2. Add a *Button* control to the page named:
    ButtonContinueToPayment

3. Set the *Text* property of the button to: **Continue to Payment**

4. Add a *Click* event handler to the *Button* control.

5. Add code to the new event handler to redirect the user to *pay.aspx*:

    Response.Redirect("~/pay/pay.aspx");

Shopping Cart

Databound	Databound	Databound
Databound	Databound	Databound
Databound	Databound	Databound
Databound	Databound	Databound
Databound	Databound	Databound
Continue to Payment		

8   Test the checkout page.

You'll need to begin at the products page and then add some items to the shopping cart.

note

Internet payment providers

The vast majority of web sites use third party payment providers to process credit card payments.

The most popular payment provider is PayPal. PayPal accepts all major credit cards and is relatively easy to integrate into your site using the skills that you've learned in this book.

As an alternative to storing your own transactions, many payment providers offer a complete online storefront, meaning that all you have to do is send your users to the correct link to buy your products.

Lesson 12-11: Create a Payment page

The purpose of this page is to record and store delivery addresses and orders before sending the user to whichever payment provider you use to handle their payment details (see sidebar).

1   Open *SmartMethodStore* from your sample files folder.

2   Open *pay.aspx* (from the *pay* folder) in *Design* view.

You can see that the controls to enter the address have already been created to save time. You could easily create this form yourself.

3   Add code to write an *Order* record to the database.

Before sending the user to your payment provider, you will need to record their order details.

1.   Add a *Click* event handler to the *ButtonContinueToPayment* control.

2.   Add the following code to the new event handler:

using (StoreDataContext Data = new StoreDataContext())
{
}

```
protected void ButtonContinueToPayment_Click(object sender,
{
    using (StoreDataContext Data = new StoreDataContext())
    {
    }
}
```

As usual, you need to create an instance of the LINQ class to connect to the database.

3.   Add the following code inside the *using* statement to create and populate a new *Order* object.

Order NewOrder = new Order();
NewOrder.OrderAddress1 = TextBoxOrderAddress1.Text;
NewOrder.OrderAddress2 = TextBoxOrderAddress2.Text;
NewOrder.OrderTown = TextBoxOrderTown.Text;
NewOrder.OrderRegion = TextBoxOrderRegion.Text;
NewOrder.CountryID =
Convert.ToInt32(DropDownListCountry.SelectedValue);
NewOrder.OrderPostCode = TextBoxOrderPostCode.Text;

This code creates a new *Order* object and populates its address details.

4.   Add the following code to set the remaining properties of the *Order* object:

NewOrder.OrderPaid = false;
NewOrder.OrderSent = false;
NewOrder.UserName = Page.User.Identity.Name;
NewOrder.OrderDate = DateTime.Now;

This code sets the *OrderPaid* and *OrderSent* flags to *false,* so the order is marked as unpaid and unsent. It also sets the *UserName* to the username of the currently logged-in user and sets the *OrderDate* to the current date and time.

In the next lesson you'll add security to make sure that a user must be logged in to place an order.

```
using (StoreDataContext Data =
{
    Order NewOrder = new Order(
    NewOrder.OrderAddress1 = Te
    NewOrder.OrderAddress2 = Te
    NewOrder.OrderTown = TextBo
    NewOrder.OrderRegion = Text
    NewOrder.CountryID = Conver
    NewOrder.OrderPostCode = Te
    NewOrder.OrderPaid = false;
    NewOrder.OrderSent = false;
    NewOrder.UserName = Page.Us
    NewOrder.OrderDate = DateTi
    Data.Orders.InsertOnSubmit(
    Data.SubmitChanges();
}
```

4 **Commit the record to the database.**

Add the following code on the next line:

Data.Orders.InsertOnSubmit(NewOrder);
Data.SubmitChanges();

This code commits the record to the database.

5 **Record the list of products for the order.**

As well as storing the address details in your database, you'll need to store the list of products that the user ordered.

To store the list of products, you will add the contents of the shopping cart to the *OrderProduct* table in the database. You can do this by using a *foreach* loop.

1. Add the following code inside the *using* statement:

    List<int> Products = (List<int>)Session["Cart"];

    This code retrieves the shopping cart from the *Session* object.

2. Add the following code on the next line:

    foreach (int ProductID in Products)
    {
    ** OrderProduct NewOrderProduct = new OrderProduct();**
    ** NewOrderProduct.OrderID = NewOrder.OrderID;**
    ** NewOrderProduct.ProductID = ProductID;**
    ** Data.OrderProducts.InsertOnSubmit(NewOrderProduct);**
    }
    Data.SubmitChanges();

```
using (StoreDataContext Data =
{
    Order NewOrder = new Order(
    NewOrder.OrderAddress1 = Te
    NewOrder.OrderAddress2 = Te
    NewOrder.OrderTown = TextBo
    NewOrder.OrderRegion = Text
    NewOrder.CountryID = Conver
    NewOrder.OrderPostCode = Te
    NewOrder.OrderPaid = false;
    NewOrder.OrderSent = false;
    NewOrder.UserName = Page.Us
    NewOrder.OrderDate = DateTi
    Data.Orders.InsertOnSubmit(
    Data.SubmitChanges();

    List<int> Products = (List<
    foreach (int ProductID in P
    {
        OrderProduct NewOrderPr
        NewOrderProduct.OrderID
        NewOrderProduct.Product
        Data.OrderProducts.Inse
    }
    Data.SubmitChanges();
}
```

This code cycles through the list of products in the shopping cart and adds a record to the *OrderProduct* table for each product. They're linked to the *Order* table by the *OrderID*.

Notice that you only need to call the *SubmitChanges* method once, after the loop has finished. This was covered in: *Lesson 10-8: Insert database records using LINQ.*

6 **Send the user to your payment system.**

There are many different payment systems available on the Internet, all of which operate differently.

For now, just mark the end of the event handler with the following commented line:

//Send user to payment system here

7 **Close Visual Studio.**

Lesson 12-12: Implement security

Using the skills that you learned in *Session Nine: Authentication,* it's time to add security to the site.

1   Open *SmartMethodStore* from your sample files folder.

2   Open the *ASP.NET Configuration* utility.

You learned how to do this in: *Lesson 9-2: Manage a site with ASP.NET Configuration.*

3   Enable roles.

You learned how to do this in: *Lesson 9-9: Set up roles.*

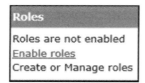

4   Create a role called: **Admin**

You learned how to do this in: *Lesson 9-9: Set up roles.*

5   Create an *administrator* user.

Create a user named **administrator** and assign it to the *Admin* role using **learnasp** as the password.

6   Create an access rule to only allow users with the *Admin* role to access the *admin* folder.

You learned how to do this in: *Lesson 9-8: Add folder-level security.*

1.   Click the *Security* tab of the *ASP.NET Configuration* utility.

2.   Click *Create access rules.*

3.   Click the *admin* folder.

4.   Create a rule to allow *Admin* users access to the *admin* folder.

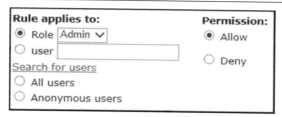

5. Click OK.

6. Return to the *Create access rules* form.

7. Create a rule to deny all other users access to the *admin* folder.

Rule applies to:
○ Role [Admin ∨]
○ user [   ]
<u>Search for users</u>
● All users
○ Anonymous users

Permission:
○ Allow
● Deny

8. Click OK.

Now only users with the *Admin* role will be allowed to access the pages in the *admin* folder.

7 Create an access rule to only allow logged-in users to access the *pay* folder.

You need to make sure that the user is logged-in when they access the p*ay.aspx* page so that you can link orders to user accounts. You can do this by creating an access rule.

1. Open the *Create access rules* form again.

2. Click the *pay* folder.

3. Add a rule to deny anonymous users.

Rule applies to:
○ Role [Admin ∨]
○ user [   ]
<u>Search for users</u>
○ All users
● Anonymous users

Permission:
○ Allow
● Deny

4. Click OK.

Now only users who are logged in will be able to access the *pay* folder.

8 Close Visual Studio.

Lesson 12-13: Publish a site

Your site is now finished, although you could add a lot of tweaks and improvements using the skills that you've learned in this book.

The final step is to publish the site so that it can be used by a web server.

1   Open *SmartMethodStore* from your sample files folder.

2   Open the *Publish* dialog.

Right-click on *SmartMethodStore* in the *Solution Explorer* and click *Publish…* from the shortcut menu.

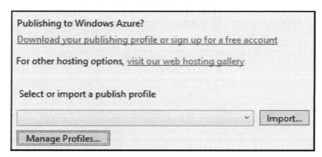

The *Publish* dialog appears. Using this dialog, you can publish your site using a variety of methods.

3   Create a new publish profile.

Before you can publish your project, you will need to create a new *profile*. Profiles store publishing settings so that you can easily reuse publishing settings later.

1.   Click the drop-down menu and select *<New…>*.

     A dialog appears, prompting you to name the new profile.

2.   Enter: **SaveToFolder**

3.   Click *OK*.

4   Publish the site to a folder on your computer.

Although you can publish the site directly to a server using the *Publish* dialog's other settings (see sidebar), it's usually easier to publish a site to a folder on your computer and then copy it to the server manually.

By publishing the site to a folder on your computer, you can also keep copies of each published version of the site.

This is a good idea, as you can quickly revert back to an earlier version if a problem is discovered with a newer version.

1.   Choose *File System* from the *Publish method* drop-down.

---

important

Only files included in the solution will be published

When you publish a site, only the files that are included in the *Solution Explorer* will be published.

Before publishing, you should always make sure that all of the images and resources that your site needs are included and use the Add→Existing Item option to add anything that is missing.

Remember that the *Web.Config* files that are created when you add access rules will not be included in your solution by default. If you want your access rules to work on your published site, you will need to make sure that each *Web.Config* file is included.

Visual Studio does not include databases in the solution by default. This is normally what you want, as the database on the live web server will be more up-to-date than the database on your local machine.

The only time you will want the database to be included is when you are publishing your site to the web server for the first time.

note

Other publish methods

As well as publishing the site to a place on your computer, as you do in this example, you can use the following other methods:

Web Deploy
A method that publishes your web site directly to the web server. *Web Deploy* is a service that isn't supported by every web host; your host should supply the required settings.

FTP
The most common way of connecting to remote web servers is using FTP (file transfer protocol). By using the FTP option, you can copy your site directly to the web server. FTP details should be provided by your web host.

FPSE
FPSE stands for FrontPage Server Extensions. It is another way of publishing directly to a web server that is supported by some hosts. As with the other options, settings should be provided by your host.

In general, the simplest way to publish your web site is either to publish to your own computer and then copy the files using FTP, or to use the FTP option to directly publish your site to the server.

2. Click the  icon next to *Target Location*.

3. Navigate to your sample files folder and click *Open*.

4. Add a back-slash and the date to the end of the path.

   You don't want the site to be published directly into your sample files folder. This will place it in a subfolder with the date you entered.

Target location:	C:\Practice\ASP.NET45\16May2013	...

5. Click *Publish*.

   The site is published to the location you specified.

5 View the published files.

Navigate to the folder that you published the site to and view the files.

checkout.aspx
Default.aspx
error.aspx
favicon.ico
Global.asax
packages.config
products.aspx
search.aspx
Site.Master
Site.Mobile.Master
Store.dbml
Web.config

You'll notice that there are no longer any *.cs* code-behind files with your *.aspx* files. This is because they have been compiled into the *bin* folder.

The site is now ready to be published to any Microsoft IIS web server. The files simply need to be copied to the server.

6 Close Visual Studio.

Session 12: Exercise

1 Open the *SmartMethodStore* project from your sample files folder.

2 Open *products.aspx* from the *admin* folder.

3 Add a *LinqDataSource* control to the page which retrieves all entries from the *Product* table.

4 Add a *GridView* control and link it to the *LinqDataSource*.

5 Add the ability to update and delete products to the new *GridView* control.

6 Add a *DetailsView* control linked to the same *LinqDataSource* control.

7 Add the ability to insert a new product to the *DetailsView* control.

8 Open *orders.aspx* from the *admin* folder.

9 Add *LinqDataSource* and *GridView* controls to display all records from the *Order* table where *OrderSent* is *false* and *OrderPaid* is *true*.

10 Add a *ButtonField* to the *GridView* control and set its *Text* property to: **Send Order**

11 Add a *RowCommand* event handler to your *GridView* control that will set the selected order's *OrderSent* property to *true* when the *Send Order ButtonField* is clicked.

The Smart Method Store

Home   Products

ProductID	ProductName	ProductPrice	ProductImageUrl		
1	Large amethyst crystal geode	150.0000	images/geode-tn.jpg	Edit	Delete
2	Small amethyst crystal geode	20.0000	images/geode-tn.jpg	Edit	Delete
3	Snowflake obsidian keyring	5.0000	images/keyring-tn.jpg	Edit	Delete
4	Large amethyst stone	5.0000	images/amethyst-tn.jpg	Edit	Delete
5	100g mixed gems	10.0000	images/mixedgems-tn.jpg	Edit	Delete
6	500g mixed gems	40.0000	images/mixedgems-tn.jpg	Edit	Delete

ProductID   1

ProductName   Large amethyst crystal geode

ProductPrice   150.0000

ProductImageUrl   images/geode-tn.jpg

New

SmartMethodStore - start   SmartMethodStore - end

If you need help slide the page to the left

Session 12: Exercise Answers

These are the four questions that students find the most difficult to answer:

Q 11	Q 9	Q 7	Q 5
1. Add a *RowCommand* event handler to your *GridView* control. 2. Add the following code: **int RowClicked = Convert.ToInt32 (e.CommandArgument);** **int OrderID = Convert.ToInt32 (GridViewOrder.DataKeys[RowClicked].Value);** **using (StoreDataContext Data = new StoreDataContext())** **{** **Order OrderToSend = Data.Orders** **.Single(Order => Order.OrderID == OrderID);** **OrderToSend** **.OrderSent = true;** **Data.SubmitChanges();** **}** **GridViewOrder.DataBind();** This was covered in: *Lesson 12-6: Create a Products page.*	1. Add a new *LinqDataSource* to the page. 2. Click *Configure Data Source* from the *QuickTasks* menu of the *LinqDataSource*. 3. Click *Next*. 4. Choose *Orders* from the *Table* drop-down. 5. Click *Where…* 6. Choose *OrderSent* from the *Column* drop-down. 7. Choose = from the *Operator* drop-down. 8. Choose *None* from the *Source* drop-down. 9. Type **False** into the *Value* box. 10. Click *Add* and repeat the process for the *OrderPaid* property with a value of: **True** 12. Add a *GridView* control and link it to the *LinqDataSource*. This was covered in: *Lesson 11-1: Use the LinqDataSource control.*	1. Open the *Edit Columns* dialog from the *QuickTasks* menu of the *DetailsView* control. 2. Add a *New, Insert, Cancel* field from the *CommandField* category. 3. Click OK. 4. Set the *EnableInsert* property of your *LinqDataSource* to: **True** This was covered in: *Lesson 11-6: Use the DetailsView control.*	1. Open the *Edit Columns* dialog from the *QuickTasks* menu of the *GridView* control. 2. Add an *Edit, Update, Cancel* field from the *CommandField* category. 3. Add a *Delete* field from the *CommandField* category. 4. Set the *EnableUpdate* and *EnableDelete* properties of your *LinqDataSource* to: **True** This was covered in: *Lesson 11-5: Add editing features to a GridView.*

If you have difficulty with the other questions, here are the lessons that cover the relevant skills:

1   **Refer to: Lesson 1-7: Manage a project with the Solution Explorer.**

2   **Refer to: Lesson 1-7: Manage a project with the Solution Explorer.**

3/4   **Refer to: Lesson 11-3: Use the GridView control.**

6   **Refer to: Lesson 11-6: Use the DetailsView control.**

8   **Refer to: Lesson 1-7: Manage a project with the Solution Explorer.**

10   **Refer to: Lesson 12-6: Create a Products page.**

Index

J

K

L

Q

R

S

Become an ASP.NET Expert with our Expert Skills book

The next book in the series builds upon all of the foundation skills you've learned.

There's a whole lot more to ASP.NET, C# and Visual Studio and you'll learn it all with this book. AJAX, web services, advanced class structures and so much more.

Search for it at **Amazon.com** or **Amazon.co.uk** or view the lessons in video and PDF format at **ASPNETCentral.com**.

You can also find links to book resellers stocking this title at the **ASPNETCentral.com** web site (click *Books* on the top menu bar).

ASPNETCentral.com

For many years I have dreamed of creating an online learning resource that would provide the same experience as my classroom courses.

My books cover the same material as my classroom courses, but it is clear that some learners need more than can be delivered via printed media. In 2013 we began the design of an ASP.NET Internet resource that aims to bring my classroom courses onto your desktop.

The site is available at: **www.ASPNETCentral.com**

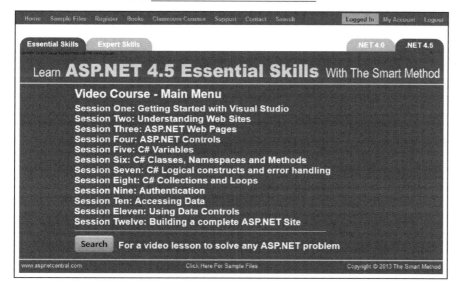

On the site I have recorded a video walk-through for each and every lesson in this book. The videos have also been indexed by keyword to provide a unique interactive ASP.NET reference resource.

Lessons can be viewed without cost by using our *FreeView* facility.

Enhanced features can also be unlocked for a small annual subscription charge.

Made in the USA
Lexington, KY
08 July 2014